Television and the
drama of crime

Open University Press
New Directions in Criminology series

Series Editor: Colin Sumner, Lecturer in Sociology, Institute of Criminology, and Fellow of Wolfson College, University of Cambridge

Current titles:

Imperial Policing
Philip Ahire

Lawyers in a Postmodern World
Maureen Cain and Christine B. Harrington (eds)

Feminist Perspectives in Criminology
Loraine Gelsthorpe and Allison Morris (eds)

The Enemy Without: Policing and Class Consciousness in the Miners' Strike
Penny Green

Television and the Drama of Crime
Richard Sparks

Censure, Politics and Criminal Justice
Colin Sumner (ed.)

Corruption and Politics in Hong Kong and China
T. Wing Lo

Reading the Riot Act
Richard Vogler

Television and the drama of crime: moral tales and the place of crime in public life

Richard Sparks

Open University Press
Buckingham · Philadelphia

Open University Press
Celtic Court
22 Ballmoor
Buckingham
MK18 1XW

and
1900 Frost Road, Suite 101
Bristol, PA 19007, USA

First Published 1992
Reprinted 1995, 1997

A catalogue record of this book is available
from the British Library

Library of Congress Cataloging-in-Publication Data

Sparks, Richard, 1961–
    Television and the drama of crime: moral tales and the place of
crime in public life / Richard Sparks.
        p.   cm. – (New directions in criminology)
    Includes bibliographical references and index.
    ISBN 0–335–09328–0 (hb) ISBN 0–335–09327–2 (pb)
    1. Crime in television–United States.   2. Violence in television–
United States.   3. Television broadcasting–Social aspects–United
States.   4. Television serials–United States.   5. Law enforcement–
United States.   6. Criminology.   I. Series: New directions in
criminology series.
PN1992.6.S66   1992
303.6'0973—dc20   91–46581
                                                                            CIP

Typeset by Inforum Typesetting, Portsmouth
Printed in Great Britain by St Edmundsbury Press Limited
Bury St Edmunds, Suffolk

We are closed in, and the key is turned
On our uncertainty; somewhere
A man is killed, or a house burned
Yet no clear fact to be discerned . . .
      W. B. Yeats (1923) 'Meditations in Time of Civil War'

Contents

Acknowledgements

There are many people to whom I would like to record my grateful thanks both for practical help and moral support during the time it has taken to prepare this book.

I am grateful to Colin Sumner, who supervised the PhD thesis on which this book is based. Thanks go to Colin not only for his acute (though always constructive) criticism, but also for his warm encouragement. I would also like to thank Geoffrey Pearson and Graham Murdock, who examined the thesis, for their many helpful comments.

My friends Ian Taylor, Ruth Jamieson, Graham McCann and Marion Smith all read most of my work in progress. Their comments and advice have helped me enormously. Tom Woodhouse and I have discussed the issues raised here many times, and his ideas have stimulated and influenced me very much. David Garland kindly read some of the manuscript at a late stage and commented on it with great tact and insight. There are a number of others who have read some of my work, especially long ago in its early stages, or with whom I have had enlightening (for me at any rate) discussions. They include John Clarke, Alan Clarke, John Thompson, Todd Gitlin, Roger Silverstone and Bob Towler. Each of these people has done much to improve this book: its inadequacies, however, are all my own work!

I count myself lucky to have enjoyed the friendly and stimulating environment provided at the Institute of Criminology by the Director, Tony Bottoms, the library and administrative staff and my fellow students. Will Hay was my constant companion through many ups and downs: I would have thrown in the towel without him. Phil Brown, John Pratt, Mike Nellis and Alison Liebling have all stretched my mind and lightened my life. Thanks also go to Judith Ayling for the life-saving loan of a word processor, and to the word processor for lasting the distance.

I want to thank my parents and my brother Jon for their constant and unconditional support. I have been extraordinarily fortunate to have known the companionship of some kind and loyal friends. Among those who have shared the long (too long) experience of the gestation of this book have been Molly Andrews, George Conyne, George Hardy, Jonathan Luke, Jon and Liz Morris, Howard Moss, Shirin Rai and Jeremy Roche, and Peter Swaab (to whom thanks also for all the gin, the squash, and the beach and for carrying out all his rights and privileges with such style).

Little Thomas timed his arrival in the world just well enough to make it on to the acknowledgements page and change everything. Last, but always really first, to Marion Smith, love and gratitude.

Series editor's introduction

This series is founded upon the socialist and feminist research carried out in the Institute of Criminology between 1980 and 1990. However, it is also concerned, more broadly, to publish any work which renews theoretical development, or opens up new and important areas, in criminology. Particular attention will be paid to the politics and ideology of criminal justice, gender and crime, crimes of state officials, crime and justice in underdeveloped societies, European criminal justice, environmental crime, and the general sociology of censure and regulation. The series will centre upon substantial empirical research informed by contemporary social theory, and will be international in character.

Behind the series is a belief that criminology must resist being limited to policy-oriented studies and must retain its integrity as an area of independent, critical inquiry of interest to scholars from a variety of disciplinary backgrounds. A criminology that wants to remain dynamic and worthy of its complex subject matter must therefore constantly renew theoretical debate, explore current issues, and develop new methods of research. To allow itself to be limited by the narrow political interests of government departments or the funding agencies' need for a parochial 'relevance', especially in an age when 'realism' is so often defined by short-run philosophies, is to promote its own destruction as an intellectual enterprise. A criminology which is not intellectually alive is useless to everybody. We live in increasingly international societies which, more than ever, require a broad, non-parochial vision to ensure their viability and health. Administrative criminology may be necessary for wise

government, but it can offer only pseudo-scientific verbiage to governments unless it remains closely and genuinely connected to an independent, critical and intellectually rigorous criminology, whose ideas, drive,
depth, topicality and legitimacy are the ultimate motor-force of all criminology. Equally, critical criminology must retain a close connection with
political reality in contemporary societies if it is to achieve real insight and
sharpness. Both, we believe, must be committed to a general drive towards increased democratization and justice, and the indivisibility of
freedom, truth and justice, if they want to avoid a drift into the twin culs-
de-sac of police science and political propaganda.

Some might argue that criminology is an outdated term in that few
people believe any more that a positive science of crime and criminal
justice administration is possible. Indeed, most of the books in this series
will look more like studies in the sociology of law, or in political sociology, and their view of science is never positivistic. We have decided to
retain the term criminology, however, because we intend this series to
contribute to the contemporary redefinition of its meaning, so that it
clearly includes work on crime matters from within the sociology of law,
political sociology, social history, political economy, discourse analysis,
anthropology, development studies and so on. Criminology merely refers
to any kind of study concerned with crime and criminal justice. It is an
umbrella term covering a multitude of topics and approaches. The task
for all of us is to give it a meaningful substance to meet the emerging
challenges of the 1990s. The cold war is almost over. Now we enter a
phase which will demand a new clarity on fundamental social values, and
a stronger vision of the kinds of social censure and social regulation
necessary to promote peace, health, growth, equity and co-operation on
an international scale.

Richard Sparks's thoughts on the subject of television crime drama
move criminology into a new and largely unexplored terrain. He not only
demonstrates the centrality of the dramatization of crime on television to
key issues in criminology, but also, by drawing upon contemporary social
theory, he enters a telling series of caveats about the kinds of conclusions
we might reach on the subject of television's influence. He considers, in a
careful, measured way, whether the 'cop shows' stimulate our fear of
crime, whether they mystify the truth of policing in suggesting that the
good guys always win and that detection rates are high, whether the
imagery built into the narratives of these very moral tales excites a more
punitive attitude to 'criminals', thus reinforcing the drift towards a more
authoritarian society begun in Western societies in the 1980s. All too often
in criminology, what television crime data does to mass audiences has
been assumed, and then these assumptions are blithely harnessed to a
sweeping political argument. What Richard Sparks offers us is a sustained, detailed survey of the arguments involved in assessing the role of

television crime drama, a survey conducted at the highest level of erudition. Few rhetorical stones are left unturned as he clarifies the role of television crime drama in contemporary Western societies, thus doing a valuable service to criminology.

Having worked closely with Richard for around ten years now, what strikes me as particularly important about his work is the clear way in which he situates television symbolism within the everyday social practices of both viewing audiences and criminal justice officials. His analyses should prevent us from ever again dividing up television and its impact into a kind of base/superstructure topography. Television and its symbolism are fully interlaced with many other social practices. One cannot therefore seriously suppose that the question of television is somehow a separate question from the question of crime (or justice). Television is heavily watched, and prime-time viewing is crime-time viewing. 'Cops and robbers' roam all over our nightly television schedules. Criminology has gone on far too long without analysing in detail the impact of these prevalent, entertaining and popular moral tales upon recurrent public images of criminality and policing, *and* upon young police officers racing around in their fast cars. For too long, it has sidestepped the difficult debates within social theory which try to detail the role of almost subliminal ideas, messages or ideology in the everyday reconstruction of social order.

Entertaining the crisis is as important as policing it; indeed, perhaps entertainment should properly be considered part of policing in its broadest sense. Publics routinely subjected to a certain kind of satisfying moral tale, which they themselves have chosen to watch, must build up ethical and juridical sensitivies – or insensitivities. As Gramsci kept telling us, most governments do not rule by coercion most of the time, they rule by assent. In the West, Gramsci clearly foretold, that assent rests partly upon the ethical capacities and tendencies developed within leisure activity. In the *longue durée* of the war of position, no line of trenches or series of bunkers is more important than the social practice of watching television of an evening, warm and secure in the comfort of one's own home. Coercion may be the state's armoury in the last resort, but, equally, it may be that the public thirst for punishment is refreshed on a daily basis by television crime drama, and that the lonely hour of the last resort never arrives.

Many years ago, Durkheim taught us that both definitions of crime and degrees of tolerance were intimately bound up with the collective sentiments and the *conscience collective*. The education of that conscience and the sensitivity of that sentiment is partly governed by practical life, or experience, and partly by reflection, or thought. The passions of moral indignation in modern societies are thus interwined with a complex labyrinth of social relations and their corresponding typical experiences, while also being located at the centre of a welter of public rhetorics about right, wrong, taste, danger, due process, and justice. It is to Richard Sparks's great credit that he has located television crime drama within the full complexity of its social position in modernity, and hopefully contributed to the final demise of simplistic approaches to television. Even if he has been only partly successful, the debates about the role of television will now move on to a much higher level of sophistication.

Colin Sumner

Introduction

What are the landscapes of fear? They are the almost infinite manifestations of the forces of chaos, natural and human. . . . In a sense, every human construction is a component in a landscape of fear because it exists to contain chaos. Thus children's fairy tales as well as adults' legends, cosmological myths and indeed philosophical systems are shelters built by the mind in which human beings can rest, at least temporarily, from the siege of inchoate experience and doubt.

Yi-Fu Tuan, *Landscapes of Fear*

In this book I treat something which is familiar and commonplace as though it were something strange, in the hope of seeing it anew. The familiar thing in this case is popular crime fiction on television, or what are generally known as 'cop shows'. I shall focus on only some of the many things it would be possible to say about this or any other cultural fragment. That is I shall concentrate on the rather long and contentious debate (in both academic and 'lay' circles) on the possibility of relations between watching television of this sort and the extent and intensity of public fear and alarm about crime. Part of my task is to pick a course through those arguments, to discard what is misleading in them and retain what is interesting and provocative. I shall therefore try to show what I think is really at stake in arguments about the fear of crime, and why they have generated so much heat. This in turn leads me to the question of the wider social and political consequences of fearfulness. I want to use our participation in crime fiction on television as a point of entry into these matters, by discussing some of the meanings which crime and law enforcement are called upon to bear in contemporary culture. I hope to develop an account of some of the ways in which these issues are important – at theoretical, practical and personal levels.

This book grew out of a quite personal experience of curiosity and puzzlement. I have always found cop shows, thrillers and detective stories involving and interesting. Watching the detectives on television has been as much a part of my own life as of many other people's, perhaps a more important part. Yet I have never been a straightforward fan. My pleasure and excitement have long been tinged with unease at what the conditions of my involvement might be and a sense of uncertainty as to the roots of the appeal they held for myself and for others.

Something similar is true for the perspective I develop here on the issues of fear and anxiety about crime. One would never guess when reading most criminological accounts of fear of crime that the authors had ever had any private perception or sensation about the matter in hand, at least prior to the intervention of feminist writers on the topic. Most discussions of the subject rely at least implicitly (as I shall go on to show) on a notional and counter-factual rational agent from whose hypothetical awareness of risk real people's fears deviate. I have never believed in such a being or even in his (for I think he is male) utility as an argumentative strategy and I certainly bear no resemblance to him myself. My scepticism on this point fundamentally influences my reading of the literature on the fear of crime which, I find, betrays remarkably little insight into the nature of fear as a dimension of experience. If I then go on to argue that non-rational factors have a part to play in explaining people's television viewing, their experience of fear and anxiety and, moreover, the connection between the two, I do not do so from a lofty and dispassionate height but rather in the belief that we are all swayed by emotions and capable of mistaken impressions and that lucidity has to be struggled for.

Stimulated by these introspections, much of this book comprises a critical review of the literatures on fear, television and the connections which have been drawn between them and it records my attempts at a theoretical reconstruction of the relevant terms. Dissatisfied even at the outset with the ways in which these issues have hitherto been posed and addressed, much of whatever I have learned in the course of writing this book has been learned in a mood of disenchantment.

From time to time, but perhaps especially during the 1970s, many criminologists and sociologists of social regulation have been concerned with public perceptions and misperceptions of crime, criminals, law enforcement and punishment. For numerous observers the reproduction of such misperceptions owes much to the alarmism prevalent in mass media, and it has often been argued that the dramatization and simplification of questions of crime and law enforcement in the media has lent weight and credence to political rhetorics demanding severity and the reassertion of 'law and order'. All such arguments implicitly depend on claims about the nature of fearful and anxious public responses to crime inasmuch as the invocation of fear through the overstatement of danger is held to have provided the motor for the persuasiveness of demands for disciplinary and punitive policies.

I remain much in sympathy with this basic view, but it has rarely been developed with sufficiently careful attention to either theory or evidence. Some of the main terms associated with these views, principally the concept of 'moral panic', have come to be used in casual and confusing ways (see my discussion in Chapter 3). Meanwhile, as the volume of evidence about the distribution of fear has increased, so some of the strongest claims made for the influence of mass media on fearfulness, especially perhaps in the work of Gerbner and his collaborators, have come to seem simplistic and overstated. In this sense, some widespread views on mass media and fear of crime have invited and deserved the counter-assertion from at least one quarter, namely 'left realist' criminology, that most fear is so plainly a product of the real conditions of existence of those who experience it as to leave no significant space for the role of mass media in accounting for it. None the less, there seems to me to be little prospect of providing any account of the demonstrable preoccupation of mass media with crime and law enforcement, let alone arriving at an understanding of any of its possible social and political corollaries, without reference to the capacity of those subjects to invoke anxiety, fear and other strong emotions.

The polemical exchanges which have so far taken place between 'realists' and those whom they style 'idealists' within criminology risk becoming a parody of scholarly argument. Much of that argument at bottom concerns competing depictions of the character and causes of fear and anxiety. Whether the kinds of fears and anxieties experienced by different groups can be regarded as 'reasonable' or otherwise, and how such feelings should be explained and understood, have become the subject of hot controversy. Moreover, there has been a growing awareness of the relation between the experience of anxiety about crime and danger and the quality of both private and public life. Fear is thus now a central concept in recent debates in the sociology of crime and punishment. Yet, for all the importance of the topics of fear, anxiety and alarm, it is questionable whether most accounts of them to date have really been adequate to their subject's more profound implications: the insinuation of fear and anxiety into daily life and ordinary routine on the one hand, its possible roles in the sponsorship of political campaigns on the other. One way into (around?) these problems is to consider the ways in which the underlying preoccupations of fear, danger, reassurance and retribution are encoded, diffused and received in networks of communication. To adopt such an avenue of approach is not necessarily to presupppose that media representations exercise a powerfully direct influence over the consciousness and beliefs of their audiences. Instead it is to look at crime and punishment as cultural forms: things which interest people and sometimes give them pleasure.

In a programmatic recent article, David Garland argues that

modern punishment is a cultural as well as a strategic affair; that it is a realm for the expression of social value and emotion as well as a process for asserting control. And that, for all its necessity as an institution, and despite all our attempts to make it positive and useful, it still involves a tragic and futile quality which derives from its contradictory cultural location and which ought to be recognized in analysis. Our framework for analysing punishment ought thus to be geared towards interpreting the conflicting social values and sentiments which are expressed and evoked in punishment as well as tracing instrumental strategies of penal control.

(Garland 1990a: 4)

Instead of identifying only 'two parties involved in punishment – the controllers and the controlled', Garland argues, we have also to consider 'the onlookers, whose sentiments are first outraged and then reassured' (1990a: 8) through the processes of crime and punishment. Therefore, Garland proposes, the contemporary sociology of punishment should reclaim that part of Durkheimian theory which recognizes punishment as an 'expressive' institution and which thus takes seriously the proposition that ' "passion" and social sentiment remain "the soul of penality" ' (Garland 1990a: 8).

It follows from Garland's position that no sharp theoretical separation is possible between the study of the practical conduct of affairs in crime and punishment and the ways in which these matters are publicly represented and perceived. My task in this book will be to discuss some of the 'passions and social sentiments' which attend the public representation of crime and law enforcement, in this case in television entertainment. The dramatic moral structure of outrage and reassurance which Garland finds in punitive action is, I shall suggest, quite plainly central to the operation of heroic fictions of crime and law enforcement. Perhaps these stories address themselves to some potentially important passions and sentiments. If so, fear and anxiety may be among the most potent.

Modern media systems undermine received distinctions between public and private life. The routine extension of access by very large numbers of people to information, opinion and imagery via mass media makes those media fundamentally constitutive of the 'public sphere' in industrial societies. However, more particularly for this book, the reception and use of television takes place primarily in private and domestic settings. Perhaps nowadays when we are fearful, anxious and uneasy, television can provide a focus for the experience of a tension between public participation and the protection of the private sphere. One possibility is that fear provides a stimulus to what I call, following Lasch (1980), 'privatism'. Answering questions about why television 'cop shows' are as they are, as widespread as they are, and as widely viewed as they are, demands attention to the kinds of appeal they mount to viewers approaching them from distinct material, geographic, cognitive and emotional starting-points. Narratives of crime, pursuit and capture encode repertoires of images of cities, heroism, wickedness and vulnerability in ways which, at a given time, may be variously regarded as being 'realistic', exciting, funny or otherwise morally and aesthetically satisfying. To seek to chart the parameters of a particular set of stories is also to delineate certain features of the intellectual and cultural field out of which they arise and to speak about the terms on which their recipients are being addressed.

This suggests to me that criminological work should be attentive to the ways in which images of crime, law enforcement and punishment are caught up in the fine grain of cultural and personal experience. This may be especially important in debating the issues of fear and anxiety, whose less manifest resonances conventional methods of inquiry may be too crude to capture. The study of the place of crime in fiction and entertainment may provide one avenue of approach to problems of this kind, perhaps thereby also facilitating the development of more refined surveys and other methods of interrogating these issues. This book therefore looks for some ways forward in understanding the expressive and emotive characteristics of crime, law enforcement and punishment in contemporary culture. The somewhat tentative and speculative nature of some of its conclusions is unavoidable given the difficulty of its subject matter. Considerations of the place of mass media in public experience are not best served by imposing a premature certainty on processes which are sometimes not the least obscure where they may be most important. This recognition should not deter us, however, from what I continue to regard as a necessary activity, namely to make available for wider discussion the emotive, metaphorical and figurative dimensions of crime and punishment, their position within everyday life and their resulting cultural salience and ideological weight.

1 Crime, television and social anxiety

We had fed the heart on fantasies,
The heart's grown brutal from the fare;
More substance in our enmities
Than in our love . . .

W. B. Yeats, 'Meditations in Time of Civil War'

What is the fear of crime?

During the 1980s the question of the fear of crime moved close to the centre of theoretical, empirical and political debates in criminology and criminal justice. The development of both national and local crime surveys (Hough and Mayhew 1983; 1985; Jones et al 1986; Crawford et al 1990) has held out the possibility of discussing the place of crime in people's everyday experience in ways which are both concrete and refined.

Meanwhile, the main focus of attention within television studies in relation to crime has finally shifted away from their historically central concern with 'effects' of viewing on offending, or more diffusely on 'aggressiveness', and towards a broader interest in the viewer's experience of crime and law enforcement through television, especially in relation to fearfulness. The debates between the proponents, most importantly Gerbner, of a 'cultivation hypothesis' (which holds that watching television 'cultivates' a 'scary' perception of the world) and their numerous antagonists now constitute an extensive literature in themselves and are of long standing (see Chapter 4). The potential bearing of this literature on central criminological concerns is considerable. It claims to have illuminated some of the same questions regarding the determinations and distributions of fears as those which now preoccupy many criminologists, and which they have debated inconclusively.

However, the developments in criminology have occurred largely in isolation from those in media studies (see Schlesinger et al 1989: 45). This disciplinary separation has inhibited the refinement of debate about fear of crime, and has had some ironic consequences. To take only one prominent example, Young's recent contributions to criminological debate insist on the real basis for fear of crime among relevant publics and largely disregard, if not actively rule out of account, any potential new evidence from media studies (Young 1987: 338). Meanwhile, those commentators within media studies who argue most strongly that mass media engender undue fearfulness (Gerbner and Gross 1976b; Carlson 1985) tend to base their conclusions on the variance between their subjects' perceptions of risk and the extent of crime as measured by official statistics. Yet it is now a commonplace within criminology that official statistics do not in themselves provide an adequate basis for such assertions (Box 1971; Bottomley and Pease 1986).

One result has been that some of the strongest claims for 'effects' of media use on fear made by Gerbner and others have become very difficult to defend empirically. At the same time, recent approaches to the fear of crime by some criminologists have unduly circumscribed the range of topics which they are prepared to recognize as having any possible bearing on the subject; this situation results in part from their inattention to television and other media. It is thus important that these debates should now be reviewed in light of one another's claims and concerns. Existing contributions have by no means exhausted the range of what it is both possible and necessary to say about television, crime and social anxiety.

Recent arguments about the fear of crime have often seemed to terminate in stalemates. One reason for this may be that they have become preoccupied with the question of whether or not fear is 'warranted' or 'rational', without having first determined in any precise way what 'rationality' might be in this context (see Reiner 1988: 281). In general it has simply been assumed that the issue of whether fears are regarded as being 'warranted' or not turns entirely on whether it is possible to find systematic discrepancies between measurable risks of victimization, subjective estimates or perceptions of such risks, and levels of expressed fear. Therefore, whether or not this is openly acknowledged, the problem of fear not only always involves difficult and often obscure kinds of empirical evidence but also commits the observer to making certain kinds of judgements about the appropriateness of cognitions and emotions. These judgements remain open to fierce dispute, however much some observers may have assumed that further data-gathering would put an end to the argument. Furthermore, questions regarding the fear of crime have assumed a heavy polemical charge in recent theoretical and political debates. 'Fear' is thus a more open-textured and debatable theoretical construct than many criminologists seem ready to admit. In particular the development of a 'left realist' criminology has in large measure consisted in the attempts of the 'realists' to differentiate their views on the fear of crime from those of either earlier radical criminologies, now styled 'left idealism', on the one hand or of the 'new administrative criminology' (Young 1988: 306) on the other.

'Realist', 'idealist' and 'administrative' views of fear

While presenting his case for a 'realist' criminology, Young (1987) offers a rather brief and dismissive summation of 'left idealism' and its influence on criminological thought. He sees a close link between the thesis of 'moral panic' (which arguably became such a widespread trope of radical criminological discourse during the 1970s as to lose much of its original force) and what he terms the 'Great Denial' of the impact of crime on contemporary urban social life. The 'Great Denial', Young argues, let radical criminologists off the hook of giving any careful attention to crimes as social facts – as events with consequences. Instead it allowed them to indulge in an abstentionist politics of radical pessimism and to concentrate largely on discourse *about* crime and deviance, especially in the mass media. Young thus now tends to regard the notion of 'moral panic', as something to which societies 'appear to be subject every now and then' (S. Cohen 1972: 28), as explanatorily evasive and misleading. He argues against

> those idealist theories which portray moral panics as media insti-
> gated events without any rational basis and against those writers
> who talk glibly of irrational fears of crime without specifying what a
> rational fear would look like.
>
> (Young 1987: 338)

For those influenced by the 'Great Denial', Young considers, any assertion of the real consequences of victimization, including its attendant fears, was regarded as prima facie reactionary and as lending weight to the extension of strategies of surveillance and control.

Worse yet, Young further insists, the radical 'denial' unwittingly colluded with a parallel denial on the part of the 'new administrative criminology'. This too claimed to find disproportions between the level of threat and the existence of fear. Untoward fear is made to fill the apparent gap between measures of actual and perceived risks. Such a position sends the investigators off in search of the 'surplus' of fear, whether in the form of 'broken windows' (Wilson and Kelling 1982) or the existence of 'incivilities' (Maxfield 1984) or other 'perceptions of neighbourhood change' (Skogan and Maxfield 1981; see also the summary provided by Box et al 1988). These notions suggest that fear is extraneous, excessive, generated by something other than its ostensible objects, and to this extent irrational. Such views imply the existence of a hypothetically appropriate level of fear, from which notional expectation real fears deviate.

Young and other realists have several objections to these positions. They argue

1 that they are empirically false and that a more thorough and methodologically adequate understanding of the true extent of victimization reduces the scale of the apparent disparities or dissolves them altogether
2 that such arguments necessarily style certain fears, perhaps particularly those of women and elderly people, excessive or undue or fanciful, and that whether or not such fears are based on an empirically precise estimation of risk, this contradicts the realist theoretical premise that they are intelligibly related to 'the day-to-day lives of the fearful' (Young 1987: 348)
3 that these arguments sustain misleading political choices by encouraging strategies aimed at 'fear reduction', either by cosmetic improvements in the physical environment or by the heavier policing of incivility, independent of the real problems of risk reduction through effective crime prevention and the provision of more adequate and accountable service delivery by the police and other agencies.

So, the realists contend, the 'idealists' and the administrators have incorporated at least some of one another's assumptions. At bottom each of them asserts that a significant number of fearful citizens are simply mistaken in the way they have interpreted their relation to the social world and their exposure to risk. So far as the question of fear is concerned it is to this that realism fundamentally objects:

> Realism . . . believes that fragments of reality are re-contextualised just as they are in criminological theory itself. To take crime seriously, then, is not to reflect the public images of crime. But it is to say that there is a rational core to public concerns and images. That is, that popular conceptions of crime and policing are, in the main, constructed out of the material experiences of people rather than fantasies impressed upon them by the mass media or agencies of the State.
>
> (Young 1987: 337)

Perhaps the most important and controversial issue here concerns women's fear of crime. 'Realist' social surveys suggest that a proper account of women's subjection to domestic, work-related and other peripherally visible forms of victimization, their experience of other harassments and marginally criminal incivilities, their unsatisfactory experience of police protection and the multiplication of each of these problems by factors of race, class and age, entirely dispels the apparent disparity between risk and fear (Jones et al 1986; Crawford et al 1990: 40). Moreover, they insist, this directly contradicts 'the Home Office argument' (i.e.

the administrative line) which in minimizing the connection between crime and fear imputes irrationality to the fearful. And so, Young asks, 'Does not a seeming irrationality become transformed when we place it in terms of the real predicaments of the individuals involved?' (Young 1987: 349).

On the other hand it is an oddity that when so much of the realist argument depends on a concept of rationality the term itself is left largely unexamined and undefined. By default the notion of rationality functions in realist discourse to stipulate that a fear is fully 'rational' only if its existence is wholly accounted for by an antecedent level of objective risk. But such a view differs from earlier orthodoxies not on theoretical grounds but only in asserting that the risk really exists. I intend to argue that this view inherently simplifies the way that people in fact respond to their social and physical surroundings. In this sense it constitutes very much the kind of derogation of lay knowledge which the realists are concerned to avoid (MacLean 1989: 13; see also Giddens 1976: 71) and in so doing it distorts the nature and complexity of our ordinary knowledge of the world in an unrealistic way. Of course the administrators are even slacker in their use of the concept of rationality – or its cognate terms: warrantability, appropriateness, reasonableness, dueness – throughout the fear of crime literature, including in the publications surrounding the British Crime Survey (e.g. Maxfield 1984; Hough and Mayhew 1985). Not only the 'realists' but also their 'idealist' and 'administrative' antagonists tend to misapply the notion of rationality in relation to risk and fear.

In his dismissal of 'those writers who talk glibly about irrational fears', Young has raised the question of 'what a rational fear would look like' (1987: 349) but he has scarcely begun to answer it. Reiner has also alluded to this problem, but discovered that it is not so easily resolved:

> When is concern, and public policy directed towards it, to be ana-
> lyzed as a 'panic', as distinct from a reasonable response to a prob-
> lem? Hall *et al* speak of 'panic' when 'the official reaction to a
> person, groups of persons or series of events is *out of all proportion* to
> the actual threat offered'. But this reference to 'proportion' makes
> the concept an arbitrary value judgement unless it is solidly an-
> chored in both agreed criteria of proportionality and convincing
> evidence about the scale of 'the threat'.
>
> (Reiner 1988: 281)

Since the end of the 1970s (the period to which Reiner refers) there has been plenty of new information about dimensions of threat and even a good deal about the nature of public responses to threats, but precious little about the 'unanalyzed notion of proportionality' (Reiner 1988: 281) in the relation between them. The equation between the 'reality' of a risk and the appropriateness or rationality of an emotional or dispositional state called fear (or worry, or anxiety, or concern) is more complicated than research into fear of crime, which has needed some sort of working rule of thumb for making such judgements, has yet admitted. Moreover, in making such attributions criminological debate, including the work of the realists, has unduly simplified its notions of what fear actually is, or is like as a mode of experience and perception. Thus the level of empirical detail which research on fear of crime has furnished has not been matched by parallel conceptual development, and scope has arisen for confusion between questions which can be solved empirically (on the basis of current knowledge or further data gathering) and those which require theoretical elaboration and interpretation.

It is questionable, therefore, whether Young is justified in asserting that the fear of crime, in whatever area, is a *rational* matter in any strong sense. None of the usual definitions of risk – for example that it is the product of the probability of an event multiplied by the severity of the harm which would result from it (Campbell 1980) – really settles the question of when it is reasonable to be worried or fearful (Douglas 1986: 20). Indeed, one of the strangest features of fear-of-crime debates is the extent to which the participants imagine that people *ought* somehow to be able to calculate what risk they run of becoming a victim. What from the point of view of an outside observer looks like an actuarially calculable risk is, from the point of view of any individual (potential victim), more like a simple case of *uncertainty*. The notion of risk strictly speaking is really intelligible only in a situation 'governed by known probabilities' (Douglas 1986: 43). At the same time, however, and for a similar reason, those who argue that the fear of crime is *undue* or *excessive* or *irrational* (see Wright 1985 for an example) are usually also too hasty. As Young makes plain, they speak as though an appropriate level of fear were empirically decidable when in fact it involves particularly difficult and contestable judgements.

Perhaps then anxiety about crime is at times as much a product of uncertainty itself as of risk. Or at least different senses of the term 'fear' may be operative for different circumstances and groups of people, so that women's fear might differ from men's, or the fears of the elderly from those of the young, not just in 'quantity' but in kind (see Hanmer and Saunders 1984; Box et al 1988; Stanko 1990). In most cases what we mean by fear of crime is not so much a calculation of probabilities as a set of 'intuitions' (J. Cohen 1981) grounded in experience. This much is close to Young's views (Young 1987: 349). However, since fear is an intuitive mode of perception we cannot restrict a priori the set of experiences which may be relevant to it: indeed the more pervasive fear is the more likely it is that its constitution is open to influences which extend beyond induction from first-hand past experience. Let us then begin by agreeing that many of our fears (perhaps especially, but not only, women's fears of male violence) are indeed well founded (Hanmer and Saunders 1984). But let us not imagine that fear of crime stands alone: that it exists only as a result of direct personal experience; that it can be separated out from other experiences and hazards and troubles. Fear, like other human interpretations of the world, generally 'exceeds the information given' (Tuan 1979). It is deeply implicated in our more general sense of well-being or otherwise in the environments in which we find ourselves. It is unevenly distributed, but it is not the prerogative of a few. Rather, the fear of crime takes its place amongst the 'anxieties which press in on everyone' in modern societies (Giddens 1990: 49).

Risk-perception

Analysts of risk-perception have long known that not all risks which are equally probable receive equal attention or concern (see Von Neumann and Morgenstern 1953). Instead, just how much any individual focuses on certain risks depends upon the place those risks hold in a given culture, where culture means, according to Douglas, an 'actively invoked conventional wisdom' (1986: 66). The risk of crime, it would appear, is more publicly salient than, say, the risks of domestic accidents: and some crimes are more salient than others. Perhaps the interest which we generally pay to the reporting of crime, or to its representation in stories, is similar to our attention to rumour and gossip: it reflects both our need for information and for conventions within which to frame and interpret our knowledge. The modes of reporting and talk with which we are familiar are 'heuristics' (Douglas 1986: 79) for framing bits of information and fragments of experience about things which concern us.

I believe that it follows from this that we need not accept a direct opposition between 'realism' (and hence rational choice and perception) and other modes of perception, however much realist criminology seems to insist that we should. Fear of crime does not necessarily become either unreal or unreasonable simply because we stop seeing the chances of falling victim to crime as its only determinant, even if most of us might want to reserve the right to see fears as excessive or damaging (and hence unreasonable) under certain circumstances. Conversely, there is no need to deny that people are indeed subject to definite risks in order to agree that crime and justice carry cultural and political meanings which precede and extend beyond our direct encounters with them. Indeed, one may conjecture, the more fearful people become, whether this is directly in proportion to the risks they run or not, the more urgent and important such meanings are likely to become for them. Douglas (1986) thus gives grounds for supposing that those people who are already fearful may also be the most likely to seek out information, gossip, rumour and stories which bear upon the things which concern them, in that they have need of such 'heuristics' for ordering and understanding their own troubling thoughts and feelings.

In this regard, in the course of an exhaustive consideration of risk-perceptions in a number of spheres, Douglas reaches the reverse conclusion from that which criminologists seem generally to have presupposed. She argues that the problem of risk-perception can *never* be wholly settled by drawing up an inventory of objective risks, no matter how precise. Furthermore, there is also always another set of questions beyond those conventionally posed in survey accounts of the determination of fears. These include: what consequences actually follow for everyday domestic and public life in settings where the fear of crime is a salient feature of people's daily awareness? To what sources of information, reassurance or distraction do people turn in seeking to cope with fear? More particularly, the question arises afresh of how crime and justice are located, represented or discussed in the wider cultural and political realms. Is there a sense in which the distribution of fears either motivates or constrains the availability, plausibility or acceptance of particular images, stories, rhetorics and political programmes? As Pearson comments at the end of his historical retrospection on 'respectable fears':

> This is why I have laboured the figurative and metaphorical dimensions of the arguments that are arranged around the criminal question, because of the way in which they focus our perceptions in such a way as to diminish whole areas of social experience, except insofar as these are thought to cause crime and disorder.
>
> (Pearson 1983: 239)

One of the benefits of focusing on particular forms of communication or representation is to refine attention to the ways in which these 'arguments arranged around the criminal question' may be channelled, taken up and used by their various publics.

Diffusion and interpretation in the construction of fear

For all their differences, 'realist' criminology and Gerbner's 'cultivation analysis' might at least agree that, in complex societies, the question of social distance, which falls between events, their representation in talk, print or pictures and their reception by disparate groups, cannot lightly be disposed of. One continuing reason for the relevance of media studies to criminology is provided by the recognition that the significance of any criminal event need not be confined to those immediately involved, but that it can be relayed to other sites within the social formation and is open to multiple interpretations. Neither Young's viewpoint nor Gerbner's can show that there is a necessary limit to these processes of relaying and reinterpreting. There remains, therefore, inherent scope for discrepancy between what criminal events mean at the moment of their commission and what they stand for once they have entered the widening circles of punishment, reporting, rhetoric and rebuttal, election platforms and the multitude of communicative exchanges which compose the public sphere. This is in fact the force of the example which Young offers of the 'suburban soul' (1987: 338) whose risks of falling victim to violent crime may be relatively low but for whom it may nevertheless be a quite acute preoccupation. Are we then to assume that only city dwellers are rational and that the suburbanite's fear can be dismissed as fantasy? If we do not make this assumption, then other considerations, of the kind Douglas points out, come into play.

It can be argued, therefore, that the main currents of concern with crime, mass media and fear within both criminology and media studies share a common limitation. Current debates centre on the realism or otherwise of fear; they calibrate levels of fear against indices of exposure to risk of feared outcomes. This is a legitimate concern, but it is by no means exhaustive. Fear is not simply a quantity, of which one possesses larger or smaller amounts: rather, it is a mode of perception, even perhaps a constitutive feature of personal identity (see Glass 1989). To be fearful, that is to say, is to approach and interpret the world in particular ways. To this extent, it is rarely fully accurate to speak of fear as having been 'caused', even by a specific precipitating event; nor is it always appropriate to interpret fearfulness solely in terms of the objects to which it ostensibly attaches. This being so, it would seem less appropriate to view fears of crime among those who are not much at risk of becoming victims as, in any simple sense, 'irrational', than to see such fears as also intelligibly summarizing a range of more diffuse anxieties about one's position and identity in the world. Equally, even among those for whom risks are very great (and perhaps with the important exception of chronic marital violence) the threat itself is not ever-present and visible, even if the sense of threat never goes away. In this respect the issue of the fear of crime always involves problems of representation and meaning: it concerns the way in which people understand the fear-inducing environment which they are forced to inhabit. The presence of specific fears also tends to presuppose the existence of more general experiences of anxiety, unease and lack of well-being. Indeed, as Tuan comments in differentiating between 'alarm' and 'anxiety', anxiety as a generalized 'presentiment of danger' (1979: 5) is particularly problematic because it is difficult to take decisive action against it. Furthermore, Tuan remarks, 'Imagination adds immeasurably to the kinds and intensity of fear in the human world' (1979: 5). This being so, I shall argue, the full social and personal consequences of fear and anxiety can never be deduced from the simple enumeration of risks. Like other human experiences they necessarily involve representation, communication and the attribution of significance, and it is for this reason that the understanding of the character and uses of mass media may be able not simply to help explain the distribution of expressed fears but also to illuminate their nature and implications.

'Crisis', crime and the media

In the course of his analysis of apocalyptic modes of fiction in *The Sense of an Ending* (1967) Kermode speaks of twentieth-century literary and social criticism as being marked by a 'perpetual assumption of crisis' whose main manifestation lies in chronic difficulties in 'the justification of ideas of order' (1967: 124). The phrase 'perpetual assumption of crisis' is an interesting one. First, there is a tension between the notions of acuteness, suddenness and immediacy usually associated with the term 'crisis', for example in medicine, and conversely the sense that the crisis is 'perpetual'. Second, there is the assertion that the crisis consists in an 'assumption'. This suggests that it is located mainly at the level of thought and feeling and seems to bracket the question of whether it derives from objective social and political conditions. These ambiguities suggest that 'the crisis', wherever it originates, is not one that admits of any conclusive resolution. A number of authors including Lasch (1980) and MacIntyre (1981) claim to locate something like a crisis in 'the justification of ideas of order' in the attenuation of agreed modes of debate and participation in a public sphere, whose place is increasingly colonized by managerial and technicist ideologies. In Lasch's view this results in a growth of 'privatism' (1980: 25). That is, involvement in public affairs tends to be supplanted by a retreat towards an introspective preoccupation with the care and development of the self. Meanwhile, Lasch argues, forays into the public realm tend to become marked either by modish and cultic enthusiasms or reactionary nostalgia. Lasch specifically views various contemporary forms of privatism (he is mainly interested in the cult of 'self-awareness' in American society) as reactions away from 'the warlike conditions which pervade American society, from the danger and uncertainty that surround us, from the loss of confidence in the future' (1980: 26). Evidently, these allegations of a rather general perception of 'crisis' are not identical with the fear of crime as such. Neither are such arguments by any means easy to validate empirically, although Lasch provides a good deal of suggestive corroboration. However, if they can be shown to have a solid basis, such considerations are likely to have a considerable bearing on questions at issue here. Much of what follows is devoted to providing support for the following suggestions:

First, public responses to crime and their expression in political contests over law and order are central to conflicts in the justification of ideas of order (see Dahrendorf 1985).

Second, the fear of crime – especially if it is acute enough to lead to the evacuation of public space – is likely to encourage some form of 'privatism'.

Third, many of the relevant issues can be conceived in terms of the relation between public and private spheres of activity. If the public political sphere demonstrates a preoccupation with the justification of ideas of order, and these are expressed for example in appeals to discipline and severity in matters of crime and punishment, the success of the relevant rhetorics may in turn be predicated on the extent of fear and anxiety within the private domain. Equally, if fear does encourage privatism and withdrawal it may be that this in turn engenders increasing reliance on television and its representations, whether for informational purposes, distraction or emotional satisfactions. The question then concerns the mechanisms which mediate between the public and private spheres, the terms on which they do so, and the consequences this has on either side of the public–private boundary. However it is interpreted, the restructuring of practices of both leisure and public participation through the extension of electronic media and other domestic technologies constitutes a real difference between contemporary social life and that of any earlier period.

Privatism and social anxiety

The massive development of television and its associated industries has historically coincided with a period of chronic, and sporadically acute, anxiety about crime and policing. Such anxieties, as Pearson has convincingly shown (1983; see also Tuan 1979), are in no sense new or unique to our own period. However, their recent scale, form and distribution none the less call for a particular and contemporary effort of interpretation. The massive preoccupation demonstrated by television and other media with crime speaks to these anxieties in certain definite ways. Such anxieties, however, are by no means equally distributed throughout the social formation: but neither is the unevenness of their distribution entirely explicable by the distribution of criminal events themselves. Hence we may suggest that different sub-populations relate to crime, to information about and representations of it and, moreover, to the media which carry those representations, in distinct ways. As I go on to show in Chapter 3, among those whose anxiety (expressed in but not confined to a sense of vulnerability to crime) is most acute, concern about social order is particularly prone to being translated into concern about crime on television. That is to say, the medium itself becomes the focus for social anxiety and political controversy, and its representations are made subject to demands for increased regulation.

Thus, for example, Mary Whitehouse charts declining 'moral standards' since the Second World War largely in terms of successive eras of television. Hence, it may be too restrictive to suppose that the involvement of television in stimulating or assuaging social anxiety can be wholly confined to anxiety about victimization as such. Crime fiction in particular characteristically makes crime and law enforcement stand for wider aspects of the world: there simply is no morally or factually neutral language in which to narrate stories of crime and punishment. Rather, the range of outlooks which, on the one hand, generate narratives and, on the other, are brought to them by their audiences stipulate, interpretations of the world, its dangers and conditions under which security can be restored. It is thus appropriate to contextualize 'cop shows' in terms of the history of moral tales which have surrounded and underwritten successive forms of penality (see Chapter 2). Looked at in this way the question of how crime and law enforcement are represented in mass media and the part played by that representation in the construction of public perceptions of crime is much less separate and self-sufficient from its surrounding cultural and political matrices than researchers have tended to assume (for example in the bulk of the research which I review in Chapter 4). My larger argument, therefore, is that the issue of the relation between television and fear is itself intelligible only when it is understood in terms of the position of crime as a discursive area in contemporary cultural life. The role of television is both important and difficult to pin down partly because it subverts our received distinctions between public and private spheres of activity.

Mass media and the public sphere

Recent contributions in the sociology of mass media have become increasingly concerned with the question of whether modern media can or do constitute a 'public sphere' (Elliott 1982; Garnham 1986; Schlesinger et al 1989). Most discussions of this topic begin from Habermas's formulation of the 'classic bourgeois public sphere' (Habermas 1974: 178). For Habermas the public sphere comes into being whenever 'private individuals assemble to form a public body' in which they may 'confer in unrestrained fashion'. Such considerations have been basic to the importance in recent social thought of the theorization of citizenship itself. Turner (1990), for example, proposes a typology of forms of citizenship which attends not only to the possession of legal rights and liberties but also to the historically variable extent of public participation and activity (1990: 209). In the most optimistic accounts, especially those of Scannell (1986; 1988; 1989), broadcasting not only replicates features of Habermas's 'classic bourgeois public sphere', but also extends their availability to an enormously larger and more socially inclusive range of people. Thus, Scannell insists that broadcasting contributes fundamentally to the 'democratization of everyday life' (1989: 135) by rendering the world 'ordinary, mundane, accessible, knowable, familiar, recognizable, shareable and communicable for whole populations' (1989: 152). Broadcasting, Scannell contends, 'brings public life into private life and private life into public life, for pleasure and enjoyment as much as for information and education' (1989: 143).

It is possible to accept, however, that broadcasting systems do indeed subvert the public–private dichotomy without sharing Scannell's lyrically optimistic view of the process. Indeed the predominant tone of such discussions has historically been morose and doom-laden (Postman 1986). Scannell passes over some serious problems in the stratification of both access and reception, and especially the consequences of continuing 'knowledge gaps' between those who are 'rich' and 'poor' in information. Garnham, for example, provides a more modulated account in arguing that the defence and extension of the possibilities of broadcasting as constitutive of the public sphere also involves recognizing its current limits and asymmetries (1986: 52–3). In particular, Garnham draws attention to the danger that television will provide the 'locus' for

> an increasingly privatized, domestic mode of consumption, by the creation of a two-tier market divided between the information rich, provided with high-cost specialized information and cultural services and the information poor, provided with increasingly homogenized entertainment series on a mass scale.
>
> (Garnham, 1986: 38)

Pepinsky (1987) has extended such an argument in a way which is directly germane to my current concerns. He argues that the very notion of participation in a public sphere rests on a presumption that a 'propensity to share information' is basic to human sociability (1987: 82). However, Pepinsky suggests that where information flows unequally or is 'blocked', then mutual fear and suspicion are among the likely results, stemming from the 'thinning' of social relations to which Christie alludes (Christie 1981; Pepinsky 1987: 83). Hence, if criminology is interested in public perceptions of crime, including such issues as the distribution of fear, then it must also interest itself in the communicative means and resources available to people and through which such perceptions and representations are actively constructed. How do the great public dramas of crime and law enforcement actually enter private life, and what process of translation do they undergo in order to do so? Thus, the questions to which criminologists and sociologists of mass communication must jointly attend include: what consequences would follow for both public and private life if the primary channels of public communication and exchange are much preoccupied with themes of fear and anxiety (see Ericson et al 1987; Glass 1989; Schlesinger et al 1989; Garland 1990b)?

Television, criminology and 'modernization'

Orthodox criminology has generally eschewed such speculations as those provided, for example, by Lasch, MacIntyre and others. Only under the impetus provided by the radical criminologies of the 1970s did the 'assumption of crisis' and its political correlates begin to receive serious attention. Cohen's innovation in *Folk Devils and Moral Panics* (1972) was to point to the discrepancy between the dimensions of threat and their wider public perception as a space in which the ideological work of mass media took place. The perspective thus initiated achieved its fullest development in Hall et al's *Policing the Crisis* (1978). However, some recognition of a relationship between television, crime and social anxiety was present at the margins of the British criminological tradition as early as Mannheim's *Comparative Criminology*. Mannheim offers an extended account of television as an indicator of social trends and harbinger of anomie (1965: 422–505). Television is seen by Mannheim as symptomatic of the shock of modernization. It both represents the gratifications of affluence and stimulates the sense of relative deprivation (see also Fyvel 1961: 108–10).

'Violence on TV' and the allegation of moral decay

What Mannheim's position could not anticipate or explain is the field of forces involved in the collision between a persistent unease over the powers which mass media, especially television, have been presumed to exert and deepening disquiet in public perceptions of crime and law enforcement, crystallizing from time to time in the recurrent ferocity of debates about 'violence on television'. Similarly, although there is a very large body of research devoted to 'effects' of television on crime it offers little insight into the conditions of existence of the debate itself. Thus, although 'TV violence' was, as Raymond Williams remarks (1974), throughout the late 1960s and early 1970s one of the most extensively researched and best-funded areas in the whole of social science, this entire body of work is virtually devoid of any comment on why this should have been so. The quantitative and technical orientation of 'effects' research precludes any systematic attention to the political matrices in which it originates. In fact the argument advanced by Klapper in 1962 that no behavioural effects of viewing could be demonstrated was for some years the orthodox view, and revival of interest in the area was almost entirely political in origin. The revival was stimulated in part by polemical remarks by J. Edgar Hoover, then head of the FBI. The issue was debated in a US Senate sub-committee chaired by Senator J. Pastore. The first wave of resulting interest culminated in 1972 with the report of the Surgeon General's Scientific Advisory Committee, *Television and Growing Up*, a document surrounded by special pleading and compromise (see Cater and Strickland 1975; Rowland 1983). The fact that its empirical claims were modest almost to a fault did not prevent a further massive renewal of interest in the area. In 1982 Pearl et al claimed to find 2,500 academic contributions on the subject in the intervening decade. To this extent interest in 'violence on television' has always extended well beyond the concerns of academic researchers. This is one reason why a debate which has often seemed repetitious and intellectually stagnant has stubbornly refused to die. It is thus insufficient for academic commentators to dismiss continuing public concern over 'TV violence' as a simple mistake since the retailing of competing findings is only obliquely relevant to the real motor of the debate. Rather, I shall argue (especially in Chapter 3) that what has often been at stake is a contest over the interpretation of the medium itself, over the meanings of its artefacts and over the sense that it is in some way related to other aspects of social change which are unwelcome to the protagonists.

As Muccigrosso argues (1979: 35), the debate over the malign effects of television effectively begins in the USA in the late 1950s: that is at the moment of 'saturation' of the entire national territory by the networks (see also Rowland 1983; Kreiling 1984; Rowland and Watkins 1984). Hirsch (1976) suggests that the most popular medium of mass entertainment at any given historical moment tends also to provide the focus of the most intense social anxiety. Thus the fears attaching to the growth of television may be historically continuous with those which in earlier eras surrounded music halls, penny dreadfuls, silent cinema and so forth (see Pearson 1983; 1984). In Britain the debate about the harmful effects of television begins in earnest a few years later, given impetus by the arrival of commercial television in 1954 and the consequent challenge to the established position of the Reithian BBC, and signalled most clearly by the initiation in 1964 of the 'Clean up TV' campaign (see Chapter 3).

To a large extent the most vociferous expressions of concern about the harms wrought by television and other media cluster at the conservative margins of the polity (Wallis 1976; Pratt and Sparks 1987). Moral enterprise about television is marked by a constant ambivalence between the need to claim to represent the 'silent majority' and an express sense of dissidence in the face of a prevailing 'permissiveness' (S. Hall 1980a). Yet the sense of unease also extends more widely than such pockets of resistance. The notion of permissiveness implies deterioration in civility, and in sexual and other conduct; such deterioration is usually viewed as finding expression in rising crime, especially among the young. The chief legal and other public battles about permissiveness have always centred on questions of publishing, broadcasting and public display: this is partly because moral enterprise itself shrewdly acknowledges its need for access to mass media, partly also because the very notion of permissiveness is a reaction to actual or presumed changes in familiar modes of representation and communication. The rhetorical weight of 'permissiveness' as a rallying cry thus requires a prior sense of unease about social order and cultural continuity (see Chapter 3).

The development by radical criminologists of both studies of crime reporting (S. Cohen and Young 1973; Chibnall 1977) and revisionist histories of policing (P. Cohen 1979: Gatrell et al 1980; Reiner 1985) has responded to and charted the growth of an entrenched presumption of a progressively degenerating 'law and order' situation. As Reiner reports, the issue of the legitimacy and effectiveness of the police, largely absent from public debate in the inter-war years, returned in a striking way in the 1960s:

> From a position of almost complete invisibility as a political issue, policing has become a babble of scandalous revelation, controversy and competing agendas for reform. . . . The tacit contract between police and public, so delicately drawn between the 1850s and the 1950s had begun to fray glaringly by 1981.
>
> (Reiner 1985: 61)

The conditions underlying such developments continue to be hotly debated by students of crime and law enforcement (S. Hall et al 1978; Lea and Young 1984; Reiner 1985; Scraton 1987). What is clear for present purposes is that shifts in the manifest public debates about law and order find echoes in the representation of crime and policing in television and other media, in fiction as well as reportage (Hurd 1979; Murdock 1982; Reiner 1985; Clarke 1986). The question is thus raised of the precise nature of the connection between these representations, and the moralities embedded within them and the wider problems of politics and consciousness around which they circulate.

Law enforcement and the 'sense of crisis'

The most extensive discussion of these topics remains that provided by Hall et al in *Policing the Crisis* (1978). Hall et al argue that it is possible to identify a concrete relation between the representation in press reporting of a specific moment in the development of public anxiety about crime, namely the 'mugging panic' of the early 1970s, and the growth of a more general sense of social and political 'crisis'. In the case in point, they argue, the events which initiate the 'panic' are dramatized against a repertoire of motifs about public safety and national identity, crystallizing in a horrified condemnation of the mugger. Thus, the reporting of crime has consequences both for the practical conduct of criminal justice (in the severity of sentencing, in the use and distribution of police time and resources) and for the politics of law and social order in a wider sense. The imagery of crime and law enforcement also broaches questions of social cohesion, solidarity and authority beyond and beneath its manifest content, especially where a 'signification spiral' (S. Hall et al 1978: 76) provides that the existence of 'crisis' becomes a given of public discourse about crime. Thus, Hall et al argue, it is a mistake to make a sharp separation between the realm of representation and that of the practical conduct of affairs:

> The crystallising of 'public opinion' is . . . raised to a more formal level by the networks of the mass media. It is true that, in societies like ours, individuals often live highly segmented lives, embedded in local traditions and networks. But it is also true that, precisely in such societies, the networks which *connect* are pivotal. Events, issues only become *public* in the full sense when the means exist whereby the separate worlds of professional and lay opinion, of controller and controlled, are brought into relation with one another, and appear, for a time at least, to occupy the same space. It is communication and communication networks that create that complex creature we call 'public opinion'.
>
> (S. Hall et al 1978: 136)

One of the most deeply embedded themes which Hall et al identify as generating the specific form of crime reporting is a persistent ambivalence about the nature of urban life:

> The city is above all the concrete embodiment of the achievements of industrial civilization. . . . The 'state of the city' is, in a sense, the 'tide-mark' of civilization; it embodies our civilization and the degree to which we are successful in maintaining that level of achievement.
>
> (S. Hall et al 1978: 145)

Where the dominant representation of the city becomes that of the stage upon which criminal events are enacted then each discrete event resounds with a general significance about dislocation, decline and the destabilizing of social organization. Hall et al's postulate that the city stands for what our civilization is means that a concentration on the city as a site of violence and danger suggests a general crisis of authority.

Hall et al seek to draw some ambitious conclusions from these reflections, namely that the diffusion throughout the social body of the sense of 'crisis' is sufficient to constitute a general crisis of the state. The state responds, they argue, through 'a modification in the modes of hegemony' registered as a 'tilt in the operation of the state away from consent towards the pole of coercion . . . an "exceptional moment" in the "normal" form of the late capitalist state' (Hall et al 1978: 217). Thus, changes in the representation of crime and law enforcement are actively instrumental in producing changes in the manifest public political sphere. Hall et al's analysis clearly provides a more stratified and sophisticated discussion of crime, the media and social anxiety than those previously offered by orthodox (or indeed radical) criminologists. They offer an attempt to identify some material consequences of the embeddedness of crime as a theme in public discourse while avoiding the usual weakness in radical criminology's characterization of moral panics as things which from time to time happen to come and go.

The sense of crisis and the place of fiction

A number of empirical and theoretical problems and omissions remain, some of which can be substantially corrected and supplemented by a new reconsideration of crime fiction and drama.

The first of these returns us to the question I raised at the outset, namely that of the real bases of fear of crime and the possible ways of explaining the distribution of fear. From the perspective of the challenge mounted by 'left realism' Hall et al are simply too hasty in assuming the unreality or excessiveness of fear and anxiety (see Reiner 1988: 281). However, it would be quite wrong to suppose that this is a conclusive objection, since it does not logically preclude the wider consideration which Hall et al aim to provide of the uses of anxiety within the political culture as a whole.

The second argument is that Hall et al equivocate in their characterization of 'the crisis': they assert a 'general crisis of the state' as a manifestation of structural contradictions. Elsewhere, however, they reduce 'the crisis' to a ruse of statecraft, a particular moment in which 'the social order *represents itself as* powerfully challenged, threatened or undermined in some fundamental way by crime' (S. Hall et al 1978: 31) (emphasis added). This leads to a confusion as to whether the range of conflicts, crimes and political oppositions to which they allude really constitute an 'exhaustion of consent' (1978: 218), and hence a crisis in hegemony, or whether they belong together only in the sense that they are yoked together in ideology (1978: 257). It is arguable that the oscillation between these points leads to a depiction of the crisis which is both too specific, in terms of time and the discontinuity of 'the moment of force' (1978: 219) from the preceding period, and too general, in terms of scope and scale. The role which Hall et al assign to the media (by which they mean newspaper coverage almost exclusively) is thus an instrumental one (see Garland 1990a). Their stress is on the *policing* of the crisis and on the justification by the media, *qua* ideological state apparatus, of increased surveillance and coercion.

Yet newspaper reporting is not the only form in which mass media present images of crime and law enforcement to the audience. A consideration of the nature of contemporary fictional representations of crime and punishment on television not only extends our knowledge of such imagery but also suggests a rather different emphasis. The fictional narration of thematics of crime and law enforcement stands in a more oblique relation to the immediacy of current concerns than do news, documentary and polemic. This does not mean that they are any the less fundamental, however; only that the effort of translation between their manifest appearance and the underlying principles of their operation is more complicated and less clear-cut, and that it is unwise to foreclose the range of meanings which they may be taken to carry. This in turn stipulates attention to irony and ambiguity. It allows that the positions which the fiction may occupy in the lives of its audience may vary markedly, even in apparently paradoxical ways. It also suggests that the infiltration, through the media, of notions of crime, law and order into everyday life cannot be restricted to their direct bearing on manifest public concerns but rather may extend deep into domestic and private spaces. Nor can the relations between these private and public spheres be specified a priori; yet neither can they easily be separated. For instance, Ericson et al (1987) show in detail that there is a demand for narrative in Press reporting of crime which to a significant extent parallels that in fictional modes: the most 'satisfactory' news story is also a literal *story*. It may thus be that the expectation of narrative resolution in fiction frames the expectations which are brought to the reporting of real events. Equally, it may be that the audience turns to crime fiction precisely in consolation for the messy inconclusiveness of the process of justice in the world and its obdurate failure to conform to morally or aesthetically satisfying patterns.

In either case it is not fanciful to argue that the 'realism' of fiction and the dramatisation of news are connected matters. In this regard it is unfortunate that Hall et al only explicitly refer in passing to the dramaturgy of crime as public spectacle when they speak of 'a modern morality play' in which the guardians of order 'symbolically cast out the devil' (S. Hall et al 1978: 66). It is easy to see how this relates to particular features of their argument, especially in so far as they are concerned with the role played by the press in the identification and targetting of such 'devils'. Yet the detail of relations between the play of social moralities in media representations of crime and the 'morality play' as such remain to be explored. More pointedly, there is no automatic relationship between the notion of a 'morality play' and that of a specific 'crisis of the state'. Rather, the invocation of the idea of crime as drama reminds us that representations which are unique to any particular historical moment can be grafted on to a structure which is more basic and more durable, and which envisions the casting out of the devil as a virtual universal of social life, endlessly repeated.

For these reasons the persuasive analysis which Hall et al provide of certain connections between modes of reporting, the diffusion of social anxiety and aspects of political rhetorics of law and order look unduly literal and causal when applied to fiction. The fundamental difficulty in accounting for the place of popular modes of fiction in everyday life lies

in tracing the transformations between the prevalence of certain fundamental forms and their realization in particular instances which at some
level claim to represent a recognizable world.

Fear and anxiety must emerge again here as they are always key terms
in the analysis of crime fiction, especially in relation to television. The
argument (which I have already raised) that for at least a fraction of its
audience the medium itself is a focus of anxiety, is thus only part of the
story. For the implications of narratives of crime and law enforcement are
always in varying degrees unnerving or reassuring, and the extent to
which they are experienced as pleasurable lies largely in the dialectic
between these terms. Thus, the debate about whether or not television
'causes' fear of crime (see Chapter 4) suffers from a failure to recognize
that the narrative is directed towards precisely the area of tension between anxiety and resolution. This is what Adorno has in mind when he
remarks that detective fictions 'charm away' the challenge of disorder
(quoted by Swingewood 1977: 17).

Television crime fiction and the politics of law and order

The ideological weight of crime fiction seems likely to relate to the kinds
of tension between transgression and retribution which narratives generate, the relations of commentary and justification in which these representations stand to the experience of such conflicts in the world and the
terms on which the narrative crisis is resolved. As the foregoing reflections suggest, not the least important elements in providing the context
for the reception of crime on television are that, first, the audience knows
full well that 'violence on television' is itself construed as a social problem
and, second, that the presumption of a progressively degenerating 'law
and order' situation is an entrenched feature of journalism and punditry.

In this regard, Clarke (1983; 1986) points to some relations, albeit uneven ones, between changing public perceptions of the dimensions of the
crime problem, the development of new styles and strategies of policing
and changes in the mode of representation itself. A number of observers
(notably Holdaway 1979; Reiner 1985) cite the introduction of the Unit
Beat System of patrol in the mid-1960s, and the consequent erosion of the
doctrine of constabulary independence (Tobias 1979), as a critical moment
in this chronology. If the supersession of beat policing by the Unit Beat
System in the mid-1960s was the single most important shift in post-war
British policing, its reverberations also rang echoes in the presentation of
policing on television. The withdrawal of the police-officer into the panda
car necessarily lessened the extent of public interaction with the police,
and presented a less reassuring image of the police-officer's role and
powers. The common law tradition of the constable as little more than an
ordinary citizen in uniform could no longer be sustained. Parallel changes

have been identified in the police culture itself (Reiner 1985), reinforcing police commitment to what Skolnick and Woodworth (1967) call 'the symbolic rights of chase, search and capture'. At the same time these very changes in the relationship between police and public, themselves the source of some anxiety, also made the public more dependent on mass media for knowledge or reassurance (see Wilkins 1964; S. Hall 1976). One need not suppose that policing in the foregoing period had really been so consensually accepted as 'Whig' historians are wont to suggest (Critchley 1978), simply that the erstwhile preferred ideal images of the 'British Bobby' have become more difficult to sustain. A number of otherwise disparate commentators agree on at least one point: if the first half of the twentieth century was a period of generally rather high police legitimacy, the return of more widespread unease and mistrust since the 1960s constituted a real and rather marked change in public perception (Reiner 1985; Jefferson 1987; Morris 1989).

George Dixon, the fictional character whom many regard as having provided the epitome of the citizen-constable, became, in a sense, obsolete during his own screen lifetime. The earlier mode of presentation ceded place to a nostalgic and wistful sense that Dixon represented a doomed species. As Clarke (1983: 45) observes, Dixon constituted a sufficiently powerful motif that the *Financial Times* could include in its account of the 1981 riots a lamentation for the passing of 'the George Dixon type of policing'. Clarke continues:

> Such is the power of media imagery that this description could still be used to summon up not just the memory of a popular entertainment but a style of policing the 'real' crime problem. In fact the nature of the common sense understanding of the crime problem seems to be peculiarly open to such connections between a little known 'real' and a widely viewed world of fictional realism.
>
> (Clarke 1983: 45)

From the very small body of work which has yet treated the cop show form on British screens with any seriousness at the levels of representation and historical development (Hurd 1979; Murdock 1982; Clarke 1983; 1986; Reiner 1985) a fairly clear chronology emerges. In the first instance British realist television productions sought to track the perceived changes in patterns of actual policing; but in the course of time the realist imperative was itself attenuated. One tends to see a decline in the prestige within fiction of the uniformed branch and increasing interest in CID (from Dixon to Z Cars) and thence to a concentration on the activities of more specialized services (Special Branch, Flying Squad). Clarke comments:

> It should be remembered that the concept of 'serious crime' had assumed particular connotations by the early 1970s: it referred to

crimes involving large amounts of money and large amounts of violence and usually both. *The Sweeney* legitimated the transition to violence as part of the routine of police work by locating the fiction within the framework of that section of the police force most likely to deal with violence in the course of its work. The Flying Squad was an ideal vehicle for this fictional representation both in terms of the internal logistics of the genre and the concerns of the law and order debate outside of the series.

(Clarke 1986: 221)

This confers two strictly dramatic advantages in that, first, it permits the creation of a harsher, more combative hero and second, the increasing distance of the sphere of dramatic action from public experience affords greater dramatic licence, more schematic narratives, more action and less contamination by the equivocations of the real. It is a particular irony that the demand for a new definition of the aesthetic sufficiency or plausibility in the representation of policing resulted in the ever greater removal of the sphere of action from everyday experience and concerns. Beyond the Flying Squad lie all manner of more or less fictitious special services whose ethos and vigorous mode of action is not seriously compromised by any reality principle (e.g. *The Professionals*: see Murdock 1982; Clarke 1986: 47).

These movements have also responded to developments originating in the United States. The American experience bears witness to a somewhat similar pattern: from the quasi-naturalism of the 1960s 'procedurals' (*The Untouchables, Dragnet*) to the 'new wave' of the 1970s (*Kojak, Columbo, Rockford, Starsky and Hutch*). Clarke claims to trace a distinct line of descent in this transition between the 'procedural' and the 'action series' from changes in conventions of depiction first seen in the cinema, especially in the later Western. The introduction of vivid violence in the films of Leone, Peckinpah and Penn, for example, suggests to Clarke and others (e.g. French 1977) a dissolution of the settled moral and aesthetic conventions of the classic Western, implying a demand for a more restless and mannered representation, often known – especially with reference to Peckinpah's films – as hyper-realism. Clint Eastwood, as Clarke points out, is clearly a mediating figure: witness the quite rapid transition from the 'man with no name' of the 1960s Spaghetti Westerns, via the ruthless Arizonan cowboy policeman displaced in New York in *Coogan's Bluff* (1968) to 'Dirty Harry' Callaghan (*Dirty Harry*, 1971; *Magnum Force*, 1973) (Clarke 1986: 221).

By the early 1970s the cop show had entirely supplanted the Western as the dominant genre of narrative fiction on US television (Barnouw 1975; Gitlin 1985), largely on the basis of its superior 'demographics'. The cop show drew an audience which was not necessarily larger but which had a younger, more affluent, urban profile. The urban audience seemed to prefer to the traditional Western myths of the foundation of the law in American frontier history the *contemporary* mythology of the enforcement of the law in the recognizable city.

The arch figures of the 'new wave' of American television policemen were perhaps Kojak and Starsky and Hutch. Television here not only follows developments in cinema and adopts elements of both technique and content (at least one episode of *Starsky and Hutch* plagiarizes the plot of *Dirty Harry*) but also tends to domesticate them. Kojak is as hard-pressed by the tide of crime as Eastwood's Harry Callaghan, but he is also humorous and graceful. It is this aspect of the iconography of policing that leads Martin Williams to observe that 'against the image of the crumbling city' (1982: 140) the cop show has created a number of liminal figures whose magical interventions not only solve the crime but also symbolically reconstitute the integrity of the social body into the bargain.

Clarke traces developments in the British context as more distant sequels of the same transitions, but inflected by specifically British concerns and anxieties. In arguing thus he concentrates on the great gulf between the policing of London as envisaged in *Dixon of Dock Green* and *The Sweeney*. (It is a great distance in sensibility but not in time: it should be remembered that, in a clear case of uneven development, George Dixon did not finally leave the screen until 1976.) For Clarke, the principal motors behind this transition are provided in part by the specific intertextual and stylistic demands to which we have already alluded but also and more importantly by a context of deepening anxiety over 'law and order'. This in turn suggests an increasingly problematic sense of place in relation to the city. The consequences of these felt or presumed social changes permit a 'redrawing of the boundaries of acceptable behaviour' for the police-officer (Clarke 1986: 221).

Some reasonably clear lines of inquiry emerge from this, which I shall pursue in the following chapters. It seems probable that both *Kojak* and *The Sweeney* assume more anxious and disillusioned audiences than some of their precursors did. Even so, there are sufficiently strong grounds for identifying them as at least distantly related members of the same family of tales. In all cases the integrity of the central character is paramount. The question is: what is the right course of action for a person of integrity under the prevailing conditions? Dixon's integrity is established in his strict observance of propriety: Regan's on the other hand is established in *The Sweeney* rather by his assertive impropriety, which encodes his disgust at bureaucratic stuffiness and hypocrisy.

There is a danger here of presenting too instrumental a view of the relations between social and political developments and the sphere of representation. Either one resorts to viewing fictions as simply reflecting the conditions of their formulation, hence mistaking them for historical documents of a more straightforward kind, or one attributes an undue role to them in bringing about the events they seem to describe. Clarke risks doing this when he argues that 'Each arrest in *The Sweeney* was one more blow to the champions of civil rights in this country, as it helped prepare the ground for official recognition of more authoritarian methods' (1983: 49). Murdock rightly advises against this, as well as against attributing a false similarity to each and every member of the 'genre' which happens to be available at any given time (1982: 116).

Evidently, the dramatic possibilities of crime and law enforcement are both sufficiently fundamental (Bremond 1966) and sufficiently various to permit a range of inflections and modes within the generic category (Reiner 1985: ch. 5) claims to differentiate twelve types of police narrative). Moreover, there is an historical logic to the distribution of these variants as they have occurred. The turn away from community policing *avant la lettre* in *Dixon of Dock Green* towards an increasing preoccupation with pursuit and capture in television crime fiction since the early 1970s has been the consequence of an intimate compound of insistent commercial pressure with a crisis in the relationship between the police and the public, against which the drama of retribution serves to offer a degree of reassurance. Yet such reassurance as narrative resolution continues to provide is premised on different grounds in the 'procedural' and in the later 'action series'. As Clarke observes, where the 'equivalence of interest' (1983: 46) between police and public cannot be assumed, the guarantor of certainty is no longer the police institution but the probity and strength of the picaresque individual, for whom violence is generally the condition of success.

Television crime fiction brings retribution into the midst of flux and anxiety. In subordinating complex institutional conflicts to the restoration of natural justice it also offers a certain consolation, as Adorno noted. The later and more fantasist schematization of the narrative responds to a more acute sense of 'crisis' than did the more domestic parables of George Dixon. Hence Reiner's identification of a 'deepening darkness of mood in police fictions' from the late 1960s onwards (1985: 166). The growing assumption of a crisis of law and order and the problem of the alleged power of mass communication, especially of television, intersect in television crime drama. As has been widely observed (e.g. Hirsch 1976; Pearson 1983) the principal medium of popular diversion has repeatedly been called to account for the felt 'crises' of a variety of historical periods. What is distinctive about the television age is that never before has this medium *also* been a principal means of information and knowledge *about* this crisis. As Stuart Scheingold observes (1984: 60), the analysis of law and order as a public issue must include not only debates about specific policies or measures but also a consideration of its value as a talisman, as a potent index of the integrity of society as a moral order (see also Murdock 1982).

The fictional representation of crime and law enforcement on television has responded to changes in policing and its social context. A sophistic- ated understanding of this process could, in part, assist in illuminating the varying symbolic values which have been attributed to policing with- in what Scheingold (1984) calls the 'myth of crime and punishment'. Yet if some such 'myth' exists it is not as a fixed repertoire of contents: rather such contents will vary according to what the narration supposes it is either plausible or otherwise interesting to assert about the world. Instead the 'myth' comprises many inflections of an underlying set of preoccupa- tions: order, community, integrity, masculinity, danger and the need for retribution.

2 Moral tales and social theory

Again there is danger, the mother of morality – great danger – but this time displaced onto the individual, onto the nearest and dearest, onto the street, onto one's own child, one's own heart, one's own innermost recesses of wish and will.

Nietzsche, *Beyond Good and Evil*

Penality and moral tales

Why is television (like cinema, like newspapers) so much preoccupied with tales of crime and policing, detection and pursuit? It is not enough to reply that this is in some basic sense what many stories have always been about, though this is plainly true and must form part of the answer. In this chapter I shall draw on some recent contributions in social theory in an attempt to outline an account of some reasons for and results of our long love affair with crime and policing. I shall consider, first, some relations between particular kinds of moral tales and the successive forms of 'penality', and second, the ways in which the television medium itself, as one of the primary tellers of such tales, shapes their characteristics and uses today.

I shall insist, here and throughout this book, that this is not an esoteric interest, nor one without practical effects. How television depicts crime and law enforcement has often been a hotly controversial topic as well as being something of durable and sometimes powerful appeal to audiences. Of course 'television violence' is only one, and by no means the most important, theme in the contemporary politics of criminal justice, however many millions of words have been devoted to it. However, it is a topic which has been chronically implicated in recent debates (Pratt and Sparks 1987). A clear view of how television is involved both in mundane experience and in explicit debates is important, if only to assist comprehension of the other topics on to which it abuts or into which it intrudes: fear, the growth of crime, the severity of punishment, the purpose and conduct of policing. As Garland observes, crime and punishment are never simply *there*, nor are they reducible entirely to their ostensible and acknowledged aims. Rather, they are involved in cultural formation, in the creation and expression of passions and sensibilities. They fascinate, motivate, frighten, enrage and excite. Hence, in punishing 'We are also and at the same time defining ourselves and our society in ways which may be quite central to our cultural and political identity' (Garland 1990b: 276).

Crime fiction has long found a place at least among the marginalia of classic social theory. Clearly, for example, it is relatively easy to extend Durkheim's concern with the demand of the *conscience collective* for moral boundaries to incorporate this topic, as Klapp claimed (1954; see also Chapter 6), and as Douglas (1986) also begins to do. Considering crime within her general analysis of responses to risk, Douglas argues that one can use public perceptions of risky or frightening subjects as a 'lens for sharpening the focus on the social organization itself' (1986: 92). The Durkheimian, therefore, is likely to regard popular tales as part of a societal 'machinery for renewing members' commitment' (Douglas 1986: 56). Hence, Douglas remarks that 'the morally punitive cosmos uses risks to uphold community' (1986: 97). The corollary of that is how often 'reactive traditionalism' (Giddens 1990: 158) and other varieties of authoritarianism focus upon the felt failure of law enforcement and punishment as morally central institutions as a primary argument for the reassertion of the forces of order (see Garland 1990b: 237).

To the extent that crime fiction, like earlier moral tales, encodes some features of society's responses to sources of danger and anxiety it would certainly appear to lend itself to being considered in these terms. Sometimes Durkheimian or 'culturalist' arguments overstress the continuity between contemporary narratives and earlier 'myth', as Bremond does (1966). Extreme versions of such arguments recognize no basic functional difference between myth, epic, fairy tale, Western and cop show (see E. Katz and Liebes 1986). One source of objection to such universalism, therefore, is that it is insensitive, failing to register the modulations within genres over time, or their changes of focus in response to momentary concentrations of social anxiety. Nevertheless, some sense that all heroic and moral tales have to do with reconvening or establishing order and equilibrium in circumstances where disorder seems to threaten is common to all thoughtful analyses of the subject, and represents a necessary starting point. Marx's observation, for example, in *Theories of Surplus Values* (1968, part 1, 387) that the criminal 'renders a "service" by arousing the moral and aesthetic feelings of the public' is not at all difficult to reconcile with this general view.

In subsequent social theory crime stories have figured, at least peripherally in *bons mots* and *aperçus*, in the writings of many scholars.

For some the fascination with crime, or more particularly with murder, is universal because it addresses a universal problem, finitude and death. On this view the murder mystery, and the enigma of motivation, stand for the fundamental human enigma of mortality. This is Fromm's view when he argues that the abiding popular fascination with crime stories corresponds to 'a deep yearning for the dramatization of the ultimate thing in human life, namely life and death, through crime and punishment' (Fromm 1956: 142). Clearly, this is also especially appealing from within the Catholic problematics of sin and free will. Hence Eric Griffiths offers an account of T. S. Eliot's fascination with murder beginning from the deep ambiguity of the line 'There will be time to murder and create' (Griffiths 1988: 30). Elsewhere the metaphor of a distorting yet truthful mirror is common. Thus Freud, comparing psychoanalysis and detection, is reported to have been fond of the image of 'a mirror of society from below, dragged along the streets' (Bruckner 1975, quoted in Mandel 1984: 2). Similarly, Kracauer (1971: 105) speaks of a 'refracted mirror' which offers back a 'caricature of that which is civilized'. The most persistent and persuasive theme, however, remains that of anxiety. In *Prisms* Adorno (1967) remarks that

> Detective fictions regularly distort or unmask the world so that asociality and crime become the everyday norm, but which at the same time charm away the seductive and ominous challenge through the inevitable triumph of order.
>
> (Adorno 1967: 32)

For Adorno (1967), Benjamin (1970) and Brecht (1967) the detective story is a fiction of alienation: it addresses itself to an experience of anxiety, yet it translates this experience into a form of entertainment or distraction, whose outcomes are finally consoling or 'charming'. Mandel reports Walter Benjamin's observation that a traveller reading a detective story on a train is 'temporarily suppressing one anxiety with another' (Mandel 1984: 9). Brecht, meanwhile, argues that under conditions of alienation 'We gain our knowledge of life in catastrophic form'. That is, he argues, behind our awareness of accidents, mishaps and mayhem, we have the sense that 'something is going on' of which we are uncertain (quoted in Mandel 1984: 72). The detective story, Brecht argues, provides a model for this query, and the unfolding of the mystery offers a palliative to the demand for answers which provokes it. Thus Mandel's rhetorical question stems from a quite lengthy tradition of reflection on the subject:

> Is it contradictory to maintain that the need for distraction from monotony lies at the root of the popularity of the crime story, and that simultaneously a deep anxiety lies buried within that need?
>
> (Mandel 1984: 9)

It is in answering these needs, Mandel and earlier Marxists have argued, that the crime story is caught up in webs of ideology, either through offering the appearance of having resolved certain conflicts, or by translating their social dimensions into a purely personal sphere. Thus the crime story serves to 'reconcile awareness . . . of the inevitability of crime, with the defence of and apology for the existing social order' (Mandel 1984: 8). Perhaps this is so, though it seems difficult now to accept the simple functionalism implicit in these arguments. However, the durability of stories of crime and punishment, their sheer preponderance as a narrative form, seems to escape comprehension unless it is seen in its close relation to things that matter to us. If these include our own senses of place and security, and the affirmation of cosmologies and moralities upon which we rely, and, moreover, the relation between these and the representation of a contemporary world that we recognize, then these can be matters which at times (and especially in hard or anxious times) do have a quite directly political resonance (see Garland 1990a; 1990b; Ericson; 1991).

Crime stories: archaic or contemporary?

Some recent contributions in social theory have tended to move away from these concerns. For example, it has been argued, most influentially by Foucault, that modern penality has ceased to depend on its commitment to the public drama of transgression and retribution, relying instead on a dispersed 'capillary' network of private and institutional 'disciplinary' mechanisms. The *mise-en-scène* of the public execution, Foucault argues (1975: 19) gives way to the calculations of *'le petit fonctionnaire de l'orthopédie morale'* (1975: 16), whose main concern is the precise ordering of the use of time in captivity: *'Le chatiment est passé d'un art des sensations insupportables à une économie des droits suspendus'* (Foucault 1975: 16). But the modern system is stricken, Foucault argues, by *pudeur*, distaste for punishment. In place of a public performance, the *'microphysique'* (1975: 31) of modern penality is imposed with due propriety and in secret. It acknowledges not punishment but correction as its justification, and it seeks not confession but docility as its outcome.

Such accounts of the history of punishment, with their primary stress on the development of disciplinary technologies and strategies of social intervention and surveillance, have tended to neglect the survival of the demand for retribution in modern culture. (David Garland has recently criticized Foucault's overemphasis on the instrumentalism of modern punishment and his apparent readiness to believe that Benthamism *is* the case (1990b: 163), thereby overlooking Durkheim's insight into the relationship between punishment and the passions (1990b: 61).) Attending to the dramaturgy of crime and punishment in contemporary popular culture calls into question the adequacy of views such as those of Foucault. This has two aspects. First, it is readily apparent that contemporary mass media continue to generate crime stories and other moral tales, some of which achieve immense public salience (the immensely marketable iconographies of Humphrey Bogart as Philip Marlowe or Clint Eastwood as 'Dirty Harry', for example; the repeated trope of vigilantism in films starring Charles Bronson, Mel Gibson or Sylvester Stallone). Second, there is the sense in which fear or horror at particular real events seems partly to be registered by recounting them in a language which assimilates them to fictional and dramatic conventions (the 'Moors murders' retold as Gothic horror, for example).[1] Even if one suspends judgement on the adequacy of Foucault's account of actual penal practice, it does not seem possible seriously to argue that crime and punishment as spectacle and as moral tale have vanished from modern culture. In television and elsewhere a version of that spectacle, which Foucault's position surely inclines him to see as archaic, persists vigorously (Garland 1990a). The question remains as to whether the 'educative' effect of these vicarious, televised or cinematic, spectacles is in any way similar to that which Foucault attributes to the pre-modern 'carnival of atrocity'.

Indeed, far from having disappeared, the crime story is in many ways a distinctively modern genre. Mandel offers an account of the rise of the crime novel from around 1850 in terms of its relations both to changing modes of official penality and to sources of anxiety for its readership. Mandel attributes this rise partly to the 'evaporation of a sense of security' (1984: 5) among the Victorian middle class, brought about by an increasing awareness of their proximity to *les classes dangereuses*. The figure of the brilliant detective originates, on this view, partly from the rising public status of law enforcers in response to anxiety about crime and partly from an admiration for positivism and for 'games of deductive intelligence' (1984: 21). The classical detective story adopts a confident, problem-solving approach to its initial premise of anxiety or enigma. It is only from about 1930, in Mandel's view, that the crime story tends to become a *roman noir*, as the genre begins to confront the existence of organized crime and official corruption. The heroes of Chandler, Hammett and Simenon are disillusioned. Their only clear continuity with Sherlock Holmes lies in their individualism and integrity. Above all they have taken on a relation of passionate ambiguity to the city and the streets. As Chandler famously has it:

Down these mean streets a man must go who is neither tarnished nor afraid. The detective in this kind of story must be such a man. He is the hero. He is everything. He must be a complete man and a common man and yet an unusual man. He must be, to use a rather

weathered phrase, a man of honour, by instinct and inevitability,
without thought of it, and certainly without saying it.
                              (Chandler 1944, quoted in Mandel 1984: 35)

Chandler is less interested in the detective as the one who finds solutions
to particular mysteries than in his capacity for stoic resistance to a general
corruption, or in his maintenance of personal integrity while standing in a
marginal or disreputable social position, as for example Sam Spade does.
Knight (1980) considers that this is characteristic of later crime stories. For
Knight the drama which takes place between police-officer or private eye
and criminal antagonist summarizes an underlying preoccupation with
the city itself. Thus in the novels of Ed McBain, Knight remarks, the city is
named *Isola*. It is too large to be known and hence is seen not as a human
institution but as a force of nature. It can thus not be changed or understood but only wondered at and regretted. It is a source of both 'romance
and anxiety' (Knight 1980: 171).

Knight makes a number of points which are worth developing in subsequent discussion of the representation of crime and law enforcement in
contemporary television. These concern the ambivalent but central place
of the city in modern sensibility and the place of the individual moral
agent in the face of social organizations too extensive to direct or comprehend. As the urban crime story displaces the Western in popularity, so
the exploration of the hidden life of cities displaces the colonization of
frontiers as the primary motif of heroic tales. The frontier and the city are
both open to being represented as situations of disorder, but the Western
allegory of the foundation of the law in the process of nation building is
supplanted by another notion of heroism whose main concern is with the
maintenance of integrity in the face of urban anomie. Under such conditions the law enforcer stands in a tense and problematic relationship to
social institutions, including the law itself. In this regard we are likely to
observe an ambiguity between private and public obligations as justifications for heroic intervention (see Chapter 6). When he is a policeman the
hero may none the less be, to paraphrase Gramsci (1971), both 'within and
against' the police force. Gitlin makes a similar point with more specific
regard to television. Television cops, he argues, stand in a tradition in
which law enforcers are 'simultaneously outcasts and knights' and which
he identifies as seeming 'both to crave strong protective powers and to
distrust governments' (Gitlin 1985: viii).

Is the crime story a 'basic' narrative form?

These observations are sufficient to call into question any implication that
the drama and symbolism of law enforcement have ceased to matter in
modern society. On the contrary it is clear that fictions of crime and

policing continue to constitute, in certain definite ways, a fundamental genre of story-telling.

This has two senses. In the first place many observers go so far as to equate the play of transgression and retribution with narrative itself (Bremond 1966). It would appear that a certain narrative economy, initiated by the breaking of a social boundary, law or taboo and moving through a series of conflicts towards a decisive act of retribution or restitution is common in many periods and cultures.[2] Many of the more abstract models of narrative structure seem at least to suggest, although they do not always make it plain (Heath 1981), that since narrative classically demands a consecutive sequence of events unfolding in time, some kind of transgressive act is necessary to initiate the story. The analogy which is commonly drawn from this between modern popular culture and myth tends to be pushed too far and too literally. Nevertheless it may be reasonable to see in the crime drama an opening through which the mythic intrudes upon the everyday, at least in the sense that it draws upon topics and structures which are both widespread and venerable.

In the second place the crime drama is fundamental in a more mundane sense: it is very widespread and popular. Together with soap opera crime fiction is one of the commonest generic forms of television entertainment in industrial societies. Through processes of syndication and serial marketing, as well as through indigenous production (especially in Hong Kong, Japan and Brazil) crime fiction on television is watched throughout most of the world (Gould et al 1984). As Gitlin observes, from the point of view of the networks 'tough cops' are clearly a ratings 'banker' (1985: viii).

Some observers attribute a further significance to this frequency. It implies, they suggest (*pace* Foucault) that this form of fiction speaks with particular resonance to contemporary anxieties and concerns. Thus, Martin Williams asserts that 'If the USA could be said to have a national literature it is crime melodrama' (1982: 121).

The resonance of crime fiction

Two subsidiary conjectures follow: first, that the police-officer and the criminal are particularly representative and interesting beings; and second, that the crime drama is likewise successful in posing a powerful and resonant image of the city, as the stage upon which conflicts are played out and out of whose dynamics they spring. Hence Williams again comments (with reference to *Kojak*) that 'against the image of the crumbling city' the policeman hero is also in part a sacrificial victim 'carrying the load of everybody's failures, everybody's helplessness, everybody's neglect, everybody's wickedness' (M. Williams 1982: 140). The outsider remains, as so often in the Western,[3] the touchstone of order and integrity.

Williams's comments are suggestive rather than systematic. They do possess the virtue, though, of attempting to return the pleasure which can be taken from fiction to its place within contemporary urban experience. Some connection of this kind is, in my view, a precondition for a critical theory of television fiction. In this regard Hebdige (1974) makes a telling point in his study of the careers of the infamous Kray twins when he refuses to disconnect gangsterism from the gangster movie. Thus:

> When Warshow concludes his essay by writing that the gangster genre: 'is a more modern genre than the Western because, like much of our advanced art, it gains its effects by a gross insistence on its own narrow logic. But it is antisocial, resting on fantasies of irresponsible freedom', he is indeed writing as much about the gangster of the 'real city', as the gangster of the 'dangerous, sad city of the imagination'. The two can no longer usefully be distinguished. Fictional form and lifestyle . . . coalesce to produce one shrunken world, one self-perpetuating, self-supportive universe – to produce, in short, a system of closure, which is a parody of the genuine struggle for completion – a tragic and unnatural synthesis.
>
> (Hebdige 1974: 10)

This seems to me very perceptive, if a little overstated. Hebdige develops his theme by examining the theatrical and extravagant cruelty with which the Krays and Richardsons explored their power: refinements of violence which could come only fron seeing oneself as an actor in a drama. This also raises the question of what it was that 'the twins' represented for their various publics. Hebdige's point is that, in this case, narrative closure matters because it carries over into thwarted moral reasoning in the rest of life, and it raises a question about the audience's guilty complicity in the heroization of gangsterism. Hebdige's analysis addresses itself to the relation between certain narrative categories and the possibility of particular feelings and actions (see Kappeler 1986).

Hebdige thus raises the questions not only of what a particular story 'says' or 'means' in a formal sense but also of the ways in which it insinuates itself into everyday life: ways which can perhaps only finally be measured at the levels of ordinary vocabulary and gut reaction. This in turn requires attention to the sense in which a television transmission (especially when embedded in a genre) seeks out its audience. It presupposes certain things about them, to which it then addresses itself. We return again to the argument that this 'implicit reader' (Eco 1979) for television crime drama is in general addressed as a rather fearful person, and one who may enjoy the reassurance of an authoritarian narrative resolution. It is in this respect, as something which stands in for the satisfactions involved in the imposition of order, that the television cop show might be said to carry a specific ideology of law and its enforcement. (Though we also know that the audience is in fact enormously various and differentiated – by geography, class, generational, gender and ethnic experience – so that the *real* reading of any particular narrative is contingent and unpredictable.)

In television crime drama a number of potentially interesting connections are therefore broached between the prevalence of particular kinds of stories, the needs or demands of the audience which they presuppose and their implicit relations to crime and law enforcement, both as real social practices and as bearers of specific social meanings. In the crime drama we are presented with a representation, for pleasure, of topics which are otherwise, in other registers of talk and imagery, widely felt as very troubling and dangerous. Such a presentation (as I detail in subsequent chapters) both foregrounds and contains this dangerousness. That is crime drama is preoccupied with vulnerability and threat, but it is also intrinsic that it provides ways in which the threat is countered and overcome. The 'good', for the most part, continue to end happily and the 'bad' unhappily. Empirical arguments about whether or not television 'causes' fear of crime have to take cognizance of these dynamics (see Chapter 4).

Furthermore, in so far as the story is carried on a particular medium, embedded in institutionalized patterns of both production and use, we are led to consider the meeting between 'fabular' tales (Eco 1979) which, if not eternal, certainly exist on a long wave of historical time, and the 'urgent contemporaneity' (Chaney 1977) of television imagery. The television schedule imposes an organization of time which is regular, episodic and repetitive. Whatever the genealogy of the moral tale, it enters the domestic setting in ways which are decisively shaped by the television medium.

One question which arises, for example, concerns the relation in which such imagery stands to the overt politics of 'law and order'. If Foucault is in some degree right in stressing the disciplinary, technological character of modern penality, yet mistaken in not attending sufficiently to the survival of moral tales, how are these domains connected? Some observers suggest that modern penality in a sense stimulates such narratives in that the continuing demand that punishment perform its older function of moral re-equilibration is driven towards vicarious, surrogate or fictitious satisfactions. This is the argument made by Jacoby in *Wild Justice* (1985) when she posits that the disconnection between these registers of language is responsible for the incoherent, convulsive and brutal obsession with personal revenge which she identifies in recent Hollywood movies (Jacoby 1985: 174; see also I. Taylor 1987). Jacoby contrasts these desolate pieces with the revenge stories of earlier periods in which, she argues, the dilemma between private vengeance and public justice could at least be posed in an intelligible way.

Two points arise which will be of some importance for the argument which I shall go on to develop. First, in so far as a 'myth of crime and punishment' (Scheingold 1984: 64) exists, its content is not fixed but is, rather, open to inflections which result from points of tension or anxiety in the relation between the audience and the law, as the practical and symbolic embodiment of social order, at particular times. Second, while it is easy enough to indicate ways in which moral tales may be 'conservative' and 'ideological', none the less their concerns may stand at some distance from, if not in open contradiction to, the posture of the state: much as vigilantism stands opposed to authorized punishment.

Such discussion of the appeal of narratives edges beyond the questions which have commonly interested criminologists. This does not make it an esoteric interest, however. Its centre of attention is in fact very close to home: its focus indeed lies within the home itself. Television provides a point of contact between public discourse and private life. The study of television's representations of crime and law enforcement is a way of gaining access to some of the places which criminal justice occupies in everyday talk and experience: the significances it bears, the fears and pleasures it provides. One consequence of the mythic pole of this experience may be that its resonance extends far beyond an ostensible subject matter, away from the 'facts of the case' and towards the play of fundamental social moralities. Another may be that this extension serves to contaminate discussion of what the facts really are. The underlying question concerns how a given population comes not only to think but also to feel within certain boundaries. This raises a second question, which is in turn at the kernel of the idea of a critical theory, namely whether those boundaries are inherent or contingent, imposed and damagingly constrained.

Television, anxiety and ideology

Orthodox criminology has been unduly cautious in declining to enter this intimate sphere of domestic life and private feeling. Recent contributions in social theory, however, have shown themselves increasingly concerned with it. They have thus tended away from the confinement of the notion of ideology to the *grands recits* of political master institutions. They suggest instead that fundamental forms of social integration and control result from ways in which frames of meaning are sustained and reproduced in everyday transactions (Giddens 1984; J. B. Thompson 1984).

This has certain consequences which I explore later. The first is that it is important to attend closely to mundane features of speech and inscription; and this attention should centre on utterances, forms of talk and texts as media of practical activity and foci of interaction (J. B. Thompson 1984: 2–5). Second, commonplace distinctions between micro and macro levels of analysis will not serve, since fundamental features of social integration, which may none the less be profoundly settled and institutionalized, exist only by virtue of their continual reproduction in such exchanges (Giddens 1984; J. B. Thompson 1984: 43). Third, this in turn requires close scrutiny of the temporal and spatial co-ordinates of social action in order to locate sources of regularity in everyday conduct and of fixity in modes of information and exchange.

Modern television systems are among such organizing media. The structural properties of television networks, and especially the division of time and co-ordination of content through the schedule, tend to constrain and direct the patterns of television use. The question thus arises of what the social and ideological consequences of the routinization of media use might comprise.

Gouldner on ideology and 'paleo-symbolism'

One of the more intriguing answers to this question is that proposed by Gouldner in *The Dialectic of Ideology and Technology* (1976). I have already suggested that the question of ideology in relation to television crime fiction concerns not only what an audience thinks but also, and more particularly, what it feels. In a similar vein Gouldner suggests that it is appropriate to draw a distinction between ideology and 'paleo-symbolism'. Gouldner restricts the use of the term 'ideology' to refer to manifest public discourses laying claim to a certain authority. However, Gouldner argues, any ideology, especially in so far as it represents a demand for a given course of action, requires a certain emotional underpinning which provides its element of 'command' (1976: 34). Thus, Gouldner introduces the notion of paleo-symbolism in order to show that even highly elaborated ideologies depend for their persuasive effect on their relation to aspects of ordinary speech which are themselves of 're-stricted communicability' (1976: 224).

Gouldner's concern in this is with the relationship between a representation or image, our responses to it, and our disposition to feel or act in a certain way. It is not difficult to see the possible bearing of this on issues of crime and punishment. For example one could interpret the analysis which S. Hall et al provide in *Policing the Crisis* (1978) in terms of the relationship it identifies between certain ideologies (about policing, sentencing and indeed the nature of the modern state) and an underlying paleo-symbolic dynamic of fear. In like manner the feasibility of any public project is likely in Gouldner's view to be constrained by its relation to the paleo-symbolic, because the emotive power of words and images sets limits on the acceptability of ideas (see Garland 1990a: 8). The particular issue which Gouldner raises in respect of television centres on what he sees as its tendency to consolidate the hold of paleo-symbolism over the viewer, at the expense of discursive self-knowledge. Gouldner

argues that because television is a participatory and iconic and profoundly *familiar* medium it asks to be viewed in a particular way. Where
the experience of viewing produces dissonance or tension (as it may in
relation to images of crime and law enforcement) it calls not so much for
'intellectual clarification' as for ' "resolution", in the sense that a drama or
piece of music may be "resolved" ' (Gouldner 1976: 169). This in turn
requires that 'such ideologies as the television watchers accept must be
successful in integrating and resonating with the residual iconic imagery'
(Gouldner 1976: 169). He concludes:

> In brief, things people could not normally speak about are now
> being affected by other things they cannot speak about, in ways and
> with results they cannot speak about.
>
> (Gouldner 1976: 169)

Gouldner's concern is thus that the element of force or command in
ideology rests on something which is never directly *said*. This has much in
common with the interest of recent semiotics in 'surplus' or 'second-
order' meaning (Barthes 1972; Genette 1982). In its stress on reiteration
and routine, however, it is also more sociologically concrete and convinc-
ing as a description of the infiltration of rhetoric into everyday activity
than are those positions which concentrate on surplus or ideological
meaning as a mechanism of any individual text. Gouldner's argument
thus suggests that the problem of the social influences of mass media can
no longer be approached either by analogy with earlier political science
notions of propaganda and public opinion (as in the tradition which
extends from Lasswell to Gerbner) or by an exclusive concentration on
the formal properties of texts construed as finished systems of signs (as
Giddens also suggests, 1976: 104; 1987: 99). Rather, the 'problem' has to be
reconsidered as having to do with the production and reproduction of
social life in everyday transactions. (This is, for example, the sense of
Thompson's observations about the inappropriateness of traditional hermeneutic and literary principles to the understanding of the multiple
forms of inscription, reproduction and storage involved in electronic
communications systems (J. B. Thompson 1984: 195).)

Crime, television and critique

A number of issues are thus raised which suggest certain priorities in
developing any analysis of the relations between television systems, their
representations of crime and law enforcement, the interests the audience
may have or develop in attending to such representations and the 'communicability' of the resulting experiences. If asked why we watch television crime drama we may readily say that we do so because we find it
pleasurable, or relaxing or exciting or something else of that sort. Most of
us, indeed, will be able to say a good deal more than this, certainly to the

point of showing that we can follow and grasp the story, and begin to comment on aspects of style, performance and so on. We may then find, however, that we push up against a boundary in accounting for why we do what we do. The questioner may, for example, be reluctant to accept that the features we identify are actually the heart of the matter, and may then begin to make attributions of latency or unconsciousness in respect of our pleasurable experience. In short, there is frequently something insufficient about accounts of actions, perhaps especially habitual actions and descriptions of pleasure.

One principal aim of a critical theory of television is to assist reflection of this kind. Within the meaning of the term as used here one of the objects of critique is both to enlarge and clarify the conceptual ground over which exchanges such as the one I have proposed can range (see also J. B. Thompson 1984: 66). This implies that the observer is committed, in certain distinct ways, to producing both knowledge and evaluation. At the level of knowledge or explanation a critical theory therefore aims to place any particular event, say an experience of watching television, within a more extensive framework in terms of its preconditions (skills implicit in watching television) but also of its unanticipated consequences (such as results of watching a lot of television). The persuasiveness of the theory then rests on the adequacy of the interpretive procedures and explanatory concepts deployed. This is what Thompson calls 'the claim to know which impels critique' (1984: 202). The evaluative level, however, is also intrinsic: it is the criterion of pertinence. The critical observer inherently claims that the knowledge so derived permits a fuller understanding of the event or process at hand in relation to some moral, political, aesthetic or cognitive standard. To this extent the critical theorist must temper the 'claim to know better' (Dunn 1985: 142) with the recognition that their account is challengeable, incomplete, 'risky and open to dispute' (J. B. Thompson 1988: 369). The critical analysis of cultural production faces tasks which are inherently difficult, in holding together its assertions of fact and its attributions of value in some sort of integral relation. It is necessary to steer a course between the 'occidental arrogance' of objectivist social science, and the 'idiot relativism' which presents itself as the easiest alternative (Dunn 1985: 143). The observer is committed to trying to elucidate aspects of real and materially important social processes, but using 'intellectual weapons' which are neither 'guaranteed nor self-legitimating in any automatic fashion' (Dunn 1985: 143). It is precisely because the kinds of significance at stake frequently pass without notice or examination and, more particularly, because their weight and effectivity are genuinely contestable that a specific activity of critique is necessary. As MacRae (1974) observes, sociology thus considered is an attempt to extend 'human self-consciousness':

Sociology both makes society clear and present to us and makes society bearable and subject to analysis by endistancing us from the stark reality of immediate apprehension.

(MacRae 1974: 16)

With these considerations in mind, I now turn towards outlining some features of a somewhat more formal model of the position of the crime drama in the lives of the members of the television audience.

Schedules, viewers and the crime drama

The 'question of function' (S. Hall 1984) in relation to television and other cultural forms includes, but is not limited to, the truth or falsity of its propositional content. Analysis of the reception of television, I want to argue, goes beyond the ostensible meaning of its stories and towards its use in maintaining ontological security, local and national affiliations and in warranting codes of conduct.

For present purposes the dynamics which situate the crime drama in the daily lives of the viewing audience can be summarized under three headings: scheduling; the role of viewing in domestic life; the nature of generic contents and styles.

Scheduling

Within a general model of television viewing the question of the schedule has a certain priority. The division of time which the schedule imposes is the mechanism through which the economic and organizational priorities of broadcasting institutions impinge most directly on the routinized activity of viewers. As a routine organization of time the television schedule represents a particular case in point of what Giddens regards as a fundamental feature of social life. Giddens has argued that routines are 'integral both to the continuity of the personality of the agent, as he or she moves along the paths of daily activities, and to the institutions of society, which are such only through their continual reproduction' (Giddens 1984: 60). Similarly, to borrow Unger's terminology, mechanisms such as scheduling provide the links between the 'formative frameworks' of production and the 'formed routines' of daily time (Unger 1987: 4).

The episodic nature of television transmissions influences not only the character of the text itself, but also the composition and disposition of its audience, that is who they are and what they will be doing at the time. The text (or performance) is carried on a medium which is itself a focal feature of the context of its reception. Indeed, the use of the terms 'text' (for programme) and 'reader' (for viewer) characteristically begs the question of how far broadcasts are in fact like texts, or in what sense viewing is like reading (see Hartley 1984). Attention to the television schedule suggests rather different priorities than those traditionally brought to bear in hermeneutics and literary criticism. It makes little sense, when thinking about television, to sharply distinguish textuality on the one hand from the time-space organization of social life on the other. However much the analysis of ideology demands attention to the specific articulations of discourse in texts it cannot undertake this analysis *ex situ*. For if, as J. B. Thompson has it, the study of ideology is the study of 'the ways in which meaning . . . serves to sustain relations of domination' (1984: 198) we cannot then disregard the sense in which television is itself a constitutive feature of the bundle of social relations in question.

To this extent, as Raymond Williams observes, 'Questions about forms in communications are also questions about institutions and about the organization of social relationships' (1974: 35). At the level of institutions the relative fixity of generic forms of television results from the sedimentation of production practices over time, but bounded on the one hand by an element of fluidity in response to audience preferences (Gitlin 1985) and on the other, by a systematic aversion to risk (Garnham 1973).

Thus, in the case of the crime drama, the salient features of the 'genre' derive less from the realization of some abstract, virtual model (Bremond 1966) than from the fact that programmes are broadcast weekly at a certain time, that each episode lasts about an hour, that it is organized around commercial breaks and that it assumes certain limits on its audience's powers of concentration (see Swidler et al 1986). Each narrative thus aims for a compromise between novelty (or information – which is interesting) and conscious reference to an existing pattern (or redundancy – which is familiar). We find intertextual references at three levels. First, each programme presupposes continuities between itself and other episodes of the same series. Second, each one is positioned in relation to other members of the same genre. Third, each genre itself occupies a place within the diurnal 'flow' (R. Williams 1974) of television. This place is established in relation to settled features of daily time. Prime-time television presupposes choices in the the use of leisure, but those choices are exercised within an ordered sequence. Thus, in one useful terminology, individual items of television 'traffic' are only analytically separable from the 'backcloth' of the schedule (Gould et al 1984).

In Garnham's view the scheduling process is mathematically predictable. The schedule, thus construed, is a cybernetic process in that the occurrence of any event is subject to systematic restraints which tend to eliminate randomness (see Bateson 1972: 405). Thus, Garnham argues:

In mathematical terms, broadcasting systems, as presently constituted, are examples of Markoff Chains, that is, a stochastic process in which probabilities depend on previous events . . . schedules tend towards a steady state – negative feedback reduces random-

ness. . . . Out of these pressures the characteristic method of audience control, known as scheduling, has grown.

(Garnham, 1973: 35)

This cybernetic language is useful, however, only if it can be translated
back into a knowledge of the practices from which the observed patterns
result (Giddens 1984: 27). The main point here is how institutional constraints direct practices of production and the extent to which this, in
turn, 'limits the range of imaginable possibilities available to an audience'
(Golding and Murdock 1979: 207). Golding and Murdock argue strongly
that it is in terms of this determination that the question of ideology in
cultural production must be broached.

However complex these processes are it is nevertheless far easier to
give an account of them at the institutional level than it is to show how
they actually impinge upon the viewing audience. Golding and Murdock
are rightly concerned to reinstate the analysis of cultural production in
opposition to those versions of semiology which suppose the self-
sufficiency of textual analysis and which proceed as though social relations could be entirely 'retrieved and explicated through a reading of the
text' (1979: 205). Golding and Murdock, however, arguably risk performing a reduction which is simply the reverse of the one they criticize.
Rather than inferring social relations from the text we may be left to infer
both text and audience as an outcome of such and such productive relations. As Counihan (1975) points out there are two ways in which it is
common to excise the audience from the analysis of television. On the one
hand lies 'an inept and reductive sociologism', on the other a 'closed
formalism . . . equally one-sided' (Counihan 1975: 35).

There are, however, a number of things which it is possible to say here
about how scheduling shapes the entry of television into the lives of its
audiences. In Giddens's view routinized conduct is basic to social integration: it is the precondition for 'trust' in the continuity of the physical and
social environment (1984: 60). The successful enactment of such daily
conduct is the primary embodiment of the actor's practical knowledgeability about his or her social setting. It is also the precondition for
maintaining 'ontological security': routine provides for the management
of anxiety by the actor, and makes possible the 'mutuality' which sustains
interaction (Giddens 1984: 53). The obverse of routine is the 'critical situation', in which discontinuity or impropriety so disrupt expectations as to
allow anxiety to 'swamp' the habitual mode of being in the world (Giddens 1984: 64). Thus Giddens (following Goffman) comments:

> That is, what from the angle of the fleeting moment might appear
> brief and trivial interchanges take on much more substance when
> seen as inherent in the iterative nature of social life. The routiniza-
> tion of encounters is of major significance in binding the fleeting

encounter to social reproduction and thus to the seeming 'fixity' of institutions.

(Giddens 1984: 72)

Like Goffman, Giddens finds that the 'intimacies of co-presence' and the certainties of routines (Giddens 1984: 68) are crucial to social integration. The question is then in what sense watching television also relates to these features of daily life.

Viewing and domestic life
Television is relevant to the 'binding of social relations across time and space' (Giddens 1984; 17) in a number of ways. First, viewing often takes place within the home or in other familiar locales, such as pubs, in the presence of intimates or peers. In this sense it is a component of the 'interaction strip' (Giddens 1984: 73) itself. Equally, to the extent that it is a topic of conversation subsequently, among colleagues at work or children in school for instance, it is still closely involved in the mutuality of interaction. It is not a wholly separate and self-sufficient activity, apart from the rest of life. So, for example, Cziczentmihalyi and Kubey (1982) show that viewing is usually not the only, or even the most salient, activity going on at any one time. People watch television while eating, talking, reading magazines, playing with dogs and so on. The screen, as it were, slips in and out of focus, while still contributing to the maintenance of continuity. Similarly, Scannell argues that broadcasting, in the way that it observes not only diurnal but also seasonal and annual rhythms (punctuated by state occasions, festivals, sporting events) serves to mediate between the *durée* of daily life and its position within the larger extension of institutional time (Scannell 1986). Sartre's notion of the 'group in so far as . . .' (1976: 259) may be relevant here. Television is involved in constituting as a group those whom it addresses as such. Even where viewing or listening takes place alone the viewer is still addressed as part of a relatively solidary group, and with the implicit knowledge that others elsewhere are doing the same thing at the same moment. The individual is thus addressed as a *member* of the television audience in a quite strong sense. In reality of course these people may lead distinct and often very dissimilar lives: the relation between what each of us has in common *qua* participant in mass-produced popular culture and what divides us in terms of local and personal experience remains profoundly unresolved. This is thankfully reflected in the less certain tone of much recent discussion in media studies and in the consequent willingness of researchers to go out and discover what different groups within 'the audience' are actually doing. For these reasons studies of the mass media have become much more responsive to social difference, more aware that the imaginative reconstruction of the text as it is received cannot be specified in

advance, indeed that the very activity of watching television may be a different one depending on who is doing it, where and with whom (Ang 1985).

Although both Goffman and Giddens are primarily interested in the organization of social encounters under 'full conditions of co-presence' (Giddens, 1984: 64) it is possible to extend this concern to incorporate interactions with or via electronic media. This is not only because television viewing itself frequently takes place in the company of others but also because broadcasting itself, in its periodicity, its 'flow' and its familiarity, has features which simulate those of co-presence. The schedule provides for 'co-occurrence' whether others are physically present or not. It is in this sense that scheduling contributes to the 'laterality' which Giddens considers necessary to 'systemness' in social life (1984: 28–36), such that engagement with communication systems necessarily has a public aspect even when undertaken in private.

Certain points follow from this. First, those approaches which focus solely on television (or film) as a carrier of ideology inscribed in texts neglect some of its fundamental processes. The relevance of textuality is constrained by the pragmatics of viewing. This does not, however, mean that the 'content' of television is in any sense a trivial matter. Rather, the involvement of viewing in the maintenance of ontological security and trust suggests a commitment to what is viewed which goes beyond its ostensible topic or subject matter.

Like all routine activity watching television presupposes certain competences, deployed in the recursive monitoring of its 'flow' (Giddens 1984: 5). This does not mean, however, that all its important features are discursively available. Indeed, as Giddens admits, habitual and familiar activities may be particularly difficult to account for or warrant or justify. In these respects the study of television viewing, perhaps especially of entertainment and narrative television, stands in what is a primary but also a particularly difficult area for critical analysis, between 'what can be said and what is characteristically simply done' (Giddens 1984: 7).

The study of television viewing is, properly speaking, a hermeneutic project in that it involves the interpretive understanding of knowledgeable conduct. However, in that like other routine activities viewing may often not be very strongly 'directly motivated' (Giddens 1984: 64) its analysis should be sensitive both to the presence of unintended consequences and to the obscurity of its appeal. This is part of what I take to be the force of Eco's analysis of the pragmatics of openness and closure (Eco 1979: see also Chapter 4). Simply put, watching television is a skilled activity, but the most refined skill may be exercised more often in habitual and acquiescent rather than in challenging ways. We know how to watch, and this knowledge is a matter of some complexity, but this is not the same as reflection about watching. We may invest more in watching than we can readily say.

The knowledge which we must have in order to view 'competently', and how we acquire such knowledge, is thus very much part of the point at issue. Eco (1979) stands in line of descent from Aristotle in arguing that the pleasure of narrative derives in large part from a knowing anticipation (even if it may be the anticipation of a surprise). Television is in the business of meeting the anticipations we have of a satisfactory conclusion. But since the anticipation is itself the result of our long experience of television it is also in the business of stipulating what our expectations should be.

Research on the ethnographic composition of the television audience indicates that audiences can and do decline 'preferred' readings. This mainly happens, however, where the viewer makes his or her primary reference to a group which is marginal or opposed to the inferred 'majority' audience. Television can then be used just as much in sustaining a deviant affiliation as in answering a 'request of conformity' (Eco 1979: 34). Such 'smart' responses seem most likely, however, and are best attested, where they take the form of rejecting the truth or adequacy of a news or documentary item (Morley 1980). It may be harder to reject a story than a news 'story' partly because it lodges a less distinct truth claim. Moreover the complexity of the conflict of interpretations is subverted by a defence from triviality: if I want to reject the sufficiency of the story this is merely the outcome of my eccentric preference, and the possibility of rational adjudication is denied in advance. Equally, since, as we have seen, television answers the needs of routine and integration my rejection may be interpreted as actively anti-social. If I persist in it I may commit an impropriety, rather like refusing to laugh at a joke.

For these reasons I consider that the interpretation of television viewing, the study of the transactions which take place between institutions, programmes and audiences, is in certain important respects more akin to the study of talk than to the study of texts. I am centrally interested in reaching an understanding of television narratives but conceived in terms of their likely 'realisations' by viewers viewing in determinate settings. In the way it enters the domestic setting television both fosters talk and, in its episodic, reiterative use of time, tends to resemble it (Conrad 1982: 9).

Generic contents and styles
The degree of fixity in generic forms of television, then, results from the conjunction between the institutional imperatives of its producers and the characteristic uses made of it by its audiences. It is not necessary to inveigh against either realism or narrative as such in the ways that much screen theory (e.g. MacCabe 1985) has done in order to argue that the operative conventions of television fiction may present some obstacles against reflection and critical judgement. Stories on television, like other fabular texts, enter a powerful 'request of conformity' (Eco 1979: 34; see

also Chapter 5). The point at issue thus concerns not so much 'realism', considered as a distinct textual process, as the 'reciprocity of perspectives' (Cicourel 1970) among viewers. Perfect congruence between a sender's intention and the disposition of each receiver may never occur *but* the sedimentation of conventions of both production and use pull towards this condition. I take up the questions of the exact sense in which television crime drama constitutes a genre, the parameters of the genre and the bearing of these on its publics again in more detail in subsequent chapters. The general point I am making here is that both the co-ordination of viewing through the schedule and the organization of television content into generic categories which occupy certain positions within the schedule are related to routinization and, thereby, to the ontological security of viewers.

However, and I regard this as central, crime drama is related to such security only in a highly ambivalent and paradoxical way; crime fictions in general aim for certain kinds of resolution and reassurance largely because they are predicated upon the prior existence of insecurity and anxiety. Television crime drama involves the routine introduction of fictive critical situations, precisely in order that they may be resolved. This is closely consonant with empirical findings (especially Wakshlag et al 1983, reported in Chapter 4) that the crime drama appeals especially to the fearful or anxious viewer. It need not, however, stop that viewer being anxious (as Wakshlag assumes). Rather it might equally well draw him or her into a cycle of anxiety, crisis and resolution which sets up a demand for its own continual reiteration. This in turn places certain restraints on the kinds of narrative which are likely to prove satisfactory or pleasurable. Moreover, they respond to a demand for reassurance and order whose origins may indeed be more diffuse than anxiety about crime as such but which nevertheless make crime and law enforcement stand for a range of anxieties and their correlative pleasures. In these respects the diversity of images in crime drama, and the contingencies of plot and circumstance are subsumed within a paleo-symbolism of crime and punishment, whose moral and emotional impact is expected, desired and difficult to discuss.

Television and 'symbolic power'

In this way television fiction tends towards what Bourdieu terms the 'doxic'. The doxic is, for Bourdieu, everything that is taken for granted and which thus 'goes without saying because it comes without saying' with the result that

> the established cosmological and political order is perceived not as arbitrary – i.e. as one possible order among others – but as a self-

evident and natural order which goes without saying and therefore goes unquestioned.

(Bourdieu 1977: 166)

As it stands this seems too strong a view and too dismissive of the knowledgeability of social actors. Nevertheless it summarizes an important preoccupation in recent social theory. (Consider its similarity to Gouldner's notion of a paleo-symbolic system, for example, or Habermas's treatment of the *Lebenswelt*.) Bourdieu contends that the doxic level of practice is most characteristic of traditional societies. In advanced societies, where diversity and antagonism manifestly exist, the doxic is brought into crisis by competing discourses, whether orthodox or heterodox. The notions of majority and minority, which already presuppose a differentiated society, are foreign to the unanimity of doxa (Bourdieu 1977: 167–71). However, if elements of doxa survive in differentiated societies then television is likely to be one of the spheres in which they reside. Bourdieu argues that an 'underlying complicity' or 'consensus within dissensus' lingers into modernity (Bourdieu 1971: 183), suggesting an implicit agreement at the level of certain basic social representations between the diverse members of any 'intellectual field'. For Bourdieu, orthodoxies (such as generic forms of television) aim, without ever entirely succeeding, at 'restoring the primal state of innocence of doxa' (Bourdieu 1977: 169). That is, Bourdieu would argue, conventionality delimits a 'universe of discourse' which in turn is

practically defined in relation to the necessarily unnoticed, complementary class that is constituted by that which is undiscussed, unnamed, admitted without argument or scrutiny.

(Bourdieu 1977: 170)

If we accept that the television message exhibits certain priorities, emphases, concerns, censures, then the extent to which we as viewers comprehend and recognize these features as familiar and unproblematic is a measure of our implication in that culture whose categories of virtue and wickedness they underwrite. As Eco argues, the ideological weight of reiteration is not that it *informs* so much as that it *reaffirms*: and what it reaffirms is a sense of membership and certainty. It may be that the doxicity which persists in television narrative acts as a kind of consolation against anxiety and dread.

The critical examination of popular fictions thus shares the aims of the longer tradition of the critique of 'public opinion'. Keane (1984) traces this tradition through the work of Tonnies (1971) and Dewey (1927) to that of Habermas (1974). This is, Keane argues, a body of thought which sees 'public opinion' as standing in danger of being reduced to 'the automatic opinion of each and the considered opinion of none' (Keane 1984: 148). In this respect a critical perspective is one which calls upon us to undertake an effort of interpretation of our own 'automatic' responses. For these reasons, one of the most basic tasks for critique is simply to notice things which would otherwise pass unnoticed and indeed be 'admitted without argument or scrutiny'. For Bourdieu and other critics, the imposition of power in communication is always bound up with dissimulation and concealment (see J. B. Thompson 1988: 370). Bourdieu approaches this issue in terms of a theory of 'symbolic violence':

> every power which manages to impose meanings and to impose them as legitimate by concealing the power relations which are the basis of its force, adds its own specifically symbolic force to those power relations.
>
> (Bourdieu and Passeron 1977: 239)

The concept of symbolic violence has a special resonance in the area of crime fiction. In addition to its general sense as a characteristic of social cognition, there is also a specific symbolism of violence as such. We are dealing with the content and the uses of a set of narratives which include representations of violence to the body and which assign certain values to it. They suggest, I shall later show, that violence can tame violence. They differentiate between the vicious and the virtuous use of violence. They lead us towards the necessity of the imposition of force.

Television, anxiety and the power of punishment

In so far as they do these things such narratives are worth thinking about in a serious way. It is not implausible that our attachment to them might constrain our reasoning about crime and punishment, at least inasmuch as a tension exists between our practical interests and the involvement of crime in more primordial, less discursively available, moral categories. Fabular narratives are ideological to the extent that they create impediments to reflection and answer needs which are not themselves fully known by social actors. The fixity which can be detected in the reiteration of narratives of crime and law enforcement results from the kinds of satisfaction they are called upon to provide for an anxious audience. Those perspectives which stress the diminution of the importance of punishment as public spectacle (as Foucault appears to do) will be severely mistaken unless they also note its vicarious survival in narrative. Meanwhile, this kind of narration tends to prefer the notion of retribution as a primary if not sufficient aim of justice, over against the more instrumental postures which are often taken to characterize modern penality. By the same token the frustration with which H. Mannheim (1965; see also Chapter 1) and others have regarded television, and their incapacity to provide an adequate critical language to address it, also results from a failure to recognize the depth at which the demand for retribution is entrenched. This is more than a matter of the audience's benighted silliness. It is something which may be reproduced and kept alive in routine and institutionalized ways. Popular narratives of crime and law enforcement tend to address us on terms which presuppose demand for the restoration of order and a desire to see punishment done (Garland 1990a).

The question which thus arises concerns whether the heroic or magical solutions of the cop show serve to provide distracting surrogates for varieties of anxiety, need or longing which have become difficult to discuss or identify precisely: this is why although crime fictions give us pleasure they may not altogether make us happy. The imposition of force by the hero may be gratifying but it is premissed on a prior sense of fear and threat. That fear must also be reiterated every week: the problem is the condition of the solution. This may help to explain why, even though its primary aim is to reassure and console, the television medium itself is also, for some, a focus of social anxiety and an object of censure.

The recent work of social theorists which I have cited is useful to the extent that it can be turned towards informing a practical concern, namely fostering our critical competence as viewers and our rational self-awareness as social actors. As Habermas (1987) points out, critique cannot be only negative, it must also be, in a certain sense, therapeutic. The life-world of everyday routine inherently seeks conditions of trust and security, but the terms on which it does so become problematic when the search for security takes place in the shadow of a particular, ideologically constituted sense of threat, and when the fragments we shore against our ruin are not answers but anachronisms.

The confinement of narratives of crime and law enforcement within a paleo-symbolic play of transgression and retribution is an elimination of complexity in favour of 'followability' (Kermode 1979). It subsumes that play within a narrative economy whose moral categories seem so natural that they can be retrieved and challenged only with difficulty. This is a limitation on our competence. One question which arises, and to which I keep returning (though without pretending to reach a firm conclusion), is whether this limitation also suggests another, namely on our competence as actors in or spectators upon the politics of criminal justice in actuality. As Clarke puts it, the question is one of how 'the fictional terrain blurs with the terrain of political debate' (Clarke 1983: 49; see also Murdock 1982). Examinations of public policy ignore the symbolic dimensions of crime and law at their peril. As Scheingold points out crime control is often only the ostensible object of law and order campaigns (1984: xi). The notion of a 'war on crime', for example, not only requires the constant 'cultural presence' of crime (Scheingold 1984: 62) but also demands its dramatization in terms of good, wickedness, dangerousness and violence, within which framework punishment is seen to be both 'morally justified and practically effective' (1984: 62).

Critique, as Geuss tersely puts it, should try to 'show us which way to move' (Geuss 1981: 54) so as to help render the social relationships in which we participate less opaque to our understanding than they presently are. I therefore want to carry forward these arguments by looking in a more substantive way at the relationship between the use of television and the apprehension (in both senses) of crime. In the next chapter I look further at some of the ways in which the medium itself has been held responsible for engendering social crises and, more particularly, at how the issue of 'violence in the media' has been postulated as a specific social problem.

3 Entertaining the crisis? Television and moral enterprise

I live in mighty fear that all the universe will be broken into fragments in the general ruin, that formless chaos will return and vanquish the Gods and men, the earth and sea will be engulfed by the planets wandering in the heavens . . . . Of all the generations it is we who have been chosen to merit this bitter fate, to be crushed by the falling pieces of the broken sky.

Seneca, *Thyestes*

Moral disquiet and the media

It seems reasonable to expect that any important social institution or practice should be widely and often passionately discussed. Broadcasting, and especially its depictions of crime and punishment, provides a singular case in point. Its cultural significance is partly defined by the fact that it has indeed attracted incessant discussion, and a fuller assessment of its social impacts requires attention as much to the meanings which have been attributed to it as to the more narrowly conceived tasks of documenting its actual 'contents' and 'effects'. This chapter thus concerns some of the attempts which have been made to define and describe the impact of television, especially where these register the growth of the television industries with a sense of unease and disquiet as harbingers of unwelcome social change. It is, in short, about words and their organization into prevailing vocabularies, inasmuch as these surround the depiction of crime on television and lay claim to influence the ways in which it should be perceived. As Cohen comments:

Words neither 'come from the skies' . . . nor can they be taken as literal explanations of what is happening. Nonetheless we must still listen to them very carefully . . . it is the rhetoric itself which becomes the problem.

(S. Cohen 1985: 115)

I shall argue here that if we look again at some of the debates and campaigns which have gathered around the medium, especially in relation to 'violence', we can see that these have in large measure been stimulated precisely by a sense of disquiet and uncertainty about the relations between the public and private spheres, and by extension about social order and political legitimacy in the television age. Among the many positions which have been taken up on these questions, I have been able to isolate two. I argue, first, that disparate commentators, associated with what has come to be called the 'theory of mass society' (Giner 1976) have been motivated both by the fear that mass media dominate public channels of communication and debate and by the view that this in turn means a colonization of the private sphere by 'mass' culture. Second, specific moral campaigns about 'television violence' and 'permissiveness', exemplified here through the activities of Mrs Mary Whitehouse, similarly posit a relationship between the decline of public morality and the intrusion of television into private life.

All this has large implications for our way of conceiving television's social 'effects'. Many commentators start from the premise that television and other media have pacifying, or anaesthetic, even narcotic effects (e.g. Winn 1977). A powerful, perhaps predominant, strand in commentaries on the impacts of mass media envisions a mainly passive audience, seeking distraction (Postman 1986). If at the same time the audience is also terrorized (Berger 1982) this serves only to consolidate the concentration on private pleasures. In the strong versions of this thesis television is 'mind candy' and a 'tool of stupefaction' (Gitlin 1985: 16). Gerbner's position is ultimately of this latter kind. The provocation of fear by television promotes withdrawal, and hence a further dependency on the medium at the expense of other modes of participation and exchange. If it also correlates with a preference for somewhat authoritarian outlooks (Gerbner et al 1984) these are nevertheless not actively pursued. Such views thus generally allege a tendency towards 'depoliticization' (Keane 1984; Ericson 1991: 234).

In this chapter I suggest that this at best only identifies a partial truth. Television is quite passively consumed at times (when people are tired, when they want to be allowed their own reveries), and generally within private space: but even this form of consumption is probably much less inert than it is often depicted as being. Indeed, my argument is that in reality people are capable of many and varied responses to television, some of them quite at odds with one another, and some of them passionately engaged. I do accept that there are many contemporary social pressures towards forms of privatism: anxiety about the safety and habitability of public space importantly among them. Television often speaks to those anxieties, focusing them, providing a vocabulary for talking about them, at times sublimating them in entertainment. But the private encounter with television can also provide a sort of connection (for some it is one of very few connections) with public life. For that reason the cultural politics of the medium itself takes on a magnified importance, because it becomes one of the main ways in which our kind of society talks about itself and its future. If we want to understand the impact of 'crime on TV' we need to look not only at what is on the screen but also at the talk which surrounds it and which it provokes.

Crime fictions address themselves to the anxieties of their inferred or target audience, by deploying narrative strategies which both evoke and yet contain the world's dangers. The picture is complex, however: the audience, being disparate, are not uniformly entertained or reassured. Those who feel most keenly that the world has become more dangerous and disorganized sometimes respond to television's fables with a tale of their own, about the havoc which television has wrought. One way of addressing the question of how and with what consequences anxieties about crime and social regulation are distributed is to look at the character of some of these responses to 'television violence'. Television, as the dominant medium of popular entertainment since the 1950s, has very frequently been taken as an index of (also in some versions as being more instrumentally related to) the state of society and of public morality. Have the campaigns about 'violence' helped form our assumptions about television's effects, or about the deterioration of 'law and order', or the link between the two?

Television and 'social censures'

Sumner (1990) uses the term 'social censures' to describe the crystallization of ideological categories into object domains with practical moral and political force, but whose purchase on reality is always doubtful. For Sumner censuring (including the making and enforcement of law, and the creation of orthodox criminological categories) is always 'a matter of moral-political judgement' (1990: 25).

> Censures are used for a variety of purposes and in a variety of contexts; that is, they are invoked or exist within the course of historically specific social practices. Their meaning is therefore usually fairly flexible, although some may have fundamental and strong roots in the human psyche. . . . Their general function is to signify, denounce and regulate, not to explain. . . . Their typical consequence is not an adequate account of a social conflict but rather the distinguishing of 'offenders' from 'non-offenders', the creation of resentment in their targets, or the cessation of the offensive matter. They mark off the deviant, the pathological, the dangerous and the

criminal from the normal and the good. They say 'stop', and are tied
to a desire to control, prevent or punish.

(Sumner 1990: 26–7)

One of the virtues of Sumner's position is that it keeps in view the relation
between particular instances of censuring or blaming and the general
realm of culture. What is at stake is the competitive exchange of meanings
– the problem of trying to make your interpretation count (to climb up the
hierarchy of credibility). Thus in Sumner's view the possession of social
power and the capacity to censure successfully tend to go together, while
conversely the struggles of subordinate groups almost inevitably include
an attempt at redefinition (at counter-censuring). Censures are thus not
something apart:

> Social censures have a profound existence: at the heart of intense
> emotional patterns, in the centre of politically and economically
> significant moral-ideological formations, and in the struggles and
> self-justifications that make history. . . . As such, they are vital forces
> in the constitution of societies.
>
> (Sumner 1990: 28–9)

I take the view that television is implicated in the circulation of social
censures in at least two ways. First, television narratives themselves propose and prefer categories of virtue, vice and threat. The ratified use of
violence is only the most evident of the means used to resolve crises in the
equilibrium of the world which the narrative projects. Hence, in subsequent chapters I offer an account of how the narrative strategies of television crime drama invoke and play upon images of fear and crime, and the
kinds of resolution they propose. We might call this censure *by* television.
Second, television's moral tales, and its use of 'violence' in telling them,
can also be taken as reprehensible in themselves. Hence the medium and
its messages are in turn prone to being considered as social problems.
This leads to censure *of* television, and is among the grounds for calls for
its more stringent regulation. At the same time the content of television is
used to warrant further arguments about the existence of a crisis of social
regulation. It constitutes, for some commentators, an index of a critical
'law and order' situation. To this extent television content can be called
upon as evidence in support of a censorious outlook on more general
aspects of modern life.

The television medium thus gathers and provokes public languages of
response. Academic research (especially to the extent that 'effects' research has been stimulated and sponsored either by government agencies
or by lobbying organizations: see Rowland 1983) is one such. An inter-
play between textual commentary and social comment is an entrenched
feature of journalism and punditry and of political polemics. If we define

'moral enterprise' as the attempt to secure acceptance for particular categories of censure and their attendant regimes of regulation – what Becker
(1963: 45) calls 'the creation of a new fragment of the moral constitution of
society' – then we can see that television has provided scope for morally
enterprising activities of various kinds. Either it is called to account as
being responsible for a postulated 'crisis', or it is called upon to provide
evidence of the existence of the 'crisis', or both together.

This generation of talk signals an alteration in the place of popular
culture in relation to the public sphere. It is an inherent, perhaps the only
truly demonstrable, 'effect' of broadcasting. The two registers of response
that I have isolated are illustrative of my concerns in the following ways.
First, the pessimistic testimony of literate observers, loosely styled the
'theory of mass society', corresponds for present purposes to the *longue
durée* of the development of modern media. It encodes a deep and lasting
tendency to censure forms of popular diversion (Hirsch 1976; Pearson
1983; Carey 1990). Second, the populist inflection of a related pessimism
as it has occurred in the campaigning activities, since 1964, of Mary
Whitehouse is more conjunctural and pressing: it recalls the connection to
which Mills alerts us (1959: 9–32) between personal 'troubles' and public
'issues'. It has set out to define the 'problem' of television as a distinct
political issue, but it has also set this argument in a wider anti-modernist
perspective which has much in common with the 'mass society' position.
Each of these constituencies has registered the rise of television in terms
of deep shock: it has been taken to signify the drift of history beyond
willed control or direction. The censure of television bears witness to the
fear of the future. It is here, in the questions of censure and the sense of
crisis, that the problems of the critical apprehension of television drama
and the immediate issues of the politics of crime and justice rejoin. In
seeking to identify some connections between television narratives of
crime and punishment and the available vocabularies of social moralities,
this chapter argues for a reconciliation between the priorities of film and
television studies and central criminological concerns: do the prevailing
modes of response to television actively impede the rational public discussion of crime and punishment?

Television and the theory of 'mass society'

As Seneca's fears suggest, the rhetoric of apocalypse is by no means new
or confined to our own period. None the less, it has been argued that
motifs of chaos and crisis have been particularly characteristic of the
intellectual production of our own century. Kermode states this view:

> The critical issue, given the perpetual assumption of crisis, is no less
> than the justification of ideas of order . . . in terms of what survives,

and of what we can accept as valid, in a world different from that
out of which we came.

(Kermode 1967: 124)

I take the view that the medium of television, particularly its violent
fictions and the 'ideas of order' which they both express and seek to
justify, is necessarily involved in the 'assumption of crisis'. If the politics
of television 'violence' are indeed articulated with particular allegations
of political 'crisis' (of the order which Hall et al claim to identify) this is
perhaps because both are predicated on a prior, more general and diffuse
set of domain assumptions about a crisis of social regulation in modern
society. The expression of anxiety about the effects of television incorporates responses which have been grafted on to some durable and
entrenched pessimistic and censorious styles of thought. The latter pre-
exist the advent of the medium, but the arrival and growth of the television
industries have been received as providing corroboration for, indeed as
intensifying, such existing anxieties. The development of television has
provided this body of opinion with fuel and energy. In particular, inasmuch as commentators have been preoccupied with 'ideas of order' and
have assumed the existence of crisis, a popular, technological medium
which devotes a significant proportion of its attention to the representation
of 'violence' offers an especially clear opportunity for social criticism and
complaint. The medium's perceived attentiveness to violence readily suggests a set of terms in which to criticize it, and by extension the society of
which it is taken to be indicative. As Barthes notes (1985: 307), the term
violence 'lends itself to dissertation', not least because 'Mass culture itself
has provided us with all sorts of ways of looking at this word'.

'Change and decay in all around I see'

For many critics the matter is taken as being quite simple. The explosion
of popular media has brought about the situation of cultural anarchy
which Matthew Arnold and others before and since had feared. Crime
fiction, meanwhile, is both meretricious in itself and is instrumental in
propagating brutality. Moreover, even this 'mass' form is taken to have
fallen off from its earlier precursors. Thus MacDonald (1981: 177) bewails
a decline from the 'rational and purposive' detective (Doyle's Holmes,
Poe's Dupin) to the 'crude man of action whose prowess is measured not
by intellectual mastery but by his capacity for liquor, women and mayhem'. In MacDonald's view Orwell has already shown, in his earlier
analysis of *No Orchids for Miss Blandish*, how

the brutalisation of this genre mirrors the general degeneration in
ethics from C19 standards. What he would have written had Mickey
Spillane's works been then in existence I find it hard to imagine.

(MacDonald 1981: 178)

These comments are illustrative of an entrenched tendency in critical commentaries on the role of crime in popular culture. Crime is central here, not only because of its prevalence as a theme within popular culture but also because of its suitability as a motif of censure. Crime fiction is regarded as both brutal and yet consolatory (or as Adorno would have it, 'affirmative').

It is also now evident that at least the early written history of critical responses to television and other popular media was recorded within the broad parameters of a more general pessimism. This has come to be termed the 'theory of mass society'. As recent observers, notably Giner (1976) and Swingewood (1977) note, the dominant inflection of literate commentaries on modernity, and especially on the role of mass entertainments within it, has been marked by pessimism, hauteur and a presumption of decadence. On such accounts 'mass culture' both unleashes *les classes dangereuses* from their traditional disciplines and supplies a new mode of incorporation in the form of the seductions of affluence and distraction (see Carey 1990).

The proliferation of pessimistic meditations on mass culture has been so great, and has taken place in such diverse circumstances, that one can question the usefulness of a single 'mass society' rubric. After all, this groups together figures as disparate as English literary and cultural critics (Eliot, Leavis) and an array of other European and American thinkers (Nietzsche, Ortega y Gasset, Weber, Jaspers, Heidegger, Shils, Bell). In many stylizations the Frankfurt school of critical theorists (Adorno, Horkheimer, Marcuse) would also be included.

However, Giner (1976: 115) convincingly identifies common preoccupations. Foremost among these is the 'wane of community' associated with the growth of the modern city whose character (*magna civitas, magna solitudo*) is seen as casting the individual 'adrift in a world of *ersatz* communities, ephemeral, shallow personal relationships' (Giner 1976: 121). Jaspers's comments are emblematic of such elegies for the *Gemeinschaft*:

> In modern times men have been shuffled together like grains of sand. They are elements of an apparatus in which they occupy now one location, now another: not parts of a historical substance which they imbue with their selfhood . . . a feeling of powerlessness has become rife, and man tends to regard himself as dragged along in the wake of events which he had hoped to guide.
>
> (Jaspers 1951: 11)

The 'mass' character of culture and communication in modern society may be attributable to demographic and technological factors (for some it is the determined outcome of these, see Ellul 1980: 311) but 'massness' always carries an imputation about a *quality*, as well as an observation about the sheer size of cities and conurbations, as Raymond Williams has well noted (1976: 195–200). The 'mass' is inherently susceptible to manipulation and to the attractions of a (perhaps covert) totalitarianism: it is this fear which draws Marxist and conservative writers most closely together.[1] The notion of massness is thus part of what Cohen calls the '*via negativa* of community'. The evocation of past communities stands in contrast to 'urban confusion and degradation'. In this sense the notion of massness partakes of a more general 'demodernization impulse' (S. Cohen 1985: 119–20).

Massness and the public sphere

A 'mass', as John Thompson points out, is a 'heap' (1988: 366). It lacks structure, order, definition. The kind of culture typical of the members of a mass will similarly lack form, purpose, distinction, refinement. At the same time, the masses are the many. They tend to predominate and overwhelm, as Nietzsche feared: 'Everywhere the mediocre are combining to make themselves master' (quoted by Carey 1990: 34). Masses may have no culture worthy of the name, but they have the advantage of numbers and they have technology and expertise, including in the modern era literacy and the 'mass media'. Thus the critique of industrialism, as expressed by D. H. Lawrence, for example, is easily elided with the anathematization of the masses who must inhabit the ant-hills of industrial production. The masses also include the 'specialists without spirit, sensualists without heart' whom Max Weber (1930: 182) sees peopling the 'cage of the future' in the closing paragraphs of *The Protestant Ethic*. Karl Mannheim follows Weber in distinguishing 'substantive' from 'functional' rationality (1940: 41). This divergence, between reason and mere bureaucratic rationale, engenders, in Mannheim's view, a return to violence, brutality and impulsiveness, because it accompanies a decline in moral reasoning. It is a short step from this Weberian duality to Ortega's identification of totalitarianism with the extension of the franchise into a politically illiterate culture (Ortega y Gasset 1976). For Ortega, as much as for Adorno (1954: 269) or Marcuse (1964: 79), the principal enemy of humaneness is ease, and the principal sources of easy, heedless gratification and pleasure are the leisure industries and especially the provision of generic, formulaic fictions by the mass media. This view seems close to what Mills (1956) called 'the professional ideology of social pathologists'. It is ironic, therefore, to see how close Mills himself stands to this view when it comes to discussing the consumption of mass media. For Mills what results is

a relatively comfortable, half-welfare and half-garrison society in which the population grows passive, indifferent and atomised: in which traditional loyalties, ties and associations become lax or dissolve completely: in which coherent publics based on different opinions and interests gradually fall apart: and in which man becomes a consumer, himself mass produced like the products, diversions and values which he absorbs.

(Mills 1956: 301)

Such comments do bespeak a deep concern. They allege the loss of a vital public sphere. Among the symptoms of this is the attenuation of commitment to agreed standards of taste and excellence. Such a position (and some such position is very widely adopted, even where it is less explicitly acknowledged) necessarily entails attention to the continuity between the spheres of the political and the aesthetic.

Criticisms of 'mass society' assumptions
Theoretical criticisms of these positions are well known, and perhaps of secondary interest here. Giner (1976: 208) argues that mass society theories are based on a misunderstanding of the 'schemes of social polarity' (mechanical: organic; *Gemeinschaft: Gesellschaft*) of classical social theory. As such they have, in striving always for a descriptive epithet for a 'whole society', failed to observe diversity, the persistence of primary group affiliations and tendencies towards social reconstruction as well as disorganization (Giner 1976: 218). That is, in equating the rise of mass culture with a crisis of social and moral regulation they have disqualified themselves from accounting for new, revised or surviving forms of social regulation, thereby severely inhibiting their own contribution to the understanding of industrial societies. Moreover, for both Giner (1976: 248) and Swingewood (1977: 75) mass society theory has infiltrated Marxism in the form of a 'radical pessimism' based on an (erroneous) assumption of the successful incorporation of the working class via the explicit use of propaganda and the anaesthetic influence of mass produced popular culture. As E. P. Thompson (1965) observes, the mass society perspective 'inevitably defines only a ruling class as hegemonic, while a subordinate class is always corporate' (quoted in Swingewood 1977: 32). More pertinently perhaps, it is evident that the over-literal enforcement of an organicist metaphor to describe socially desirable ends (society should resemble a well functioning organism) has its necessary correlative language of pathology (morbidity, syndrome). The particular proneness of crime to this kind of treatment is well documented (see Pearson 1983; S. Cohen 1985.)

Furthermore, mass society assumptions are particularly prone to the quest for Golden Ages (see Pearson 1983: 207–13; R. Williams 1973: ch. 4). The dislike of the masses and their mass-mediated distractions; the opposition between present massness and past community: each of these looks like an example of what MacLuhan (1964) calls 'rear view mirrorism', namely the tendency to deprecate emergent cultural forms in a language inherited from earlier traditions. In this sense the mass society notion is inherently given to nostalgia, which Cohen understands to entail

> a look back at a real or imagined past community as providing the ideal and desirable form of social control. This impulse is reaction- ary and conservative, not in the literal political sense, but in always locating the desired state of affairs in a past which has now (usually *just* now) been eclipsed by something undesirable.
>
> (S. Cohen 1985: 118)

However this may be, my main purpose here is to signal the prevalence and tenacity of the rhetorical motifs common in mass society theory both in attempts to characterize modernity and in the weight of presumption accorded to the malign influence of popular media within it. If, as Ellul (1980) and Giner (1976) both suggest, one characteristic of the modern era is obsessive self-examination and hence a continual 'naming' of the state of society (mass, industrial, advanced, post-industrial, technological, technetronic, spectacular, etc) it may well be that the mass society perspective has indeed provided much of our most current and resonant imagery and vocabulary (Giner 1976: 246). Indeed, it may be that at least some of the propositions which underpin the notion of 'mass society' are not at all easily disposable. As Giner concludes

> The quasi ideology of mass society is right and 'true' at least in one sense: it is accepted by a collectivity because it responds in some authentic way to their mental and moral needs. In its ambiguities and varieties it has satisfied the demands of cultural philistines, incurable reactionaries, disappointed left-wingers and latter day enemies of the new modes of oppresssion of the technocratic and technological world.
>
> (Giner 1976: 259)

This points to two principal theoretical requirements. The first is to assess the truth-claims of the interpretation of modernity which under- pins the mass society critique of popular culture. The second is to offer an account of its persistence and popularity. The refusal by professional social scientists of large claims about television's malign causal 'effects' on behaviour on technical and methodological grounds, while necess- ary, is only obliquely relevant. It can challenge the mass society perspec- tive's claim to factual veracity but cannot necessarily defuse its rhetorical potency. This is largely because the theory of mass society speaks a 'mixed discourse of force and meaning' (Ricoeur 1970: 65–9), of causality and aesthetic valuation, and declines to differentiate between these. Indeed, as Cohen remarks, 'Nostalgia does not depend on intellectual rigour: what matters is the symbolic evocation of a lost world' (S. Cohen 1985: 118).

Mass society and moral panics

These reflections, however, suggest a degree of inadequacy in certain terms claiming to describe relevant rhetorics. Principal among these in recent social science is the notion of 'moral panic', which is intended to designate a periodic tendency towards the identification and scapegoating of 'folk devils' (S. Cohen 1972) whose activities are regarded as indicative of imminent moral breakdown. Such moments are characterized by the disproportionate demand for the punishment or disciplining of deviant subordinate groups. Cohen's original formulation of the term was a modest and descriptive one, beginning by simply noting an observed tendency: 'Societies appear to be subject every now and then to periods of moral panic' (1972: 9). One danger in attaching too much weight to this idea would be that, while usefully drawing attention to the recurrence of themes of social anxiety and their association with rhetorics of crisis, it elides all such 'panics' under a single heading, representing them as a consequence of some (hypothetically universal, endlessly cyclical) feature of social life, namely panickyness. The aim, then, is to counter or subvert the allegation of crisis by an account of its repetitious and historically relative character (Barker 1984a; 1984b). In such usages the notion of moral panic comes close to being 'obsessed with debunking' in the way that Cohen has since warned against (1985: 156): it sets out with the formed intention of reaching an agnostic conclusion. This kind of argument sometimes fails to apprehend that the very fact of the recurrence of 'moral panics' might suggest not so much a persistent irrationality as the expression of fundamental contradictions in social relations, that is a 'crisis tendency' in something more akin to Habermas's sense (1976): why do some panic-prone themes crop up repeatedly? Conversely, in assigning each present 'crisis' to the inclusive category of moral panic it risks disregarding the particular features of the language and imagery, origins and implications of each: why for example do some 'panics' gain weight and momentum and others not? What is thus not given due weight by such analyses of these rhetorics is the depth and continuity of the fear and loathing of modernity which they represent, nor the specificity of the constituencies from which they emanate. What is at stake is not a series of discrete 'panics' about crime, or about television, or even about these two conjointly, but rather a continuing and intrinsic involvement between these terms and the impulse to refuse the present time.

More than this, the tendency within both the theory of mass society and what I shall call populist conservative fundamentalism to seek comparisons and justifications by reference to an ideal, organic past community, however vaguely specified, is not an arbitrary fiction. It is easy to establish that tradition can be invented and that, to be politically service-able the past is subject to acts of appropriation; but such appropriations are not always merely fanciful. As Cohen observes, the images of com-munity which nostalgia generates are 'deep and historically resonant enough to have been genuinely believed as well as genuinely influential' (1985: 121). In this sense nostalgia records, perhaps sentimentally, a vari-ety of responses to the fact that the world does indeed change, and it can use an expression of commitment to the past as a way of rejecting the present. Karl Mannheim pertinently comments

> Thus modern society is a world of rifts and dislocations, contradic-tory views and moral codes. . . . In a word, the modern world is beset by the contemporaneity of the non-contemporaneous.
>
> (K. Mannheim 1940: 41)

The experience of dislocation may have distinct origins and inflections among different classes or 'taste cultures' (Shils 1978). Yet these may coalesce in taking popular media, whose predilection for violence is both the most evident and the most charged of their alleged misdeeds, as emblematic of and/or instrumental in bringing about the most shocking and frightful aspects of modernity. For the mass society perspective, given its intimate association with and constant appeal to a canonical tradition of literary texts as the embodiment, in Arnold's dictum of 'the best that has been thought and said', one dimension of the experience of dislocation is the displacement of writing by other, and intrinsically in-ferior, technologies of inscription. Where the criterion of aesthetic value is given by the 'transcendent masterpieces of world literature' (Shils 1978: 207) television is automatically deprecated (see Schiach 1988). Within this perspective, the growth of crime is explicable both in terms of the diminu-tion of informal social controls (local loyalties, deference, respect for el-ders) and of the substitution for an educative discourse of mutual obligation and aesthetic value, of a schematic moral universe centring upon acquisitiveness and revenge. The fear of mass society and the fear of television go hand in hand.

Mary Whitehouse: television and the corruption of culture

Why then have I thought it necessary to rehearse this litany of complaint against mass media and popular diversion? First, because although the mass society preoccupation is principally the prerogative of literate elites who fear that high culture stands in danger of being overwhelmed by vulgarity, it has also come to represent a body of received ideas which have more popular inflections. The polemics and campaigns which have marked Mary Whitehouse's public career can be understood as one such. Second, Whitehouse is mainly of interest as an example of one for whom television provides the 'crystallising focus' (Pearson 1983: 230) for the 'pulse of our contemporary anxieties' (1983: 210). At the same time, if we are to do more than accept a 'flat earth' (Pearson 1983: 207) or merely 'debunking' (S. Cohen 1985: 121) account of the recurrence of television as a theme in anxious social commentary, then Whitehouse's career requires a more strenuous effort of interpretation than it has generally received. The vision of mass society provides part of the intellectual context for such an interpretation.

The notion of a populist version of a mass society critique appears to be a contradiction in terms. How can the critique of mass society emerge from the 'mass' itself? In one sense this merely signals an incoherence in the whole mass society idea: 'mass' designates nothing, except the derogation of 'the vulgar' as amorphous and indistinct. As Raymond Williams notes, 'the masses' do not exist:

> I do not think of my relatives, friends, neighbours, colleagues as masses: we none of us can or do. The masses are always the others, whom we don't know and can't know. Yet now, in our kind of society, we see these others regularly in their myriad variations: stand physically beside them. They are here and we are with them. And that we are with them is, of course, the whole point. To other people we also are masses. Masses are other people.
>
> (R. Williams 1976: 282)

'Mass', then, is a complex word. 'Massness' records the experience of the writer's position in relation to the collective image of others in the 'enlarged state of society'. In a similar spirit, John Carey argues:

> The mass is a metaphor for the unknowable, the invisible. We cannot see the mass. Crowds can be seen; but the mass is a metaphor for the crowd in its metaphysical aspect – the sum of all possible crowds, and that can take on conceptual form only as metaphor. The metaphor of the mass has the advantage, from the viewpoint of individual self-assertion, of turning other people into a conglomerate. It denies them the individuality which we ascribe to ourselves, and to people we know.
>
> (Carey 1990: 44)

The idea of 'mass communication' both encodes a dismissive elite valuation *and* a self-actualizing tendency in practice, namely the superimposition upon the reality of technologies of multiple transmission to an indefinitely large audience of the idea of 'masses'. Williams's understanding of the consequences for communication of a presumption of massness is clear. The intention of transmission is decisively restricted towards manipulation (see Keane's account of early theorists of 'public opinion', and their view that 'the empirical art of politics consists largely in the creation of opinion by the deliberate exploitation of sub-conscious, non-rational preferences': Wallas 1920, quoted in Keane 1984: 148).

For Whitehouse and other moral campaigners (I shall argue) anxiety resides partly in *being addressed* as if one were a part of the mass, when in fact one is a member of something far more dignified, namely a 'silent majority'. This is not merely (although it is also) a self-serving ratifying appeal. Rather it is an attempt to salvage the sense of belonging to a coherent, bonded public. As A. Smith (1974: 180–209) records, Whitehouse's concern has thus been as much directed towards structures of accountability and access as to denunciation and censure. For Wallis (1976: 276) this concentration depends on the conviction that whereas her organization is small in itself it *represents* widespread opinion, while the media (though widespread) represent elite, non-accountable views.

The 'moral career' of a 'moral entrepreneur'
Whitehouse's public career began in 1964 with the 'Clean up TV' campaign. The concerns of this movement were later placed on a more permanent footing in the form of the National Viewers' and Listeners' Association (NVALA). The chronology of this career is well documented by Tracey and Morrison (1979), A. Smith (1974) and, in a eulogizing biography, by Caulfield (1975).

Tracey and Morrison (1979: 33) argue (following Fussell 1977) that one can view twentieth-century history as 'a series of watersheds in the fracturing of common memory'. Whitehouse's project may be interpreted as an attempt to reinstate one version of the 'common memory'. As such it includes a preoccupation with the history and trajectory of and the prognoses for modernity and offers an account of these. Viewed in this light Whitehouse's views are more coherent than is often taken to be the case: given her preoccupation with the secularization of modern culture and its subjection to spectacular consumption she has been, in a sense, acute in taking television as the main focus of her concerns.

For Whitehouse, with an unusual explicitness, the history of television and the history of the post-war world are indivisible. Indeed her periodization of British cultural history is presented in terms of eras of television, and especially of the BBC. The long, settled years of the Reithian BBC (educative, consensualist, interested in continuity and stability) are counterposed to the turbulence of the BBC of the 1960s under Hugh Carleton-Greene. Later, in 1974, at the peak of her celebrity – immediately following an influential submission to the Annan Committee on the Future of Broadcasting (1977) and an invitation to address a Council of Europe seminar on 'Television in a democratic society' – Whitehouse stated her position succinctly. Television is a pedagogic medium. Yet those who control it observe no substantive moral code. They therefore 'teach' amorality:

What we have seen over the years is the unthinkable being made thinkable by the media; the thinkable becomes seeable and the seeable doable.

It is a short step from the doable to the done; and from the done to the done thing: for if a thing is done often enough it has a strong tendency to become acceptable and accepted . . . the public should be free from this assault on their sensibilities.

(Whitehouse 1974a: 4)

In the next edition of her organization's journal another author writes:

Broadcasting and the media are breeder reactors. They help to generate the kind of activity on which they thrive.

It is perfectly obvious that much violence and evil behaviour would lose its glamour if it were not publicised and brought into our homes in all its action and glorious colour. . . . This is what is rotting away the standards of life today.

(B. Mead 1974)

For Whitehouse and her circle the struggle over the direction of television in the modern world takes place within an orientation towards ultimate values. There is a necessary association between television and violence, on this view, but it is not a causal thesis as a social psychologist would frame it. Television is both the index and the agent of the abandonment, in modern society, of the basic disciplines which make a stable and orderly society possible. Hence, Whitehouse speaks of 'the Christian faith and ethics upon which the stability, culture and democratic nature of western society has been based' (quoted in Tracey and Morrison 1979: 87). In this conceptual universe discipline is the only guarantor of liberty, because it is our only bulwark against our own sinful natures. Only self-abnegation and restraint stand between us and the vertiginous plunge into barbarism. This is often asserted with scant regard for the niceties of historical accuracy. As Whitehouse's admiring biographer would have it:

The thin veneer of civilization that has kept the brute within all of us at bay has been deliberately [sic] cracked and we are back in the eighteenth century.

(Caulfield 1975).

The most vehement expressions of distaste and anger are reserved for the BBC, for intellectuals and mandarin civil servants. The refusal among these groups to take seriously the urgency of the message can only indicate either excessive detachment or bad faith. These elites practise 'inverted censorship'. They constitute a 'progressively illiberal establishment of the *avant garde*'. It is here that the responsibility for moral debilitation lies:

Exclusion, ridicule, misrepresentation are very effective censors, and they were applied ruthlessly to the values which, right through the centuries, had been accepted as basic to a stable and responsible society, and to the people who fought to maintain them.

(Whitehouse 1974b: 5)

The values of the 'whole Judaeo-Christian Tradition' are also the 'words and ideas which characterised the common people' to whom are counterposed a 'small, fanatical group' (1974b: 5).

Accountability is therefore an intrinsic strand of Whitehouse's argument. The technocratic insulation of the elite and the absence of a binding public morality are, in her view, inextricably linked. The broadcasting companies (especially the BBC) are bureaucratically high-handed in their treatment of the viewer ('just an audience rating cipher'). Whereas they have no understanding of the public she 'represents much of the broad middle class' (Caulfield 1975: 132). A persistent theme of this concern is a view of television as an *imposition* upon the people and, worst of all, an invasion of the familial home. Television is thus open to description in terms not only of contagion, rot, putrefaction but also of violation (Caulfield 1975: 137) of the 'sacrosanct hearth' (Tracey and Morrison 1979: 199).

Whitehouse experiences a sense of being besieged by television, and her argument suggests that it has eroded the 'buffers' which might protect the private sphere from unwelcome public intrusion (S. Cohen 1985: 135; see also Lasch 1977). As Tracey and Morrison observe:

Violation was, however, very much a corollary of the rise of television, since beamed into the heart of the home were beliefs which were held to be neither valid nor legitimate because they were ungodly, and it was to that violation that Whitehouse responded.

(Tracey and Morrison 1979: 197)

Hence the tone of Whitehouse's response has been one of pained surprise as well as of anger:

There is some strange dark force at work which protects the media. When the chips are down and the choice is between what people call freedom on the one hand and the welfare of children and society on the other, then the intelligentsia, the opinion formers, those responsible for film and television, close ranks and defend their own highly specialised version of 'freedom'. Why? Why? Why? Is it money? Is it intellectual pride and an authoritarianism that cannot brook contradiction? Or is it, as in some cases it most surely is, a commitment to cultural and political anarchy? Otherwise how does it come about that minds are so closed and intellectual integrity so prostituted?

(Whitehouse 1978: 15)

A quite particular sense of desertion attaches to the fear that the master institutions of cultural continuity and identity have, as it were, gone over to the side of modernity, of scepticism, of the heterogeneity of belief and experience. The discourse of Protestant moral conviction, whose legitimizing principles include a certainty of centrality and orthodoxy, finds itself marginal and in dissent.

Television and permissiveness

This returns us to my opening argument that the strength of feeling which is generated within arguments about the regulation of television stems from an anxiety about the relations between the public and private spheres which the issue of 'television violence' is taken to encapsulate in a special way (Ericson 1991: 238–9). For Whitehouse and others such violences are specifically the outcome of 'permissiveness', construed not just as a general social trend but as the orthodox position of the state. 'Permissiveness' is thus a *period*, initiated most visibly by the *Report of the Committee on Homosexual Offences and Prostitution, 1957* (Wolfenden Committee) (Home Office 1957). Wolfenden's conclusion that 'we are not charged to enter into matters of private moral conduct, except insofar as they directly affect the public good' provides one of the early benchmarks of social alarm about official 'permissiveness'. As S. Hall (1980a) remarks Wolfenden's 'scandal' was its agnosticism. It suggested a revised notion of the state's role in social regulation by implicitly reducing it to an arbitrator of orderly exchange between freely contracting individuals and therefore not itself obliged to propound substantive views. This was closely followed by the inadequacy, in Whitehouse's view, of the Obscene Publications Act 1959, which in any case did not apply to television. Television was therefore to be regulated by internal codes of practice, elaborated by precisely those people to whom Whitehouse felt the greatest antagonism. The exclusion of television from the provisions of the legislation was defended on grounds of privacy: yet television had precisely breached Whitehouse's sense of privacy, depriving her and her supporters of any refuge from the acknowledgement of their insecure social position.

Although, as S. Hall (1980a) has argued, the 'first wave' of permissiveness (under R. A. Butler's Home Office) did little more than rationalize legal regulation in the direction of existing current practice, it nevertheless signified a drift which was unacceptable to Whitehouse. The grounds for the beginnings of Whitehouse's interventions are thus provided by the conjunction of events of the turn of the decade, especially as they crystallized around the television medium: the beginning of officially sponsored liberalism, the arrival of ITV, the mass ownership of television sets. The 'second wave' of 'permissive' measures under Roy

Jenkins's tenure at the Home Office (relating to abortion, divorce, homosexuality and capital punishment and which were in any case more pronounced) provided further stimulus to a reaction which was already underway.

Insightful observers of Mrs Whitehouse and the NVALA have noted the inherent ironies of this position. As Wallis remarks:

> The members of moral crusades may feel that the very foundations of society are threatened by some form of behaviour, but they organize in defence of that view for the very reason that it lacks consensual acceptance.
>
> (Wallis 1976: 272)

Wallis relates the aggressive championing of traditionally respectable civic virtues (thrift, deferment of gratification, religious observance) as well as the insistence on representativeness to the insecurity of certain fractions of the middle and 'respectable' working classes, especially those excluded by virtue of age or geography from the forefront of economic and technological change, in the face of the increasing functional superfluity of those commitments: spectacular consumption replaces thrift as a social obligation in a technological, mass production economy.

Other observers broadly concur in this assessment of the depth of the offence which is thus given to Whitehouse's 'this-worldly asceticism' (Wallis 1976: 285; see also Tracey and Morrison 1979: ch. 10; Pratt and Sparks 1987). Tracey and Morrison (1979: 188) likewise recognize that the urgency of Whitehouse's mission stems from the marginalization of her constituency. In their view the dynamics of industrial society precipitate the traumas of an ever more complexly differentiated occupational structure and of 'disenchantment'. Diverse groups and value orientations are protected from the full force of these convulsions by their partial isolation from one another until television's decisive breaching of the walls of the home finally destroys all possibility of refuge and necessitates, for some, a more belligerent posture of defence. As Pratt and Sparks also argue (1987), Whitehouse's arguments have rarely been sufficiently analytic to produce substantive knowledge of television's involvement in historical change. Yet, from her vantage point in an intense ideological contest, she has located an appropriate enemy.

Television in law-and-order mythology

The certainty with which both academic observers inquiring into television's effects and polemicists castigating the modern era by reference to television, have claimed to know exactly what social influences television exerts has been delusive. As Cohen has observed:

Any topic of interest in social science has a peculiarly amorphous quality. It looks distinct, tangible, separate – empirically or conceptually – but the closer you examine it, the more it merges into the surrounding space. . . . We move into spaces which are not just amorphous but imagined and imaginary.

(S. Cohen 1985: 197)

One confronts a situation in which either the fixity of an excessively formal model or a rhetorically exaggerated account of television's implication in events risks doing violence to the fluid complexities of social process. Whitehouse's passion is itself an 'effect' of television, whether or not the claims she makes (which may in principle be empirically investigable) can be substantiated.

It is apparent that Whitehouse has a good deal in common with the critique of mass society, in the association which both forge between the historical trajectory of the modern era and the history of the mass media. Ironically, at the same time as the notion of television 'effects' enters the common currency of our everyday speech, the critic of television is forced to present herself as being always against the current.

The interest in recounting the history of Whitehouse's interventions lies not in their being dominant (they are rather the reverse emanating from a growing sense of marginality) but from the fact that they nevertheless indicate in a concentrated way some of the ideological weight which television and 'violence' have been called upon to bear. Albeit in more sporadic and attenuated ways elements of these anxieties also permeate more central debates about crime, law enforcement and moral regulation.[2]

Hence, for example, the *Daily Mail* (13 November 1985), reporting Mr Norman Tebbit's Disraeli Lecture of the previous evening, asserted that

If a week's peak hour viewing could be retrieved from the archives of 1960 . . . and compared to the diet of gratuitous violence, sex and swearing that in 1985 passes for family viewing we should all of us be able to see how far standards have plunged.

Even this language is insufficiently florid for some observers; witness *Cambridgeshire Pride Magazine* (August 1985):

It was Winston Churchill who pointed out to the British people the need to stand up to an aggressor – or plunge forever into the abyss of a new dark age. . . . The good fight was fought and won, but the new dark age has nevertheless descended upon us with the grim inevitability of predetermined fate. Today on any television news bulletin . . .

Television, therefore, occupies a special place in the demonology of populist conservative fundamentalism. Not only is it an evil influence in itself, but also it provides a token or symptom of modernity which seems to allow comparison with images of order and stability drawn from some indefinitely specified point in the past.

Both crime and television function as metaphors for contemporary troubles. Their intersection in television violence is thus doubly resonant. Television is both the bearer of bad news and bears responsibility for it. The constant reiteration of characteristic generic forms of television, within a relatively predictable schedule (Garnham 1973; Gitlin 1985) lends credence to the ordinary critical stances built around it. The fixity of these perspectives suggests the possibility of addressing concrete events and processes through television yet, in reality, displaces the discussion on to a plane whose purchase on actuality is ever more tenuous.

*Truly, though our element is time, / We are not suited to the long
perspectives / Open at each instant of our lives. / They link us to our
losses   (Larkin 1964)*

Myths of crime and punishment are very ancient. The particular features of their inflection through television are very recent, but none the less deeply entrenched. It is through the appeal that these tales make to the modern audience that the myth of crime and punishment (see Scheingold 1984: 64) infiltrates the fine grain of our cultural experience. In particular we can see the vehement enthusiasm with which certain constituencies within the general population re-tell the narrative as though it showed the way the world is now (S. Hall et al 1978: 158). This secondary narration, inherently moral and rhetorical, conservative and yet dissenting, adds a myth of television to the levels of myth which television itself propagates. In so doing it corresponds very closely to what Nisbet sees as the defining appeal of conservative popular belief:

> But when men become separated or feel themselves separated from traditional institutions, there arises, along with the spectre of the lost individual, the spectre of lost authority. Fears and anxieties run over the intellectual landscape like masterless dogs. Inevitably in such circumstances men's minds turn to the problem of authority.
>
> (Nisbet 1970: 108)

The rhetorical critique of violence on television is a 'story of change' about the loss of community (S. Cohen 1985: 115). The persistent force of the story which Whitehouse wishes to tell and the reason for its ultimate failure both derive from its 'de-modernizing' rhetoric (S. Cohen 1985: 122). If, Cohen asks, the ideal form of social control is always in the past, has always been spoiled by modern trends, how, even where the vision has some claim to authenticity, can one 'recreate mimetically' something for which, on one's own account, the conditions no longer exist in industrial society? One is left retailing myths of purification and, as Sennet observes (1970: 98), the 'essence of the purification mechanism is a fear of losing control'.

Implications for the study of 'violence' in the media
There seems little prospect of diminishing the rhetorical force which attaches to 'violence on television' simply by introducing a sceptical argument about alarmism and moral panic. The 'passions and social sentiments' (Garland, 1990a: 8) involved are deeply engrained, and it is a measure of television's importance as a medium of exchange that people engage with and against it passionately. Never mind that professional social scientists sometimes sound pained at the imprecision with which 'their' topic is spoken about; they should first note that it is spoken about with feeling. There is an analogy here with the indeterminacy of crime statistics themselves (Pearson 1983: 218). Although it seems more oblique, we can actually study the record of what has been thought and said about television and violence with more certainty than we know its supposed 'direct' or 'objective' effects.

There could be little scope therefore for a magisterial sociology of the mass media which, in attempting to ground its claim to 'know better' (Dunn 1985: 142), sought to disregard the rhetorics in which its subject matter is 'always and already' (Keane 1984: 176) enmeshed. There are many empirical claims to be settled, but the politics of television violence are not reducible without remainder to these terms. Populist conservative fundamentalism poses in an acute form Kermode's problem of the 'justification of ideas of order': perhaps one can respond only by seeking to recover some criteria of reasonability for such justifications.

It seems that the channels whereby crime is introduced into everyday speech and belief are not conducive to the growth of such reasonability. The prevailing (and the marginal) understandings of crime and television in their relation to social change must be both accounted for and objected to as a precondition of an informed public discourse. The analysis of public representations of crime is not adequately treated either by content analyses which merely enumerate factual errors and distortions (as it often appears in Gerbner), nor is it properly understood as a technical operation in discourse analysis (Pecheux 1982). However, it is necessary to insist that media imagery and public vocabularies are part of the object domain of criminology, at least to the extent that these inform and drive public perceptions and define the position which 'law and order' occupies as a term in public debate.

On what then does a more reasonable discussion depend? As Arendt argues (1970: 64), following Chomsky, rationality is not the opposite of emotion. Rather, the opposites of emotion are the 'detachment and equanimity' of a spurious objectivism and the 'sentimentality' of inauthentic responses. The positions which Mrs Whitehouse and the critics of mass society variously adopt are disreputable not because they are normative, or even rhetorical, but because their rhetoric is inadequate, inappropriate and therefore sentimentally irresponsible. As Arendt comments, 'Rage and violence turn irrational only when they are directed against substitutes' (1970: 64).

Both television crime drama, as a schematic fable of purification, and the nostalgic critique of modernity through television, are directed at substitutes in just this way. Schematic texts have permitted schematic criticism. Thus when Holbrook (1976) writes 'Our industrial-commerical culture is the culture of hate, and it is spoiling human society everywhere', he counterposes a mythical past to a paranoid present and winds up talking nonsense in the way that Pearson identifies as characteristic of law-and-order mythology (1983: 212). Holbrook's language is excessive and offers no cogent orientation to the future. Marcuse writes:

> The word becomes cliché, and as cliché governs the speech or the writing; the communication plus precludes genuine development of meaning . . . the sentence becomes a declaration to be accepted – it repels demonstration, qualification, negation of its codified and declared meaning. . . . This language, which constantly imposes images, militates against the development and expression of concepts. In its immediacy and directness, it impedes conceptual thinking; thus, it impedes thinking.
>
> (Marcuse 1964: 79)

It is an irony that the iconography of television violence and the critical vocabulary which opposes it speak, in a profound sense, the same language. They employ the same rhetorical figures of order and disorder, they appeal to the same anxieties. If we are to talk responsibly about crime and punishment, then we must make the attempt to disentangle ourselves from this rhetoric, which we can only do by understanding and accounting for it. If, as Hall fears, we stand in danger of 'drifting into a law and order society' (S. Hall 1980b) the colonization, in our society, of the main channels of communication (both fiction and reportage) by an imagery of order and symbolic threat may be one dimension of this movement. In resisting such tendencies the recovery of articulate discussion of social order and the cultivation of sophisticated critical responses to the mass media are necessarily related tasks. The responsibility of critical examination is that of 'finding and exposing things that otherwise lie hidden beneath piety, heedlessness or routine' (Said 1980: 188). Between the piety of Whitehouse and the heedless routine of everyday television a great deal is hidden which is dangerous. One point at issue is thus the way in which connections have been posited between the regulation of television and the overt politics of 'law and order' in such a way as to collapse any distinctness between these spheres. Another concerns the difficulty for analysis in describing this assimilation without sacrificing its own prerogative of critique. This poses questions for both the objectivist theory of media 'effects' and the relativist notion of 'moral panic'. Is either of these capable of postulating a normative theory of 'television violence' which is both empirically grounded and morally persuasive?

For the time being, however, I must draw back from these big questions. In the next chapter I consider in more detail recent empirical debates about television, the fear of crime and more diffuse forms of social anxiety and seek to infer what theoretical and methodological requirements these stipulate for the examination of television content and its likely impacts on audiences.

4 Television, dramatization and the fear of crime

L'agression ne touche le corps qu'à travers les media, c'est dans ce sens que la médiatisation generalisée est à l'image d'une violence virale. Tous les faits d'agression et d'angoisse sont signifiés par avance, pris en charge par les discours et les récits des média.

H.-P. Jeudy, *La Peur et les média: essai sur la virulence*

Television and the 'scary world'

For many years a debate has continued (often ill-temperedly) about whether watching lots of television (and especially 'violent' television) provokes an increased level of fearfulness in at least some members of its audience. I have suggested (see Chapter 2 and following Giddens 1984) that, like other routine ways of spending time, watching television can in fact be seen as involved in maintaining security in the face of a range of anxieties. However, I have also suggested (Chapters 2 and 3), that the ways in which television might perform this task, and especially the extent to which its narratives of crime and law enforcement address a tension between anxiety and security, are problematic. In particular I have argued, that for at least a fraction of the audience television is felt to subvert not only the 'sense of place' (Meyrowitz 1985) but also, and more specifically, to violate a sense of propriety. In this respect the medium itself is a focus of anxiety, and is viewed in its felt relation to a range of social problems. Any such response tends to deploy interpretations of television content, and seeks to secure acceptance of those interpretations and not others. For these reasons it is impossible to accept an opposition between theories of the medium and its reception on the one hand (Meyrowitz 1985; Morley and Silverstone 1988) and theories of the ideological weight of television content on the other. Perspectives which stress the position of television in everyday life, and hence the active choices and uses made of it by a differentiated audience, will be incomplete unless they also attend to features of that which is chosen and used. Why do audiences prefer particular forms of television, and with what consequences? With what other dimensions of their social experience does television viewing intersect?

The question of the content of crime fiction on television is best construed in terms of the appeal it mounts to viewers in concrete social contexts. I shall argue here that one dimension of this appeal relates to viewers' prior beliefs about and anxieties concerning crime. This also gives rise to the conjecture that the representation of crime and law enforcement in television fiction also acts as a surrogate for other and more diffuse kinds of anxiety. One interesting feature of crime fiction, therefore, is the possibility of displacement (Knight 1980: 192; M. Williams 1982: 140). Crime fiction may permit ulterior uses of crime and disorder, in both arousing and placating social anxieties whose primary origin may or may not stem from criminal events as such. This may in turn influence the conduct and direction of political discourses about crime which, unlike the narrative itself, explicitly claim the force of truth. These include electoral law-and-order campaigns, as well as the activities of censorship lobbies and their associated beliefs about social trends.

The problem of 'content' and fear of crime

Disagreements about the significance of television, and in particular about the analysis of television content, in this area centre on three main issues, namely

1 the attribution of excessiveness or inappropriateness to the indices of fear elicited from viewers
2 the adequacy and pertinence of the measures of content which are proposed
3 the degree of determining influence which is claimed for characteristic kinds of television content over viewers' views of the world.

Most students of the depiction of crime and law enforcement on television have deployed quantitative techniques of content analysis (Gerbner et al 1969; Gerbner 1970; Dominick 1973; Gerbner and Gross 1976a; 1976b; Pandiani 1978; Krippendorf 1980). However, some observers, for example Gunter (1985), now argue that systematic content analysis necessarily tends to privilege its own readings of television content and hence to assume that viewers' orientations towards that content will more or less resemble one another. This objection has some force with respect to the kinds of content analysis which have hitherto been undertaken, especially by Gerbner and his collaborators. These tend to argue that crime fiction is troubling because of its variance from or distortion of reality, while acknowledging no special problem in recovering what that reality is like.

Such an approach seeks to isolate a determinate and measurable effect of viewing through multivariate statistical analysis. It also assumes a correspondence between measures of content, secured only by internal reliability between recorders of content scores, and viewers' responses. That is, it explicitly seeks to ground the objectivity of the analysis of content without particular regard to the variety and complexity of ordinary contexts of viewing.

Gunter's objection, however, is by no means insuperable in principle. His critique of content analysis accords poorly with his own repeated references to 'objective features of content'. Indeed, it is difficult to see, as Counihan for example shows (1975: 32), how it is possible to talk about the audience's preferences for particular kinds of programming without reference to at least an implicit theory of genre and meaning considered as inherent properties of texts.

There is no need, however, for the analysis of content to remain faithful to Lasswell's (1953) model (sender, message, receiver and channel) which relies on a literal enforcement of a 'conduit metaphor' of communication (Reddy 1979), and which was developed by Lasswell and others for the analysis of wartime propaganda (see Rowland and Watkins 1984: 16). Rather, the model of viewing which I have sketched in Chapter 2 stresses the importance of the sedimentation of genre over time, the role of scheduling in integrating generic forms within routines of domestic leisure, and the sense in which any genre opens on to other discursive areas which it may corroborate more or less closely. Equally, the way of interpreting television content which I shall propose (Chapter 5) seeks to be sensitive to stylistic questions as well as to taxonomies of events and episodes (see also Baggaley and Duck 1976: 31). There remains an obstinate coincidence between distributions of fear, correlative political attitudes, and patterns of viewing – a coincidence which it is the business of this analysis to make intelligible. However, as Christians and Carey (1981) observe, relevant issues do not turn simply on the enumeration of causal sequences but rather on the question 'what are the interpretations of meaning and value created in the media and what is their relation to the rest of life?' (1981: 347).

Traditions of research into fear and anxiety

Research into the fear of crime and its consequences, which sees fear as being in any important respect more than a simple product of the incidence of criminal events, is a comparatively recent emphasis in criminology. Most such research makes some reference to the role of mass media as one way of accounting for what are generally interpreted as discrepancies between comparatively low levels of risk and rather high reports of fear. Early considerations of the topic were conducted in the United States in the 1960s under the stimulus provided to survey research by the President's Commission on Law Enforcement and the Administration of Justice. The Commission funded attempts not only to estimate the scope of the 'dark figure' but also to achieve descriptive accounts of the impact of crime on the experience of particular localities (Lewis and Salem 1986: 4). Thus Biderman (1967) elaborated what he termed an 'Index of Anxiety'. Ennis (1967), meanwhile, introduced the now orthodox differentiation between fear (for self) and estimates of risk in general.

Attention to the fear of crime received a second profound stimulus from critiques advanced by radical observers (notably by Box 1971) of official statistics as an adequate basis for either research or policy conclusions. Radical criminologists argued forcefully that variations in official crime rates, especially where these appear to disclose dramatic surges or 'waves' in offending, are more often contingent upon variations in allocations of police resources and in practices of reporting and recording than upon changes in behaviour as such. Such work has been especially valuable in making manifest the dimension of differential *visibility* as between the commission of crimes in public and private space, and hence the disproportions in attention, anxiety and ease of enforcement which impinge upon the activities of socially marginal and disempowered groups, especially working-class youth (Pearson 1983). Considerable historiographical (Gatrell et al 1980) and ethnographic (Young 1971a) work has been devoted to demonstrating the chronic consequences of these disparities. This has focused, in particular, on the influence of mass media in equating the crimes of the powerless with crime as such (Young 1971b), in subsuming political dissent within general rubrics of deviation (Sumner 1982) and in constructing the ideological preconditions for policies of reaction and containment (S. Hall, 1980b).

Radical criminology's problematic of deviancy amplification envisaged a necessary concentration on the channels through which crime became and remained present to public attention and concerns. It thus produced a 'wave' of its own, of studies of the content and production of representations of crime, especially in the press. Fishman's statement of the theme is in some degree classic, if only for its concision:

When we speak of a crime wave, we are talking about a kind of social awareness of crime, crime brought to public consciousness. It is something to be remarked upon at the corner grocery store, complained about in a community meeting, and denounced at the mayor's press conference. One cannot be mugged by a crime wave, but one can be scared. And one can put more police on the streets and enact new laws on the basis of fear. Crime waves may be 'things of the mind', but they have real consequences.

(Fishman 1978: 531)

Notwithstanding its critical provenance, however, the awareness of these areas of difficulty (problems of criminal statistics, the oblique relationship between fear and incidence and the possible role of mass media as in-stigators of fear) has in some degree been recuperated by 'administrative' criminology (Young 1988). It is now more or less orthodox amongst sur-vey researchers in both the USA (Garofalo 1980; Skogan and Maxfield 1981) and in Britain (Hough and Mayhew 1983; Maxfield 1984) to argue that neither fears for personal safety nor people's general assessments of crime-related problems can be uniformly or readily inferred either from actual experiences of victimization or objective indices of risk. Skogan and Maxfield summarize some empirical difficulties in this area:

> Fear is indeed a consequence of crime, but . . . most consequences of crime – including fear – are indirect. While victims of crime are more fearful as a result of their experiences, many more people have indirect contact with crime. The sources of this vicarious experience include the media, personal conversations with victims and others and observations of neighbourhood conditions. These convey a great deal of information about crime, and most urban dwellers cannot get through a day without being touched by it in one way or another.
>
> (Skogan and Maxfield 1981: 11)

Given these complexities most totalizing models of the nature and deter-minants of fear, most particularly perhaps those which have made the largest claims for the influence of mass media (Gerbner et al 1978) may seem crude and premature. Most researchers stress that a high level of fear, where fear is construed as a perception of threat to personal safety sufficiently large to influence whether one would go out alone after dark, is in general confined to larger urban areas. Overall levels of fear do not vary significantly between cities of similar size, but within urban areas fear is most intense in localities which suffer the highest rates of interper-sonal violence and housebreaking (Maxfield, 1984: 38). To this extent fear and risk are indeed, unsurprisingly, closely coincident.

Meanwhile, it is true that anxiety – although not, according to some observers, risk (e.g. Hough and Mayhew 1983) – is compounded by gen-der and age. This finding leads some authorities to attribute excessiveness to the fears of women and elderly people. Other recent commentators (e.g. Maxfield 1984: 39), however, question the appropriateness of this attribution, arguing that physical vulnerability and the seriousness of the conseqences of victimization where it occurs, as well as more persistent (though not always criminal) forms of harassment and threat, should all be included in the calculus of the determinants of fear. Jones et al (1986: 75) claim that offences against women, especially sexual offences and domestic violence, remain under-reported even in (official) victim surveys. Equally, Maxfield argues (1984: 40) calculations should be broadened to include worry about the safety of others, such as children or elderly relatives. Each of these arguments undermines the claim that women's fear of crime is excessive or unrealistic. Hence, although as S. J. Smith (1986) indicates, a major focus in research on fear of crime has been its *independence* from victimization, with consequent readiness to attribute this disparity to the operation of mass media (see Fishman 1978), detailed examination of specific inner urban sites suggests that not only are fear and risk closely connected but also they are further compounded for relevant sub-populations by antagonistic or otherwise unsatisfactory contacts with police (Kinsey 1985; Jones et al 1986).

Recent contributors have therefore become reluctant to attribute any significant role to mass media in influencing the level of fear. Skogan and Maxfield (1981: ch. 8) examine this issue. Like all other observers they note the extreme concentration of both national and local media on crime, as well as the very high proportion of people who come into contact with media representations of crime on any one day (1981: 130). Yet they are unable to locate any independent influence of such representations on fear. There are a number of reservations to be noted however. The very consistency of this presence makes it unlikely that it will appear as a statistical *variance*. Similarly, it is questionable whether the multivariate techniques applied, which seek above all an *independent* 'effect', are appropriate to disclose the level at which media use is constitutive of daily routines. In general, the broader the scope of the survey, and the less concentrated its focus on realistic apprehensions of danger in inner urban locales, the more likely are attributions of excessive fear, stemming especially from media influences. This question of generality may account for some part of the disagreement between Hough and Mayhew (1983: 26) and Jones et al (1986: 81). Complications arise, however, and the bearing of the media on the constitution of public consciousness of crime is broached once again, where fears for personal safety and perceptions of risk in an immediate locality are differentiated from subjects' broader apprehensions of crime as a social problem and from perceptions of risk in other areas. It is at these levels that networks of communication retain a particular importance.

Crime, 'incivility' and the sense of place

S. J. Smith (1986) presents relevant issues lucidly by relating the spatial distribution of fear to other features of local social relations, in the context of the economic and political marginalization of an inner urban area. Smith concludes that if fear of crime is realistic in this setting it is because 'victimised populations and fearful populations (which anyway overlap) are structurally bound together by their shared location in social, economic and physical space' (1986: 117).

Equally, however, Smith (1986: 117) is concerned to show that whereas fear and risk do tend to coincide, they do not coincide uniformly; the sense of living in a dangerous place also has to do with awareness of economic and political marginality and of decline. These perceptions may crystallize in imputations of dangerousness across group (especially racial, but also age) boundaries, where the presence of incomers is experienced as an incursion upon previous familiarities and stability (S. J. Smith 1986: 111). In a similar way, Maxfield ventures (1984: 25; see also S. J. Smith 1986: 129) that fear may result from 'incivilities', where the behavioural improprieties of some groups, which may not be specifically criminal, are viewed by others as indices of social disorganization and of threat. In these senses diffuse anxieties result from social representations of the social and physical environment, whose sources are broader than the risk of victimization as such. Both Lewis (1980: 22) and Skogan and Maxfield (1981: 127) refer to these 'environmental' features as 'signs' of decay or trouble: yet neither goes any further in elucidating the nature of the *signification* in question.

One problem with the notion of 'incivility', therefore, is that it has been too narrowly conceived. In most usages it is a commonplace which is deployed either as a secondary way of censuring young people's use of public space, or else it is reduced to a simple set of 'cues' from the physical environment: the so-called 'broken window hypothesis' (Wilson and Kelling 1982). Each of these generates correlative policy strategies directed towards 'fear reduction' (Maxfield 1984; see also Bennett 1989), whether by increased surveillance of troublesome groups or by cosmetic improvements to the physical environment. Young's frustration with such measures (to which I alluded in Chapter 1) is that they constitute knowing manipulations of public perception, predicated on a presumed disparity between fear and risk (Young 1987; 1989).

Lewis and Salem (1986) propose a broader and more interesting notion of 'incivility'. For them the term incorporates a more general sense of disorder which in turn undermines any sense of well-being in the relation of specific publics to both their social and physical environments. In this respect 'incivility' also summarizes a problem in the relation of these publics to political authority since it derives from the failure to sustain adequate levels of public provision and participation, that is the preconditions for *civility* (Lewis and Salem 1986: 20; see also I. Taylor 1988). To this extent the incidence of crime and the fear of crime are not co-extensive but they share some of the same prior causes. These broader considerations also raise once again the question of the representations of crime in television and print, and the degree of attention which is paid to them in so far as these are informed not only by the fear of crime as such but also by the fear of disorder from which the former in part results (Lewis and Salem 1986: 22).

Communication and fear in everyday life

S. J. Smith (1986) shows that whether information circulating about crime is accurate or not, the fact of its circulation, the channels it follows and the motivations people have to attend to it remain important. The special significance of local news media, she argues, following Garofalo (1981), lies in the opportunity they provide for 'information seeking' consequent on the awareness of risk (S. J. Smith 1986: 117). The spatial distribution of events reported, as well as the specifically social proximity of the victims, both strongly influence the salience of reports of crime for any one individual (Skogan and Maxfield 1981: 74). This point of view is consistent with the more sophisticated outlook on risk-perception in general outlined by Douglas (1986; see also Chapter 1).

It is through such reports, and more particularly the networks of rumour and gossip for which, as forms of 'improvised news' (S. J. Smith 1986: 124), they provide the raw materials, that crime is constituted as an aspect of the social experience of a locality. Smith indicates a dual importance for rumour and gossip. At a manifest level rumour is a form of talk which mediates the transmission of crime-related information, on the basis of which strategies for the management of danger may be instituted. More obscurely, rumour is also consequential in defining and continually reproducing local social relations. Crime-related rumours flow most easily between socially and spatially proximate individuals. In so far as the sharing of a rumour is also a confirmation of this proximity rumours have multiple purposes and dimensions: they intrinsically exceed the information given. Members of particular networks agree on 'maps' (S. J. Smith 1986: 124) which designate both *sites* of danger and origins of danger in other sub-populations. Information about crime is thus integrated into local structures of affiliation and suspicion and the confirmation of their associated norms of propriety and censure. Such 'mapping' necessarily includes the potentiality for the overestimation of danger especially where demand for information exceeds its availability or where rumours refer to spatially or socially distant places or persons. It is in these terms that Smith understands the occurrence of 'fantastic rumour', where the ostensible topic of the rumour acts as a surrogate for more diffuse, discursively unavailable or socially unacceptable anxieties. In her own study of north-central Birmingham, Smith argues that the operation of fantastic rumour frequently results from mutual misperceptions across group boundaries, tending in this instance towards the exaggeration of race and crime issues (S. J. Smith 1986: 127).

Clearly Smith's analysis is consonant with the widespread finding that, even in high-crime areas where fear is arguably based on reasonable estimates of risk, subjects none the less tend to overestimate the dangers of other, further removed neighbourhoods and cities (Maxfield 1984: 28).

Even those observers who are most concerned to argue that fear of crime is realistically grounded in the inner cities (e.g. Kinsey 1985) acknowledge that those who live in areas with a lower incidence of interpersonal violence and robbery may none the less overestimate *both* overall dimensions of crime problems as they affect the whole society and, more particularly, the dangerousness of inner urban locales.

The apprehension of danger is, in part and for some people, closely consequent upon real risks. Yet to the extent that fear of crime is both more widely distributed than are risks and is bound up with other sources of social anxiety and stress it is also related to representations across social boundaries. In these respects fear is a function of *distance*. For these reasons the vocabulary and imagery in which these representations are encoded, the media through which they are disseminated and the political rhetorics and strategies within which they are subsumed remain important, notwithstanding the 'realist' challenge (Lea and Young 1984). Smith distinguishes between the levels at which fear impinges upon the experience of living in inner urban environments and at which it is co-ordinated in a national politics of law and order. To the extent that the latter is also 'mapped', as it were by a global rumour, it tends to ratify the surveillance of sites of agreed danger (Jones et al 1986: 62). Through the dynamics of distance and proximity inner urban residents (objectively exposed to the greatest risks) are doubly marginalized: subject, that is, not only to fearfulness but also to strategies of policing and investigation ulterior to their needs, stemming from the diffusion of anxiety throughout the social formation.

Given that media use and crime-related talk are diffuse and ramified it is premature to restrict the range of resources on which they are considered to draw. Just as information about crime in the news and elsewhere is differentially sought out, attended to and integrated into forms of talk and strategies for coping, so models of criminal process and more especially, paleo-symbolic systems of justification which are less clearly 'informational' may also receive attention and be put to use (Gouldner 1976). It is with regard to these two aspects of fear, the dynamics of distance and the modes of experience with which it coalesces, that the relevance of the narration of crime and law enforcement on television should be understood.

Television, crime and the 'cultivation hypothesis'

In view of the complexity of the distribution and determinations of fear, and of its embeddedness within locally sustained social relations, any attempt to attribute a significant degree of this variance to any one source or medium appears both grandiose and reductive. Nevertheless, two decades of research by Gerbner and his associates have addressed exactly this proposition, in the form of a hypothesis of the 'cultivation' by television of fear and a concomitant set of social beliefs.

As a general argument about the location of television in the cultures of the industrial societies, the 'cultivation hypothesis' asserts:

> We begin with the assumption that television is the central cultural arm of American society. It is an agency of the established order and as such serves primarily to extend and maintain rather than to alter, threaten or weaken conventional conceptions, beliefs and behaviors. Its chief function is to spread and stabilise social patterns, to cultivate not change but resistance to change. Television is a medium of the socialization of most people into standardized roles and behaviors. Its function is, in a word, enculturation.
>
> (Gerbner and Gross 1976a: 115)

Gerbner's 'violence profile' (Gerbner and Gross 1976a) applies this view to the representation of crime, law enforcement and violence on television. In Gerbner's terms the frequent reiteration of violent episodes 'cultivates' a misleading and exaggerated view of their incidence in the world. This distortion differentially affects those who watch most television. Gerbner's method, therefore, is annually to subject the whole of one week's prime-time broadcast television, available in one major American city, to an elaborate content analysis. This enumerates, among other things, violent incidents, the identities of their perpetrators and victims (demographic characteristics, relation to law enforcement agencies) as well as how often the use of violence is associated with a successful or happy outcome. On the basis of the index thus derived the researchers infer a set of 'television answers' to survey questions about the prevalence of violent crime, perceptions of personal vulnerability and the justifiability of policing strategies, especially the use of force and firearms. 'Heavy' viewers of television (those who watch four or more hours of television daily) are more likely, they suggest, to affirm the 'television answer' than they are to conform either to known facts of crime rates or to other sources of information discrepant with television (Gerbner et al 1978).

Carlson (1985) replicates Gerbner et al's investigations, and also expands on them. Following criticisms of their statistical manipulations (e.g. Doob and Macdonald 1979; Hughes 1980), Gerbner et al have introduced two refinements to the cultivation hypothesis, which they term 'resonance' and 'mainstreaming' (Gerbner et al 1980). By 'resonance' they understand an increased susceptibility to cultivation effects among those viewers whose social experience is most closely congruent with television's depiction of a 'mean' or 'scary' world, that is those who have most experience of victimization. That is, they claim, these viewers are subject to a 'double dose' of fear-inducing messages (Carlson 1985: 173). 'Mainstreaming' meanwhile refers to the claim that the messages of television entertainment are closely consonant with widespread and dominant world outlooks. In those whose views already fall within the cultural 'mainstream', therefore, cultivation processes are not visible as distinct and measurable 'effects'; rather they provide for the continual reconfirmation of an already given social identity. What *is* arguably visible is the 'mainstreaming' of those whose social position might place them outside the 'mainstream' but who are yet heavy viewers of television (Carlson, 1985: 8). Hence, it is argued, television tends to efface social difference, tugging all its viewers in the direction of a somewhat authoritarian consensus, underwritten by the uniformity of television content.

'Cultivation' and political socialization

Carlson (1985) emphasizes that the issue of the cultivation of a 'mean' or 'scary' perception of the world has a clear bearing on questions of political socialization (see also Gerbner et al 1984). Carlson finds little support for the notion of 'resonance'. In common with other investigators, notably Tyler (1980), he argues that first-hand experience of victimization *predominates over* rather than confirms mass mediated perspectives. On the other hand, Carlson (1985) argues that 'mainstreaming' is indeed strongly active. Briefly, Carlson claims to show that heavier viewers are comparatively ill-informed about legal processes and that they place a higher value than do those who view less on a starker version of a norm of compliance – that they are 'anti-heterodox' (see Weigel and Jessor 1973: 88; Corbett 1981: 330). He thus argues that they have a correlatively lower regard for civil liberties and that, in terms of Packer's two models of criminal justice, they therefore tend to favour 'crime control' at the expense of 'due process' (Packer 1969; Carlson 1985: 193). Heavy viewers believe that the world is a dangerous place. Yet they also entertain the contrary view that the police are effective in combating crime. Carlson further argues that there may be a 'spillover' from these kinds of orientations towards crime into more general and diffuse support for existing political arrangements and confirmation of the legitimacy of actually existing distributions of power (Carlson 1985: 191).

Carlson's argument is suggestive. In part its interest derives from its broadening of the scope of the 'cultivation' argument in the direction of the wider concerns of social theory with political socialization and social reproduction. It stipulates, that is to say, that the 'effects' of television, especially with reference to criminal justice, are interesting primarily in so far as they intersect with other dimensions of social being and political conduct. This being so, however, their visibility, *qua* effects of television, will be attenuated and conditional on these interactions. Nevertheless, given that Carlson's theory and method are wholly derived from

Gerbner, his argument is still vulnerable to the same series of conceptual and empirical objections which apply to the whole body of 'cultivation' research. These can now be briefly stated.

Theoretical criticisms of 'cultivation'
The authors of *Policing the Crisis* (S. Hall et al 1978) might well be gratified by Carlson's conclusions, although they never undertook empirical work at a comparable level of detail. Equally, however, Carlson does not develop his political sociology with their sophistication. Rather he allows his conceptions of authority and legitimation to rest on an undifferentiated structural-functionalist notion of social control, historically unspecific and evasive with regard to the weight accorded respectively to economic, political and ideological conditions.

To this extent Carlson's argument, like Gerbner's from which it derives, finally rests on certain very weakly defended propositions. For example, Carlson claims that

> To the extent that audiences share values that are system supportive, successful programs will be likely to be those that reflect viewpoints that contribute to the maintenance of the social and political order.
>
> (Carlson 1985: 2)

Carlson never specifies, except negatively with reference to passivity, what 'values that are system supportive' consist in, how strongly they need to be held nor whether they may coexist with other, potentially antagonistic, commitments. Evidently we are dealing here with what is more traditionally known as a theory of ideology, but it is not at all clear whether Carlson's conception of ideology is generic and neutral (i.e. that all belief is socially generated, all dominant social beliefs are inertial) or restrictive and critical (i.e. that ideology equals beliefs which underwrite sectional interests). In so far as all the important terms in his formulation (system, reflection, maintenance) go unexplained Carlson never emerges from his plausible circularity: like other functionalists, he merely presupposes the 'system persistence' (1985: 2) he purports to investigate. Under the guise of a bland and inoffensive suggestion a highly contentious, binding presumption of consensus is smuggled in: the claim that social order is 'maintained' is surely much stronger than the more contingent notions of transmission or reproduction across time and space. Carlson can thus offer no rejoinder to the objection that the mere survival of a given social system over time in no way presupposes the 'consolidation of consensus' within it, but rather only that its 'structural principles' remain recognizably similar (Giddens 1984: 180).

Similarly, cultivation research never adequately specifies either motivations to engage in television viewing, nor affiliations towards what is viewed. Carlson rests his case as to why people watch television on a second thesis which also contrives to be both banal and presumptuous: 'If people choose the television programs they view, they are unlikely to choose those that will make them uncomfortable' (1985: 6). Again, the definition of viewing appears to be modest, established by plausible exclusion, but its covert purport is more ambitious, imposing an arbitrary restriction on the range of possible reasons for viewing and foreclosing the need to speak of them. The world is full of examples of people choosing to be made uncomfortable for reasons of pleasure, as anyone who has ever been pot-holing, let alone engaged in more recondite forms of masochism, knows (see Tuan 1979: 202 on the concept of 'eustress').

For all its wealth of empirical detail about alleged outcomes of viewing, the cultivation perspective is not at all enlightening about how viewing is constituted as a situated activity nor, consequently, about how differently it may be engaged in by viewers in diverse social locations

The text, the world and the viewer

Both these problems stem in large measure from the notions of 'reflection' and 'distortion' which underpin cultivation analysis and which provide the grounds upon which its criticism of the television medium is based (see Newcomb 1978). The causal force which is attributed to television in determining viewers' perceptions of the world is derived from a crudely 'reflectionist' notion of representation. Simply put, television 'reflects' dominant values for the very reason that it fails accurately to 'reflect' the real. Starting from this premise content analysis tends to take the form of an actuarial exercise in counting categories of events and their various combinations. The origin and salience of the categories themselves is not viewed as being especially problematic: neither, correlatively, are viewers' responses to them understood as being particularly contextually variable or complex. At the level of the text content analysis proceeds in virtual ignorance of issues of either narrative or discourse (Chatman 1978; Genette 1982), modes of narration (Browne 1982), or the stylistics of openness and closure (Eco 1979; J. Taylor 1980). Cultivation analysis presents itself as a theory of the colonization of the contemporary cultural field by television, yet it pays no attention to the particular features of the medium as a technology of inscription, storage and diffusion (Giddens 1987: 101).

Similarly, at the level of the audience, cultivation analysis is insensitive to the importance of the positioning of the viewer in leading to particular strategies of disambiguation (Pateman 1983). The principal difference between the content analytic notion of 'distortion' and that of 'systematic distortion' (S. Hall 1975) is that whereas the latter does infer a 'preferred reading' of any narrative it specifically also entertains the possibility of aberrant or oppositional readings. Pandiani (1978) offers a particularly clear instance of this problem within the cultivation perspective. Pandiani's interest in the place of crime within television entertainment lies in what would follow 'if all we knew was what we saw' (1978: 437). Since there are good grounds for supposing that what we see on television is not all we know of the social world and that, in any case, one thing we do know about television viewers is that they differentiate rather precisely between the two (Gunter and Wober, 1982; Gunter 1985) Pandiani's question holds little interest, even if it is presented as a counter-factual one.

Recent attempts to supplement and refine this kind of analysis have not altogether resolved these problems. For example Surette (1984) rightly notes that the simplicity and directness of prevalent attributions of effects of viewing can no longer be sustained. However, in the face of the challenge of delineating a more adequate 'model' of the place of televised crime in the lives of its viewers Surette continues to seek safety in a terminology which still does little more than nod in the direction of viewing as situated and reflexive activity:

> the path by which media influences its audience is not a direct or simple one, but rather it is a multi-stepped transactional process that is mediated through psychological and sociological variables.
>
> (Surette 1984: 324)

This clearly looks like a technical language, but it is still mainly a descriptive rather than a theoretical one: it does not guide us with respect to the level of generality at which it is appropriate to speak. It is revealing that even as he reminds us that contemporary media are complex and diverse Surette lapses into the use of the singular verb. This imprecision matters: how unitary, how systematic is the message system in fact?

The really vexed questions of media analysis lie beyond and beneath the largely descriptive statements which cultivation analysis has so far generated. The description of television content does not in and of itself illuminate the ways in which it is viewed. Why are television crime fictions pleasurable? What socially given needs do they answer? (See Baggaley and Duck 1976: 164.) Unless it attends to these questions content analysis tends to remain uninterestingly pedantic and to observe silence about the kinds of reality claims which television fiction lodges, the regimes of representation it deploys and the modes of participation in which viewers are invited to engage.

Substantive criticisms of 'cultivation'
Substantive objections to the empirical claims made by cultivation research about television viewing and the fear of crime are broadly of three kinds.

First, there is an argument that while the constellation of social beliefs identified as linking television viewing, the fear of crime and punitive

attitudes to criminal justice may indeed exist as a set of statistical correlates, the isolation of television viewing as the causal factor is spurious.
As Wakshlag reminds us (Wakshlag et al 1983: 227; Weaver and
Wakshlag 1984: 4), Gerbner's thesis relies on a causal claim about television's responsibility for this variance. If that claim cannot be sustained
then this is sufficient to refute it in its present form. This is the argument
advanced by Hirsch (1980; 1981) who indicates that apparent cultivation
effects disappear when additional statistical controls are applied. Indeed
Hirsch claims to show that non-viewers of television (whom Gerbner
aggregates with light viewers) are more fearful than are either category of
viewers (Hirsch 1980). Similarly, Hughes (1980) also reanalyses data used
by Gerbner and his associates (Gerbner et al 1978). Hughes (1980: 293)
argues that the strongest determinant of viewing is the amount of time
available in which to view, which is in turn strongly related to prior socio-
economic conditions, notably to age and gender. In Hughes's adjusted
controls television viewing is much less strongly related to fear than are
either gender or size of city of residence (1980: 296). Most interestingly
Doob and Macdonald (1979) acknowledge that television viewing and
fear of crime *are* correlated but argue that *both* are contingent on place of
residence.

Second, one can argue that the kinds of correlations isolated by cultivation researchers may exist at some times and in some places but that they
are much less general than Gerbner would wish to claim. Cultivation
effects do not travel well. All attempts to replicate them in a British
context (Gunter and Wober 1983; Gunter and Wakshlag 1986) have failed.
That is, irrespective of whatever role television may play in some American instances, if it does something else somewhere else this undermines
the force and generality of the underlying causal mechanism which is
alleged.

The third and most important argument against Gerbner's strong version of a cultivation claim builds on the outcomes of the first two. As
Hughes (1980) observes, given the inherent difficulties of content analysis
it is by no means so obvious as Gerbner and Gross (1976b) seem to
suggest what a 'television answer' would actually be in any given case.
One can therefore argue that even if some version of a cultivation effect,
more modestly conceived, does indeed exist, researchers have been premature in stipulating its likely strength and direction (Hughes 1980: 299).
Drawing on the findings of Doob and Macdonald (1979), Wakshlag et al
(1983: 229) argue that the present state of knowledge is less consonant
with a basic cultivation hypothesis than with a thesis of selective preference for crime drama, predicated on prior anxieties. The finding by
Boyanowski et al (1974) that under particularly intense conditions of
perceived threat (immediately following the murder of a female student
on a university campus) attendance at a violent film increased dramat-

ically, in comparison with a light romance, seems to be suggestive of a similar conclusion. On these grounds Wakshlag et al (1983) suggest that, if it is indeed plausible that some kind of 'cultivation' results from the repeated viewing of somewhat similar narratives, there may nevertheless be equally good grounds for supposing that television cultivates security as fear and that this is in any case contingent on the motivations people have for using media in the ways they do, which may in turn be far more complex and variable than previously allowed.

The recognition, following Doob and Macdonald (1979), that both levels of fear and of television use may be contingent on place of residence, and by extension on the proximity of the experience of crime in a given locality, leaves open the possibility of a further relationship between the two. That is, it is at least conceivable that heightened perceptions of vulnerability dispose people towards a greater reliance on television. This may be for the simple reason that fearful people are more inclined to remain at home watching television (Gunter and Wakshlag 1986: 22), or it might also suggest that television is specifically helpful in *alleviating* anxiety (Weaver and Wakshlag 1984: 5).

Fear and viewing preferences

Research on the ways in which audiences selectively use and prefer particular kinds of television content thus makes at least two major alterations to the cultivation hypothesis.

The first is in the propositions such research introduces about television content. Zillman and Wakshlag (1987) points out that the vast majority of television crime drama emphasizes 'justice' in its outcomes. Hence, although crime drama programmes do include a high incidence of violent and transgressive action they are viewed in the expectation that order will be restored. Zillman (1980) posits that this dynamic holds a particular appeal for apprehensive individuals. This is both because the heightened experience of fear is met by a similarly greater pleasure at a happy outcome (Wakshlag et al 1983: 211) and because this encounter, which takes place under conditions of safety allows apprehensive viewers to experience a sense of the mastery of an initially 'scary' situation (Zillman and Wakshlag 1987: 13). On this view television crime drama permits a strategic manipulation of the viewers' sense of their relation to their environment in the direction of relief from anxiety (Wakshlag et al 1983: 229; Weaver and Wakshlag 1984: 26). In this sense attention to selective exposure to communication also suggests a renewed interest in content analysis, but in a form which emphasizes the organization and outcome of television narratives, as opposed to the mere enumeration of what they include. Given the predominant structure of television crime fictions, it is argued, instances which are simply conducive to the cultivation of fear will be rather rare.

Second, hypotheses of selective exposure construe the audience for television as being both more differentiated and more active than does the cultivation hypothesis in its original or strong version. For example, in experimental manipulations, Wakshlag et al (1983) suggest that apprehensive subjects incline markedly more than others towards crime drama which includes a 'just' resolution. The same subjects, moreover, are by no means drawn towards drama which includes violence in the absence of such a resolution. On these grounds the investigators conclude:

> The most compelling – and parsimonious – explanation for the present study's findings considers victimization and justice restoration in crime drama as a functional unit. . . . When suspenseful drama featuring victimization is known to contain a satisfying resolution, apprehensive individuals should anticipate pleasure and enjoyment and prefer such material. The initial distress that emerges from viewing the building of suspense in a program is clearly, then, conceived to be a critical part of eventual enjoyment.
>
> (Wakshlag et al 1983: 238)

Findings consistent with this thesis have now begun to proliferate. Thus, Wakshlag et al (1983) note heightened physiological indices of arousal as well as verbal expressions of involvement in crime drama among apprehensive viewers. Meanwhile, Weaver and Wakshlag (1984: 26) conclude that viewers who have been or who know vicitims of crime use television drama as part of a set of strategies for coping with and alleviating anxieties about the future. Moreover, and in contrast to the conclusions of Gerbner et al (1978) and Carlson (1985), it is easy to reconcile these findings with the predominant foci of research into the wider distributions of fear of crime (Skogan and Maxfield 1981) since they acknowledge that viewing is situated in relation to, and indeed perhaps encouraged by, the fear and incidence of crime in specific locales.

Similarly, the recognition of complexity in the use of crime on television also permits a more subtle treatment of the fears to which it relates. One reason why cultivation analysis has been unspecific at the levels of practice and experience is that it fails to distinguish dimensions *within* the general rubric of concern or fear about crime (Weaver and Wakshlag 1984: 24). Weaver and Wakshlag argue that it is possible to distinguish three component factors within perceptions of personal vulnerability which are related to the use of crime on television. These they summarize as concerns for personal safety in 'hypothetical' situations similar to those found in television crime drama, concern for the safety of the immediate residential environment and, third, the likelihood of becoming a victim at some future date (Weaver and Wakshlag 1984: 23). Like Tyler (1984), Weaver and Wakshlag argue that whatever then remains of a cultivation effect is operative at the level of abstract and global perceptions of crime – that is where these are not countermanded by personal experience (Weaver and Wakshlag 1984: 25) – and where television drama remains one of the resources on which viewers draw in actively constructing their view of the world.

In sum, the argument from 'selective exposure' is useful in that it reconsiders both the interpretation of television content and the interpretation of the audience. It acknowledges that viewers are not passive 'dopes', and that the uses viewers make of crime drama are contingent on their relation to social experience. Furthermore, this argument goes some way towards reconciling a serious interest in the nature and quality of television's narration of crime with the general concerns of research into the fear of crime. That is, it differentiates influences on the apprehension of the general and abstract from the experience of the personal and particular. Although the subsequent findings of Gunter and Wakshlag (1986: 21) are in some important ways at odds with those of Tyler (1984) they still seem to corroborate the overall thesis, including its emphasis on distance and proximity. In general, heavy viewing remains a statistical predictor of fear, although this is construed as an effect rather than a cause. Secondly, for a British population, crime drama in a British setting, that is one that is fictionally 'close', seems more closely related to personal fears than American counterparts are. Equally, however, British viewers consider New York and Los Angeles to be far more dangerous places than any British setting (Gunter and Wakshlag 1986: 11).

These conclusions are consistent with S. J. Smith's (1986: 124) interest in people's subjective 'maps' of their social environments. It may be that people's perceptions of spatially and socially distant places are stark and clear both because the available information about them is similarly simplified, and because these views are rather casually held. For a British viewer a lesser intellectual and emotional commitment is involved in expressing a view about the dangers of New York than about somewhere closer to home. Nevertheless, as Smith emphasizes, the views one holds about distant places are not, for that reason, of no consequence. It is perhaps in terms of such mapping that the known world is defined and differentiated from the alien, the foreign and the dangerous. Equally to the extent that crime is caught up in totalizing political rhetorics it is also intrinsically concerned with aspects of the world which are not directly known, and with the dangers that lurk in these penumbra. It has always been at the edges of maps that dragons and sea monsters live.

Some criticisms of 'selective exposure'

The return to Smith's argument, however, also highlights some important shortcomings of even the most sophisticated work on selective exposure to television crime drama. In the first place, as Weaver and Wakshlag (1984: 24) insist (following Hawkins and Pingree 1982), if there is a significant relationship (of whatever kind) between fear of crime and television viewing, it is highly likely to be 'content specific'. In this regard the authors highlight the importance of just and unjust resolutions in narrative. Clearly, Gerbner's stratagem of aggregating violent incidents from various different genres of programming is mistaken, since we are interested not in violence 'as such' (whatever that might be: see Pringle 1972) but in its co-ordination within the economy of a particular genre of stories. One of our aims, then, must be to indicate the parameters of this genre, its norms and expectations. Yet work within the selective exposure problematic never does more than broach this issue: it does not provide the new and refined content analytic scheme on which, nevertheless, its propositions implicitly depend. For example, Zillman and Wakshlag build their entire argument about the importance of just and unjust resolutions on nothing more than an assertion that justice predominates (1987: 11).

Yet what justifies 'justice'? How is it known, recognized and established as just? How completely does the triumph of justice resolve the conflicts of the plot? These questions are scarcely raised, let alone properly addressed. The authors follow Zillman (1980: 160) in arguing that 'television drama distorts reality more toward security than toward danger'. They continue:

> It projects too just and perhaps too safe a world. . . . Such drama continually conveys the message that good forces (i.e. police, private investigators, vigilantes) are out there mopping up the scum of society. Their relentless good efforts make the streets safe again. This kind of message should be music to the ears of troubled citizens. They can relax and put their worries about crime and personal safety to rest.
>
> (Zillman and Wakshlag 1987: 11)

It is paradoxical, indeed frankly contradictory, to build an argument about the complexity of the viewer's response around such a crude and presumptive summary of programme content. Like Gerbner, Wakshlag and Zillman privilege their own reading of crime drama texts: but unlike Gerbner they provide no systematic justification for this reading, even if prima facie it seems more plausible. Since all their empirical investigations are based around these presumptions the investigators simply never say what *else* and what *more* than this viewers may be capable of finding in and retrieving from what they view. Television drama does not, in any simple sense 'convey a message that good forces . . . are out there'. It is not, strictly speaking, a report or 'conveyance' of anything. Rather it *constitutes* these forces as 'good': in the act of showing it also provides the properties of what is shown. Similarly, this perspective tends to throw out the baby of the political correlates of television viewing with the bathwater of the cultivation hypothesis. It is all very well for psychologists to construe television viewing in terms of 'belief in a just world' (Gunter and Wakshlag, 1986: 4), but to what notion of justice does this refer?

When Mills (1959: 1) simply says that 'Nowadays men feel that their lives are a series of traps' he begins to elaborate an idea about personal 'troubles' which acknowledges that they originate in more diffuse sources than their ostensible objects would seem to suggest. Weaver and Wakshlag's method cannot elicit the ways in which their subjects are 'troubled' by fears that they may know quite well have no empirical referent or basis. Equally, if television does console the fearful in the face of their real anxieties what are we to make of this form of distraction? What kind of *dependency* on television does it suggest? Weaver and Wakshlag beg these questions by merely positing that the alleviation of anxiety is 'beneficial' (1984: 6), whereas anxiety of course is 'maladaptive' (1984: 20). In open, but parallel, contradiction, Tyler (1984: 35) argues that public education campaigns around crime should seek to cultivate fear, because fear stimulates 'avoidance behaviours' and therefore prevents victimization. In either case the viewers are available for manipulation in their own best interests. Meanwhile, Weaver and Wakshlag (1984: 12) follow Zillman (1980) in thinking that because television 'distorts' reality in the direction of reassurance 'it trivializes crime and, with repeated exposure, diminishes the impact of previous experience and alleviates the victim's worries'. Is this 'trivialization' likewise a beneficial process? Weaver and Wakshlag themselves note that

> the volume of contradictory evidence accentuates the fact that crit-ical questions concerning whether and how the latent messages of crime and violence are perceived by the television audience and how, if perceived, they are responded to, must be addressed before the proposed linkages can be adequately understood.
>
> (Weaver and Wakshlag 1984: 6)

Quite so: but both the theory and practice of the 'selective exposure' posi-tion suggest that the message, and its latent functions, are primary here, without providing any procedures for knowing them. In their eagerness to refute the cultivation hypothesis, advocates of a 'selective exposure' posi-tion have leapt too hastily to an opposite pole. Their inference that crime drama is 'beneficial' because reassuring is a simple inversion of Gerbner's views. It still takes insufficient account of the lived experience of fear-of-crime problems and is based on similarly reductive interpretations of texts.

Some conclusions

In this chapter I have mainly sought to evaluate, however briefly, two kinds of arguments which are current in research on television and the fear of crime, namely that television either 'cultivates' undue fear or, conversely, provides (undue?) comfort to an already anxious audience. Neither of these positions seems to me wholly satisfactory, although the latter claim is clearly the less extravagant. 'Cultivation' has a rather mechanistic notion of viewing, slight understanding of story-telling and a simplified approach to some vexed criminological issues. 'Selective exposure' wins the argument easily, but gives away its gains by substituting another notion of narrative almost as inane as the first. One source of weakness for each, therefore, is their reliance on poorly defended interpretations of television content. In order to produce any more interesting or plausible hypothesis about viewers' responses to the depiction of crime and law enforcement on television it is first necessary to elaborate a more subtle and fertile view of the 'content' of those depictions. As a preliminary to future research of that kind, my argument must therefore take a step backwards – towards the message of television – and attempt to further elucidate its implicit categories of justice and resolution, and the regimes of representation within which they are deployed. The next chapter is devoted to a refinement of the available ways of inquiry into these matters.

5 A piece of the action: approaches to content in television crime fiction

The battle is for the survival of the right party and the death of the wrong. Over against the enemy we reach the ultimate form of self assertion, whether it is the patriotic rational self, or the institutional self, or simply the self of the hand to hand mêlée. It is the self whose existence calls for the destruction, or defeat, or subjection, or reduction of the enemy. It is a self that finds expression in vivid, concentrated activity and under appropriate conditions of the most violent type.

G.H. Mead, 'The Psychology of Punitive Justice'

The viewer, viewing

In Chapter 4 I summarized and began to evaluate empirical investigations into the location of television, in conjunction with other media and sources of belief and opinion, in the construction of fear. In reviewing this research we find that very few contributions to date have sufficiently grasped either the interaction between direct and vicarious experience of crime (especially where 'vicarious experience' includes the knowing use of fictions) or the frequently paradoxical dynamics of security and insecurity. One area of particular difficulty, I have argued, is that differences at the level of substantive claims or conclusions are related to disagreements over the interpretation of television content. Proponents of a 'cultivation hypothesis' claim that people who watch a great deal of television inhabit a disproportionately 'mean' world, *because* television texts are such as to cultivate this perception (Gerbner and Gross 1976b). Those who advance a 'selective exposure' thesis want to suggest that this relationship does not hold, at least not independently of other aspects of social experience. They further argue that what viewers draw from television's depiction of crime and law enforcement may have at least as much to do with the maintenance of a sense of security as of danger.

There are, then, at least two principal bones of contention in respect of television content. The first concerns the strength, predictability and transparency which the 'cultivation' perspective attributes to the message of television in shaping the world outlook of the viewer. This stands opposed to outlooks which stress the viewer's capability both to distinguish the television image from social reality and to take from the encounter with television only what is desired, relevant or useful – notwithstanding the sense in which the categories of desire, relevance and utility are themselves socially generated. The second area of disagreement is more explicitly concerned with the content of television crime fiction, namely whether or not it is the kind of thing likely to be linked to the incidence of fear. In either case it is clear, as I have indicated, that the most interesting empirical lines of inquiry certainly do broach the problems of describing, recording and understanding television content. The arguments cannot be secured without reference to it. However, recent contributions have not adequately justified the suppositions they make about such content. Furthermore, existing research perspectives have largely failed to draw sufficiently subtle connections between fear or anxiety as features of individuals' outlooks and the more general cultural salience of particular ideological categories implicit in the depiction of crime, law and punishment.

In this chapter, therefore, I shall extend this discussion towards what I regard as a more appropriate language for describing characteristic features of crime fictions on television. I will argue here that while it is now securely established that a more complex model of the activity of viewing and of the viewer's posture towards what passes across the screen than that offered within 'cultivation analysis' is both necessary and possible (see Gunter 1985; 1987), this has not yet generated similarly sophisticated accounts of television texts themselves. Thus, the so far unmet challenge of the 'selective exposure' position is to state what relationship exists between television texts and their reception (even between a 'plural' text and an 'active' viewer) such that some responses to them are more likely than or 'preferred' over others (see S. Hall 1975). If we accept, with Eco, that the object of enquiry is the 'actual communicative effectiveness' (Eco 1972) of television in a given context, then the division of labour, presented as an opposition, between the study of content and the study of reception appears false, or at least too starkly drawn. Content analysis is of interest not *ex situ* but in terms of the consequences of pattern and order in television content for the 'realization' (Eco 1979) of the text by the viewer viewing.

Television and the real world

As McQuail (1984) has argued, the links between descriptions of content and allegations of 'effect' have become 'attenuated' (1984: 124), to the extent that sophisticated studies of the effects of television have 'seemed to do without equally sophisticated content study' (1984: 124). In part this is a legitimate reaction against the pretensions of much early (and indeed recent) content analysis, which seems to presuppose a necessary and simple correspondence between content and consequence, between what is seen and what is known (e.g. Pandiani 1978: 437). Krippendorf (1980) notes that in its early history content analysis envisaged a form of 'social accounting', in which the distributions of topics with the output of various media are taken to reflect underlying social trends (Krippendorf 1980: 14). This recalls some of the more reifying of Durkheim's usages: 'currents', 'forces', 'social facts'. Gerbner's terminology of 'cultural indicators' perpetuates these objectivist presumptions (see Rowland and Watkins 1984; Schlesinger et al 1989). Are these 'indicators' in the same sense that one has economic indicators, such as trade balances or inflation? If not then what is their status? The continued use of a language of 'reflection' generates analyses which are inadequate both at the level of the produced text (and its actual relation to the object world to which it purportedly refers) and at the level of the audience (and the real complexities of the activity of viewing).

With regard to the first of these, the notion of 'reflection' or 'expression' introduces a correlative notion of 'distortion', which is in turn used as the basis of analytic and critical activity. 'Distortion' is construed as failed or inadequate reflection: it does not call the issue of reflection itself into question at a theoretical level. The power of the cinematic or televisual image to refer to or represent the world remains an implicit given. Thus Carlson begins his analysis of television crime drama by asserting that

> The messages transmitted through television are not accurate reflections of reality, nor are they neutral with regard to social and political values. Television programming does not accurately reflect the real world because those who transmit the images are constrained by a wide variety of factors including societal values, the need to maximize audience size, organizational procedures and personal values.
>
> (Carlson 1985: 2)

Carlson appears to construe messages as 'things' which occupy channels or media in the same way that fluids occupy conduits or containers. Distortion is introduced into the message by extraneous factors – much as pollutants may be introduced into a water supply. In these terms the 'neutrality' of the message's reflection of the world is taken as the main criterion of its correspondence to truth. This glosses over the fact that such adequacy is itself the outcome of conventions of depiction, and that realism is therefore an 'effect' of a mode of narration and inscription (of technologies of recording, storage and performance, of techniques of editing and so forth).

Content analysis and 'realism'
To this extent the critique of 'classical' content analysis coincides with the critique of 'realism' in film and television. MacCabe (1985) argues that realism is a 'metalanguage' which appears to 'let the identity of things shine through the window of words' (or in this case of words and images) (MacCabe 1985: 35). According to this view, realism seeks to 'anneal' the distinction between what is said and the act of saying, through 'denying its own status' as writing or inscription. In film and television, MacCabe says, the 'knowledgeability' (of narrative prose) is recast in the narration of events: 'The camera shows us what happens' (1985: 37).

The allegation here, then, is that the language of reflection fails to grapple with the relevant processes of televisual realism. The pretension of showing the world as it is is actually a concealment: the realist text both conceals its own work of representation and, in so doing, conceals from the 'viewing subject' the way in which s/he is thereby situated and addressed. MacCabe's fundamental objection is to the fixity which ensues from these practices, both for texts and for the stances which viewers are able to adopt towards them: 'The reactionary practice of the cinema is that which involves the petrification of the spectator in a position of pseudo-dominance' (MacCabe 1985: 55). That is to say, realism encourages a 'natural attitude' of pleasure in the consumption of a finished object. In so far as it does not recognize the problematic status of the concepts of realism and representation, content analysis in fact tends to sustain the dominion of realism as the predominant mode of narration in film and television, even as it complains against the 'distortion' and inaccuracy of its products.

In another essay MacCabe reminds us that the term 'discourse' is derived from the Latin *discurrere*, 'to run around' (1985: 85). 'Realist' discourse, it is argued, places an inhibition on the subject's motion, in particular his or her capacity to question or investigate the truth conditions of a text or representation. Heath (1981), meanwhile, follows Metz (1974) in describing cinematic realism in terms of the operation of 'suture', of the 'imposition of coherence' (Heath 1981: 14). Where the contradictions of the world are imaginarily resolved, the world is metaphorically 'stitched up'. In Heath's view the consequence of this cognitive operation of ordering and simplifying (an operation of 'adjustment, centring, framing') is the prescription of the viewer's disposition. Realist discourse stipulates a 'moral attitude', a 'correct position' (Heath 1981: 11). The realist narrative tells us everything we need to know, and it cannot be mistaken. The argument from film theory, then, is that unless content analysis is sufficiently sensitive to problems of narrative structure and stylistics it will fail to identify the most important features of the relation between the viewer and the screen (see Baggaley and Duck 1976: 7).

A first argument against the presumptions and procedures of classical content analysis thus concerns its inadequacy at the level of the text. A second ground of objection centres on its premature and erroneous stipulation of the activities and responses of viewers or readers, that is of audiences. The two arguments come from rather different sources. The first originates in semiotics and film theory. The second is largely the concern of empirical social psychology (Gunter 1985). Notwithstanding these different origins, however, the two sorts of arguments coincide in offering critiques of 'transparency' in the analysis of texts and their reception. Film theory suggests that content analysis, as practised by Gerbner, Carlson and others, treats texts as being, in some simple sense, the symptom or reflection of an underlying and intersubjectively shared set of values or beliefs. That is it sees a transparent relation between the text and the ensemble of social relations of which it is the product. The second argument, meanwhile, detects a parallel assumption of transparency in respect of the alleged consequences of and for its reception by an audience.

As I have shown, the advocates of a 'selective exposure' hypothesis go some way towards making good the shortcomings of the 'Cultural Indicators Project' (the larger endeavour within which the cultivation hypothesis originates), by paying close attention to the diversity of needs and responses among a differentiated audience. This argument is taken further by Gunter (1985; 1987). Gunter employs a notion of 'ecological validity' (1985: 31). He argues that even if Gerbner's 'message system analysis' could be said to provide an exhaustive inventory of the elements and events of a set of television programmes, this in no way guarantees that the audience's responses correspond to the most frequent statistical distribution of these events. The frequency of events does not in and of itself denote their salience from the audience's point of view; nor does the numerical aggregation of events 'show' the structural principles of their organization (see McQuail 1984: 124). Gunter shows that the kinds of judgements which viewers are able to make about the 'dimensions' of television 'violence' are simply too sophisticated and too plural to be grasped in terms of Gerbner's prescription of a correlation between amounts of television viewed and perceptions of a mean or scary world (Gunter 1985).

It is thus entirely reasonable of Gunter to call for a more complex understanding of viewing and of the viewer's involvement with television (Gunter 1987: 34); but it is quite premature of him to suppose that this somehow disposes of the problem of textuality altogether (Gunter 1985: 31), especially when he suggests that the different reactions he records are none the less reactions to 'objective features of content' (1985: 252) while providing no criteria whereby such features might be 'objectively' known. Similarly, Zillman and Wakshlag (1987; see also Chapter 4) claim to illuminate audience behaviour; but in so doing they fail to secure their suppositions, first, that the dynamic of 'good' and 'evil' is the only, or even a principal mechanism at work within the text and, second, that the dialectic of pleasure and aversion is the only, or even a principal, motivation to view.

In these ways the 'selective exposure' thesis appears to dispense with the notion of the viewer as an innocently credulous 'cultural dope', but then proceeds to reintroduce this figure, modified only in that its behaviour is seen as subject to a somewhat larger and more complex range of prior variables and conditions. In so far as these authors are claiming to illuminate the questions of preference and involvement it is difficult to see how such a reduced, schematic and a priori notion of what constitutes the text contributes to this end. For these reasons the advocates of 'selective exposure' are vulnerable to the same criticism as they in turn lodge against Gerbner, namely that their findings are artefactual. They strain, that is to say, to produce categories which are clear and distinct enough to be correlated together (viewing – violence – fear), while an alternative reading may generate categories too diffuse and slippery to be amenable to these manipulations. In saying this, however, we simply acknowledge that viewers' responses to television are subject to the same inherent complexities as every other feature of mundane social activity (see Giddens 1984: xxiii). They are not straightforwardly separable from the contexts in which they take place and they are, in any case, only recoverable through procedures of interpretation. Advances in the understanding of television's narration of crime and law enforcement must recognize the necessity both of a scheme for the interpretation of television texts (as Gunter appears reluctant to admit) and of the interpretation of the audience (as neither Gerbner nor the film theoretic alternatives of Heath or McCabe sufficiently do). At present there is a tendency for observers to give such priority to one moment of the communicative exchange (*either* the text, *or* the audience) that the other is taken to follow from it alone. Social psychology generates no non-obvious and interesting interpretations of texts. Content analysis and film theory offer no empirical account of how actual viewers diverge from the privileged reading.

In television each text is part of a recurrent 'flow' (R. Williams 1974; see also Gould et al 1984: 18). The flow of television encourages a sedimentation of decoding strategies (Eco 1972; see also Bateson 1972: 428). Both production and reception tend to pull each other towards an orderly pattern, but one which is occasionally interrupted, transgressed or broken. What follows here is, avowedly, a contribution to the interpretation of television texts: but its objective is also to facilitate approaches to the television audience, because it recognizes that the crux of the matter is the point at which they act upon one another.

What is 'television violence'?

The problems inherent in previous studies of television crime drama are nowhere clearer or more serious than in their analysis of, or failure to analyse, the notion of violence. The term 'violence' has long been a touchstone of television studies: indeed concern about violence (whether on the part of lobbying organizations, government agencies or television networks) has been the largest single rationale in the sponsorship of research.

As a result of this inheritance, the claim to illuminate the issue of violence has often been the main criterion by which any research project has had to establish its claim to practicality or relevance. Within this field Gerbner's position is particularly curious. 'Cultivation analysis' explicitly addresses itself to the *representation* of crime and law enforcement. However, while it served to broaden the scope of research during the 1970s away from the issues of imitation, modelling and so forth and towards those of political and attitudinal correlates of television viewing it has not, in so doing, also broken with the problematic of 'violence' as television's central topic. Gerbner's project thus continues the emphases of the Surgeon General's Report in that the regular production of a 'violence profile' (Gerbner and Gross 1976a) is construed in part as an exercise in the monitoring, regulation and supervision of the networks and their schedules. There is thus an uneasy link between Gerbner's apparent debt to critical theory and this technical and actuarial (one might say technocratic and administrative) emphasis. This is most clearly evident in Gerbner's definition of violence as a particular category of event, amenable to being counted. Violence is

> the overt expression of physical force against self or other, compelling action against one's will on pain of being hurt or killed, or actually hurting or killing.
>
> (Gerbner 1970: 70)

One of the problems with this definition is that it tends to disconnect the issue of 'violence' both from the context of its occurrence (because the 'violence profile' comprises everything from cop shows to cartoons) *and* from the issue of its justification within any particular narrative. Thus it defines violence before it has defined the genres in which it takes place. Gerbner's later work implicitly recognizes that this definition elides violence with power or coercion (Gerbner et al 1979) yet the operational, external and behavioural definition is allowed to remain. The apparent clarity of the behavioural definition of violence, claiming to be valid for all instances, is somewhat spurious, submerging the relational questions of transitivity (the 'who–whom?' of the violent transaction) and of justification. Indeed there are now many such unhelpful definitions of violence available. For example Cumberbatch (1988: 10) has defined violence as 'any action of physical force, with or without a weapon, against oneself or another person, animal or inanimate object, whether carried through or merely attempted and whether the action caused injury or not'. This seems pretty comprehensive. Certainly it would include most sports programmes and probably extends to gardening and cookery also.

For many political philosophers (Ellul 1968; Arendt 1970; Benjamin 1979) violence is not a category of event, but rather a problem in the relation of means to ends. As Pringle observes, the removal of violence from its context only exacerbates the 'uncertainty of its polemical charge' (1972: 152). The proper understanding of 'television violence' is inseparable from the issues of instrumentality and outcome. There is a link between the use of violence and the distribution of outcomes, in which some 'violences' are ratified while others are censured. It is misleading to seek a behavioural definition of violence which makes no reference to the range of normative and associative themes which the term subtends and which compose its semantic field. These include rage, fury, excess, animality, unreason and so forth (Newman 1979: 2–5). Yet, in the context of an heroic narrative, it appears that something which is taken to be generally impermissible can be exempted from this ban, even to the point of being profoundly valued. In so far as the allegation of violence is characteristically a censure, the ratification of certain uses of violence also tends to deny or mask their nature as violence. The 'violence' of villains and heroes signify quite different things. The superficial coherence of the term, which constitutes its attractiveness to behavioural researchers, disperses under the most cursory examination of its placement in both ordinary and technical discourses.

Benjamin comments on the 'law making character' of violence (1979: 138). He means by this that the violent act seeks *both* to establish its ostensible aim *and* its own legitimacy (see Arendt 1970: 52). Benjamin argues that the reason why the state cannot tolerate violences other than its own, even when it can contain them, is that every act of violence inherently contains the possibility of 'making a new law' (Benjamin 1979: 138). La Fontaine (1974) in 'The Fable of the Wolf and the Lamb' puts the issue more pithily: 'The reason of the strongest is always the best' (see Serres 1980; 268).

This being so, it would appear that the relations between violence, power and justification in television narrative have not yet been fully explored. Gerbner is surely wrong, for instance, to assert that the only differentiation between heroes and villains in television is power or success (Gerbner et al 1979). He arrives at this conclusion by enumerating the incidence of certain events and their antecedents (i.e. by showing a correlation between the use of violence and survival or success), rather than, as the viewer can, seeing this sequence from within the horizon of genre and expectation. Gerbner seems to suggest that we do not know who the hero is until after the last shot has been fired, much as some behaviourists claim that we know we are happy because we smile. It is more precise to say that there is a reciprocal 'ordering relation' (Serres 1980: 263) between heroism and the successful imposition of violence and, hence, between power and survival (see Canetti 1986). Gerbner might have said instead that television crime fictions suggest a ruthless social Darwinism, in which the capable use of violence is a condition of heroism and success, and that the 'moral' which the narrative points is thus a questionable one, but this is already a somewhat different proposition. Similarly, when Zillman and Wakshlag note that cop shows 'feature the triumph of justice' (1987: 11) they allude to the fact that these are narratives, unwinding towards resolution. When they suggest that this 'triumph' is pleasurable and that it relieves anxiety, they are saying, albeit in a mechanistic way, that the outcome of the narrative is something which is willed or desired. The condition of the viewer's involvement is that s/he participates in this desire, at least to the extent of finding it plausible or appropriate for the purposes of the fiction. There is, then, a necessary connection between the narration of a sequence of events and categories of justification: the world of the text and the world of the viewer meet, however momentarily and contingently, on this terrain. The narrative function is inherently a moral one.

Previous research in this area has paid insufficient attention to narrative. It has consequently become confused between normative and technical imperatives. Gerbner's outlook seems somewhat misdirected, while Zillman and Wakshlag's is oversimplified. I introduce notions of narration (story and discourse), style and resolution in order to elaborate a scheme for inquiring into television crime fiction which is more adequate to the internal organization of the stories as well as more suggestive both of the kinds of activity through which viewers may 'accomplish' or 'realize' their meanings (see Eco 1979) and, further, of how they stand in relation to other features of consciousness and belief.

An example: Eco on heroism in popular narrative

The analysis which Eco provides of Fleming's James Bond novels offers a partial model for the kind of investigation I envisage (Eco 1979: 144–70). This model is appropriate partly because these are stories of heroism, violence and the 'triumph of justice' (1979: 147) and partly because the thirteen novels in the '007 saga' share some of the features of repetition and seriality which are important in understanding television series.

Eco suggests an analysis of narrative structure at five levels:

1 the opposition of characters and of values
2 play situations and the story as a 'game'
3 a Manichaean ideology
4 literary technique
5 literature as collage.

The contribution which each of these levels makes to the whole can be summarized briefly.

The actual permutations of characters are few and simple, consisting of relations of alliance and opposition between Bond, his controller 'M', the Woman, the Villain and their subsidiaries. Each of the characters, however, carries significances which allow them to stand for more abstract categories to do with, for example, nation, duty, ideals, strategy and loyalty (Eco 1979: 147). For instance, one of the most frequent oppositions is between Bond's virility and the villain's deformity and sexual impotence, resolved finally in the latter's death and the former's possession of the woman (1979: 149–54).

At the second level, Eco is interested in the organization of these elements into sequences of 'moves'. The scheme of the novels is invariant in the sense that all the elements and each of the moves is always present, although they may occur in different orders. Eco's point is that the end of the game cannot fail to be achieved because of the rules which generate the sequence of moves, which Eco jokingly summarizes as 'Bond moves and mates [sic] in eight moves' (1979: 156). Eco concludes that

> In fact, in every detective story and in every hard-boiled novel, there is no basic variation, but rather the repetition of a habitual scheme in which the reader can recognize something he has already seen and of which he has grown fond. Under the guise of a machine that produces information, the criminal novel produces redundancy: pretending to rouse the reader it in fact reconfirms him in a sort of imaginative laziness and creates escape by narrating not the Unknown, but the Already Known.
>
> (Eco 1979: 160)

What the detective story exploits, for Eco, is the pleasure of 'foregone play' (1979: 161).

Eco finds that the third level, that of Bond's Manichaean ideology, has little to do with Fleming's private opinions, whatever these may have been. On the question of Fleming's racism, for example, Eco argues that the distribution of good and bad, and otherwise 'typical' characteristics to certain characters results from the 'rhetorical purposes' which Fleming pursues. The narrative apparatus *demands* binary and archetypal oppositions (1979: 161). Fleming is 'simply Manichaean for operative reasons: he sees the world as made up of good and bad forces in conflict' (1979: 187). In his use of elementary oppositions Fleming chooses what Eco calls 'the path of fable', and 'A man who chooses to write in this way is neither a fascist nor a racist; he is only a cynic, an expert in tale engineering' (1979: 161). In short the reactionary character of the Bond stories derives from their use of stock characters and dichotomies, a refusal of ambivalence which is 'always dogmatic and intolerant':

Fleming is conservative as, basically, the fable – any fable – is conservative, his is the static, inherent, dogmatic conservatism of fairy tales and myths, which transmit an elementary wisdom, constructed and communicated by a simple play of light and shade, by indisputable archetypes which do not permit critical distinction. If Fleming is a 'fascist' he is so because of his inability to pass from mythology to reason.

(Eco 1979: 162)

These points are also relevant to Eco's treatment of the fourth and fifth levels of narrative structure. At the level of literary technique, Eco reminds us, Fleming may use simple elements but he is a virtuoso in their arrangement. Part of the success of the Bond stories stems from their capacity to invite 'smart' as well as 'naive' readings (1979: 8), so that the sophisticated reader is permitted to 'distinguish, with a feeling of aesthetic pleasure, the purity of the primitive epic impudently and maliciously translated into current terms' (1979: 163). In stylistic terms Fleming plays upon a distinction between the epic simplicity, as well as the extremity and violence, of his narrative situations and a restrained externality in his descriptions. Through his extended discursive elaborations upon the familiar and everyday Fleming can 'solicit our capacity for identification' (1979: 167) within a narrative sequence which is far from everyday:

Our credulity is solicited, blandished, directed to the region of possible and desirable things. Here the narration is realistic, the attention to detail intense; for the rest, so far as the unlikely is concerned, a few pages and a wink of the eye suffice. No one has to believe them.

(Eco 1979: 167)

Again the key point is how this narrative strategy 'makes us fond' (Eco 1979: 167) of what it presents. Fleming's style, Eco argues, performs the same function as repetition and invariance do at the level of plot. It favours redundancy rather than information. 'The greatest pleasure arises not from excitement but from relief' (1979: 167).

Eco's term 'collage' refers to this 'unstable montage' through which Fleming appeals both to his readers' most simple-minded and visceral impulses, as well as to exoticism and irony (1979: 170), in a blend of 'the literary inheritance and the crude chronicle'. Clearly Fleming does offer the possibility of a 'disenchanted' reading. However, and Eco clearly feels that this is more frequently the case, 'to the extent that it provokes elementary psychological reactions in which ironic detachment is absent, it is only a more subtle, but not less mystifying, example of soap opera' (1979: 172).

Open/closed: the relevance of Eco's categories

Quite apart from its many substantive insights the relevance of this example to the study of television crime fiction is clear. Obviously, Eco's analysis is concerned with a 'saga' of novels and not television programmes. The differences between the forms of narration in and participation with these different media are quite large. Nevertheless, Eco provides one of the few investigations into popular narratives, especially narratives of violence and excitement, which strive to be adequate to their reader's or viewer's experience. He construes the text as a form of address which, while it may be 'taken' in a number of different ways, is nevertheless far more likely to be read in some than others. No text, in this respect, is ever wholly 'open' or wholly 'closed' (1979: 8). Every text exists in a state of suspension between these ideal poles: it necessarily envisages a more or less sophisticated implicit reader. Its active social meaning, therefore, always 'depends on the concrete social circumstances of reception' (1979: 172) and there is indeed a real and sobering difficulty in recovering what these are in any individual case. Thus

> When an act of communication provokes a response in public opinion, the definitive verification will take place not within the ambit of the book but in that of the society that reads it.
>
> (Eco 1979: 172)

What Eco's intervention does establish definitively, however, is that this concrete 'realised' meaning can never be ascertained on the basis of an interpretation of texts which is *less* sophisticated (in the way that content analysis typically *is* less sophisticated) than those which the 'cultural dopes' themselves routinely achieve (see Giddens 1984: 345). Eco's position thus refuses to separate the internal organization of texts from the 'pragmatics' of their reading or reception. That is, he opposes to the 'textual isolationism' (Harari 1980: 41) of classical structuralism the issues of stylistics, or the means whereby the 'overcoding' of the text (Eco 1979: 22) leans towards its being 'taken' in one way rather than another. Eco distinguishes between 'empirical' (or real) and 'model' readers. Whereas the empirical reader may be unavailable for comment, the model reader is the text's hypothetical or implicit addressee. Thus

> To make his text communicative, the author has to assume that the ensemble of codes he relies upon is the same as that shared by his possible reader. The author has thus to foresee a model of the possible reader (hereafter Model Reader) supposedly able to deal interpretatively with the expressions in the same way as the author deals generatively with them.
>
> (Eco 1979: 7)

A closed text, such as television narratives tend to be, *both* envisages an 'average addressee referred to a given social context' *and* aims 'obsessively' at arousing 'a precise response on the part of more or less precise empirical readers' (Eco 1979: 8). These are texts which make an important 'request of conformity', such that

> They apparently aim at pulling the reader along a predetermined path, carefully displaying their effects so as to arouse pity or fear, excitement or depression at the due place and at the right moment. Every step of the 'story' elicits just the expectation that its further course will satisfy. They seem to be structured according to an inflexible project. Unfortunately the only one not to have been inflexibly planned is the reader. These texts are potentially speaking to everyone. Better, they presuppose an average reader resulting from a merely intuitive sociological speculation – in the same way in which an advertisement chooses its possible readers.
>
> (Eco 1979: 8)

Such texts will succeed more completely in eliciting the co-operation of more readers (that is, loosely, in bringing the model and empirical reader closer together) the more they can appeal to an existing 'common frame' (1979: 21) of which the target audience has already been 'made fond' (1979: 160). It is easier and more pleasurable to read co-operatively than to 'code switch' (1979: 22) and refer the text to another convention. Thus the text tends to secure its own acceptability by its adherence to genre rules (1979: 19). The text is thus a rhetoric which invites co-operation by appealing to what Eco had earlier called a common 'patrimony of knowledge' (Eco 1972), whether at the level of common frames for the understanding of real events or 'intertextual frames' which place the text within the 'treasury' of narrative schemes (1979: 21).

This has a close bearing on the ideological weight of the text. Eco argues that texts which order their 'disclosures' in accordance with a known intertextual frame and their 'discursive structures' (Eco 1979: 23) similarly in accordance with a shared common frame of reference do not require, and tend to discourage, further inquiry. The text and the reader are, in this case, 'complicit' (Mercer 1986). They seem to share the same 'basic dictionary'. They do not make conflicting inferences: rather the author 'disguises his own productive activity and tries to convince the spectator that he and him are the same' (Eco 1979: 41). The 'hidden catechization' (1979: 22) remains unstated: the 'veridiction' of the text goes unchallenged.

For these reasons, to read uncooperatively can be to read *well* (Eco 1979: 9), because the 'macropropositions' which underlie the text (which are, in Eco's jargon, overcoded into micropropositions of its expression plane) are made available for interrogation (see S. Hall 1984). It is a legitimate part of criticism to make the text 'say more than it apparently says':

in this movement . . . even the most closed texts are surgically opened: fiction is transformed into document and the innocence of fancy is translated into the disturbing evidence of a philosophical statement.

(Eco 1979: 22)

Any text, but especially every fictional narrative text, can thus be construed as an attempt at persuasion: it seeks to have its premises accepted. Stylistic features, particularly in the present context those of televisual realism, are intrinsic to this effort. Texts are rhetorical forms of address. The weakness of classical content analysis, however, is that on the basis of a weak understanding of narrative and an ignorance of style, it proceeds to make strong claims about the possibility of a 'science of persuasion' (see Billig 1987), which takes the 'effects' of certain texts to be precisely calculable. Eco's argument (see also S. Hall 1975) suggests that just as every text stands at some point on a continuum between openness and closure, so every reading may be more of less 'naive' or 'smart'. This does not make the 'naive' reading of the 'closed' text any the less cognitively and morally problematic in terms of what it allows to pass unchallenged at the level of *endoxa* (Eco 1979; see also Bourdieu 1977: 167). In answering the 'request of conformity' we are always in danger of going beyond simple 'co-operation' towards compliance and passive obedience.

Seriality and 'closure' in television narrative

I have set out to establish whether (and how) the degree of closure in television crime drama is such as to foreclose or 'fix' (T. J. Taylor 1980: 70) the viewer's response to an essentially moral dilemma, namely the resolution of the narrative 'crisis' by the imposition of legitimate violence. This in turn poses a further question, whether a resolution habitually achieved at the level of the fable (i.e. an intertextual frame) is likely to have any bearing on the social representation of real situations (i.e. a common frame). These are the terms on which it seems to me most appropriate to broach the questions of the ideological weight or other 'effects' of television. Certainly it is a more oblique language than has been current in this field but, I think, a more valid one for that very reason. It seeks to avoid unnecessary conflations (enjoyment with credulity, fiction with propaganda, fantasy with belief) while still taking seriously the possibility that the routine introduction of conventional fictions into the rhythm of everyday life is not ideologically neutral or irrelevant.

The key terms in this analysis will be those of generic rules, the degree of variation in narrative sequences and the frequency and regularity of their reiteration. I am trying to make plain the relations between television schedules, narrative structure and the prevailing mode of address to the 'implicit viewer'. Content analysis succeeds in 'showing' the frequency of certain programme categories, containing certain elements, at certain times (Dominick 1973), but it does not show how they are 'taken': it places the viewer's activity inside behaviourism's 'black box'.

Any stylistically informed analysis of narrative must try to deal sensibly with the relationship between story and discourse, roughly speaking the 'what' and the 'way' of story-telling (Chatman 1978). Genette (1982) takes issue with the conventional opposition between narrative and description. Even if one could envisage 'pure description' the reverse is unattainable: the verbs and substantives of the simplest narrative 'are never quite exempt from descriptive resonance' (Genette 1982: 134). If recounting and describing use the same linguistic resources the 'pure' state of narrative is nowhere to be found (Genette 1982: 141). This is important since it brings us back to the issue of 'veridiction' and to the link between intertextual and common frames. The impact of realist narrative, from the point of view of its audience derives from its organization of discursive elements into a given 'phraseology of action' (Chaney 1977) which is 'followable' (Kermode 1979: 117).

In television crime drama this means the co-ordination of contemporarily recognizable representations of settings (especially of urban environments) and actors (especially police-officers and criminals) within a particular sequence of events about transgression, crisis, resolution and retribution. The narrative structure, moreover, is positioned within temporal structures, both in terms of the internal movement of the episode and of the seriality of its emission: the time it takes to tell and the times at which it will be told. The question of 'form' is in this sense indivisible from the concrete facts of the tale's being broadcast and received.

Oddities of television narratives

The paradox of television is between fixity and evanescence. The form may be quite constant, but the episode is here and gone. For this reason Ellis (1982) notes a stylistic convergence between fictional and non-fictional modes of television. They are more similar to one another, he claims, than either is to classic models of narrative in prose and cinema (1982: 145). In Ellis's view the television narrative differs from the classic cinematic model of a consecutive sequence of events ending in definitive and stable resolution in that the stability is provided by the series, rather than the episode. The individual episode can only provisionally resolve the dilemma which gives rise to the action because we must return to it again next week or next season. The episode's resolution, or 'clinch' (1982: 152) thus returns us to the basic dilemma, a repeated situation which 'provides a kind of groundbase, a constant basis for events rather than . . . a final totalisation' (1982: 147). The stress is less on a linear development around a 'narrative enigma' than on the multiplication of somewhat familiar characters, exchanges and events (1982: 152–3). Resolution occurs but at a 'less fundamental level' than in other media, since the premise of the series is 'a problematic that is not resolved' (1982: 154) within a known social setting, and centring on a 'state of permanent or semi-permanent relationships between a stable but antagonistic group of characters' (1982: 155). The series provides a 'continuous update, a perpetual return to the present' (1982: 147).

It is through this organization of time that, in Eco's terms, we are 'made fond' of reiterative television. It is a form of textuality suspended between the closedness of the classic narrative on the one hand, and the open and extended nature of talk and personal interaction on the other (see Scannell 1986). This in turn should alert us to the ideological import of the television crime series. The episodic 'clinch' set against an unresolved 'problematic' suggests an ethic of stoic resistance in the face of intractable circumstances: the heroic and violent solution will always be necessary because the final moment of victory over the forces of transgression and disorder is always postponed. In television crime fiction the text's 'disclosures' are not usually very surprising from the point of view of the knowledgeable audience. Rather they serve to return us to a known, premised situation of which we have already grown fond. Within this world only certain sequences of events are really plausible or justifiable.

Investigating crime fiction: some methodological issues

A close analysis of this world and the moral tales it generates should (I suggest) adopt a dual procedure. First, it will seek to sketch the boundaries of the genre by indicating its common elements. That is it will seek to show a common stock of situations, settings, events, outcomes, persons and so forth. Second, it will show how these resources are drawn upon and organized in particular narratives.

At the first level the procedure resembles (and learns from) what is inoffensive and sensible in content analysis. That is it attempts to co-ordinate a large amount of material and to indicate the patterns into which it commonly falls, in order to generate a corpus of texts which can sensibly be said to be coherent. To this end quantification, or at least attempting to show that the patterns are really there, is clearly necessary. I do not set out primarily to count and report events, however. Rather I set out to record the occurrence of what I have already suggested, following Eco and Ellis, are the most theoretically interesting and salient features of narrative structure. Such a procedure is by no means exhaustive, but it does claim to make manifest a real pattern. It aims to show the dimensions of a discourse out of which many stories (but not just *any* story) can be generated (and of which many readings, but not just *any* reading, may be possible).

Gould et al (1984) show in great detail that the validity of content analyses is constrained by the levels of generality they envisage. They rightly note, furthermore, that similarities between the underlying themes and contents within the 'traffic' of television programmes are not confined to genres of programming advertised as such. Obvious examples include points of contact between crime drama and soap opera or situation comedy. A particularly vexed case in point would be the relations between crime drama and certain kinds of dramatized documentary (see Sparks 1987: 6). The most significant coincidence is, evidently, between crime drama series and the broadcasting of feature films. However, I have been at pains to argue that a major weakness of most content analysis has been its tendency to record 'violent' incidents with too *little* regard to their placement within particular genres of programming. To the extent that I am concerned not with 'violence' *tout court* but rather with its use and justification within a particular regime of representation my analysis is not compromised by having a selective focus.

I thus recorded British and American (plus one Italian) series and serials which advertised the activities of police-officers, private investigators and criminals as their primary focus, broadcast in one English television region between May and July 1985. This generated roughly 100 episodes. (Any which were, for technical or human reason, inaudible or incomplete were discarded: this left approximately 90 usable television programmes.) The resulting sample is both bounded and representative. It has a certain unity in that all these programmes clearly have key thematic elements in common. Its representativeness is established, first, by its size, and second, by the fact that the programmes included are there simply by virtue of having been broadcast within a given and, so far as I could establish, typical period of time, rather than because they are specially expedient in corroborating any particular a priori argument.

The results and emergent patterns of this preliminary analysis are recorded and discussed in Chapter 6. Within this body of material I devote somewhat closer attention to a number of particular examples and illustrations. Some of these conform rather closely to the overall dimensions of the sample as a whole and are fairly typical of its outlines. They reveal what is commonly known as the 'formula'. Others were chosen for closer analysis because they are in one way or another odd or aberrant. They emphasize or heighten some feature which is more or less recessive in other cases. They reveal the boundaries of the corpus, as it were, negatively, either by transgressing them or by following their logic to an extreme point. These include *Hill St Blues, Miami Vice, Cover Up, Hunter, The Detective* and *Octopus: Power of the Mafia*. The selection of this informal sub-set permits closer attention to narrative structure, and facilitates examination of the way in which any given narrative draws upon, uses and plays with the common discursive resources.

My aim is therefore to provide an initial and qualitative exploration of what seem to me to be the salient features of this body of stories. In so doing I look both at the settings and situations from which they begin, as Ellis (1982) advises, and at the kinds of sequences of events which take place within them. These two dimensions (the stock of discursive resources of character, relationship, setting and place on the one hand, and their stories on the other) provide the starting-point from which I shall look at the 'tale engineering' of the genre (Eco 1979; 161). Although not itself quantitative the analysis which I present below could be regarded as preliminary to any further attempt to describe quantitatively the units and categories which are operative within the body of stories.

It is important to see the practical advantages of the theorizations provided by Eco and Ellis and on which I draw. It is true that Gerbner, for example, expresses a legitimate, tough-minded concern with the immediate, concrete, political correlates of television viewing. However, 'content analysis' on the Gerbnerist model is not necessarily an appropriate tool for the job: in failing to penetrate the formal and stylistic structures of the text it also fails to show how, in practice, the viewer is addressed. It does not come close to the experience of viewing and its relation to pleasure, posture, consumption or reasoning. The point is, rather, that the pleasure of the narrative and the reiteration of the offer of the violent solution opens on to the issue of subjective experience and the currency of given social categories. Our positioning within the webs of representational discourse is a moral as well as an aesthetic matter. It is not, or not simply, a question of the statistical distribution of 'attitudes', but rather of whether we are also bound into a more primary level of moral reactions and dispositions, which Gouldner terms a 'paleo-symbolic system' (Gouldner 1976: 224).

Up to now I have commented on some recent debates about the relations between images of crime and law enforcement on television and public perceptions of crime. These have predominantly been concerned with the questions of fear and anxiety and their possible ideological effects. I have argued that all such arguments implicitly rest on assumptions or propositions about the 'content' or 'meaning' of televisual representations. Empirical debates frequently turn on such conflicting interpretations of meaning. However, the criteria on which such interpretations have been based have often been rather inexplicit and in any case usually too crude to bear the weight of inference placed upon them.

The business of 'reading' television is necessarily attended by certain difficulties. The more certain categories, those which one can count, may not be the most informative; the more interesting ones may involve elements of conjecture and interpretation which defy ready demonstration.

My own ambitions in the analysis I offer in the next chapter are therefore duly modest. I claim only to identify and summarize some broad parameters of a body of stories, and to warrant my arguments about them using illustrations and examples. I seek to alert the reader to some features which seem to me characteristic of them (and which I believe illuminate the question of their appeal) and to invite further consideration.

One virtue of Eco's position, which I have outlined here, is that it offers an account of the existence of generic features of narratives without recourse to essentialist notions of a crystalline 'deep-structure' (Lévi-Strauss 1966; see also Murdock 1982 for a critique of the reification of 'genre'). A further benefit is that it suggests a reconsideration of commonplace separations between the levels of production and the 'produced text' on the one hand and the audience on the other. I follow Eco in arguing that the most fruitful way of examining any popular cultural 'text' is *both* as the outcome of a specific process of production *and* as therefore necessarily involving a particular construction of its presumed or hypothetical audience.

Thus that traditional question in communication studies 'Who says what to whom in what channel with what effect?' must be revised to include a supplementary question: who does 'who' think 'whom' is, such that they choose to address them in this particular way (McQuail 1984: 4–5)? Such considerations are now basic to the analysis of advertising and political rhetoric, but they are equally crucial to the understanding of storytelling and other forms of entertainment. Recent developments in the study of the construction of deviance in news production, notably those by Ericson et al (1987) and Schlesinger et al (1989), are also consonant with this view. Ericson et al (1987) have shown that whereas journalism presents itself as merely tracking the contingency of events, it is in fact an exercise in the construction of stories, with strategic intent. It is thus a process of narration, in which presumptions as to the impact of particular themes, tropes and stylistic devices on the audience are a constitutive feature of story construction.

This recognition introduces additional complexity into the question of the boundaries between news and fiction as modes of representation (see Ericson et al 1987: 336). It thus invites reconsideration of the precise relations in which they stand to one another. In respect of news production, Ericson et al (1987) argue not only that deviance is a fundamental criterion of newsworthiness (1987: 4) but also that it is only made present to the audience's awareness through a process of 'visualizing' (1987: 167). Any instance of the visualization of deviance results from and encapsulates a preoccupation with the nature of social order and how it can be breached and repaired (1987: 12). The 'adequacy' of a story to these purposes is contingent on its amenability to being considered within certain existing scenarios of deviation and the disruption and restoration of order.

To this extent the analyses of crime news and crime fiction raise related sets of concerns. The two fields overlap both intertextually, in the construction of adequate or satisfactory stories, and organizationally, in respect of their positions within time-tables or schedules and other elements of 'mediatic logics'. As Ericson et al (1987) also point out, news of deviance need not be of momentous public or political significance. Rather, much of it is composed of the *faits divers* of social life: stories of heroism, pathos, embarrassment or misfortune. It is about that which is curious, amusing, troubling or otherwise humanly interesting. Deviance is thus clearly a category of entertainment as well as information. At the same time, as Ericson comments (1991: 224), the dramatization of deviance, whether in news or in fiction, raises stories of crime and law enforcement (some of which are mundane, some very troubling) to a more elevated level and lends them 'ceremonial force'. Such stories are haunted by the possibility of disorder (Ericson 1991: 239). They hanker for the restoration of order and authority and delight in the assertion of retribution and justice. I now turn to the substantive examination of some of the ways in which I consider such resources of anxiety and pleasure to be encoded and organized in television fiction.

6 The moral world of television crime stories

If we tore down all the laws, where should we hide from the Devil, and the winds that would blow then?

St Thomas More, *The Essential Thomas More*

Some questions, propositions and provisos

Why are 'cop shows' appealing, popular, widespread? Why are we 'fond' of heroes, anti-heroes, villains and others? How has it come about that we, the audience, know the contours of the projected world so well that we are able to move about in it as *habitués*? How do cop shows achieve 'followability' (Kermode 1979: 117)? I propose that they achieve followability by fencing in a dominant representation of the city and of its sites and sources of danger. In so doing they stipulate courses of action and justified responses. They thereby also hedge away the constant possibilities of dissolution and chaos; but at the same time they sometimes act against complexity and heterogeneity also. The 'violence' in 'television violence' cannot be isolated, from its perpetrators, from its victims, from its positions within 'codes of conduct in action' (S. Hall 1975; Ericson 1991: 235), from its metaphorical and allegorical resonance. To analyse 'violence on television' is thus to take issue with a whole rhetoric: What does it posit about the world? What does it want us to feel? What does it urge? Whom does it censure? Whom does it praise and reward? To look at the issue in this way qualifies both the happy empiricism of content analysis and the more grandiose pretensions of classical structuralism and formalism. It suggests instead a more sociologically concrete as well as a more critical enterprise. Is it the case that at the level of our daily pleasures some forms of narration act against lucidity by superimposing on the real sources of our needs and anxieties a simplistic, diverting closure?

I do not regard these as easy issues and I have discovered no definitive answers to my questions. Indeed I consider that the premature certainties of objectivist content analyses, and the presumed self-evidence of the category of 'violence', have muddied the waters around the difficult questions of representation and reception and have tended to foreclose more insightful approaches to the placing of crime and law enforcement in contemporary culture. It is worth stressing again therefore that I regard the interpretations offered here as being provisional and illustrative, rather than exhaustive and final. They are undertaken from a particular point of view: they seek out the features of 'content' which I have identified as being of interest for present purposes. They form a part of the larger argument that I have been developing. That is, I believe that crime fiction presupposes an inherent tension between anxiety and reassurance and that this constitutes a significant source of its appeal to the viewer. Furthermore, it is in the dialectical play between these terms that anything resembling a specific ideology of law and its enforcement is to be found in crime fiction. More particularly, it is in the satisfaction which comes from seeing that 'play' enacted and resolved that such importance as these fictions may hold in the lives of their viewers should be sought. As I have already suggested these satisfactions may have to do with the displacement of an indefinitely large range of anxieties, which in turn may be either manifestly or obscurely related to crime and law enforcement and the personal, moral and social significances they carry. Fabular and allegorical stories often begin from a premise of anxiety, though many of them go on to impose a pleasing order and coherence on a shifting and troubling world. It would be an easy matter to show that this imposition of order is false, or simplistic or unreal. What is more interesting is to ask why we should find it pleasing, and how our finding it so stands in relation to our everyday conditions of life.

It is imprudent to lay claim to conclusive answers to questions of this kind. This is all the more obviously so here since the interpretations I am undertaking effectively deal with only one 'moment' (namely the formal or discursive analysis of media content) in a complex and ramified chain of connections between conditions of production, distribution and reception (J. B. Thompson 1988: 377–8). To claim to know all the ideological consequences of a discourse on this basis would be, as Thompson puts it, to 'take for granted what needs to be shown' (J. B. Thompson 1988: 360), while paying 'insufficient attention to the specific social and institutional conditions within which, and by virtue of which, media messages may be ideological' (J. B. Thompson 1988: 376). In so far as what I am attempting here is, properly speaking, an effort of interpretation, it is at once more limited (in forgoing the claim to enumerate the 'objective' features of a message system) and more ambitious than is content analysis as classically conceived and practised. As Thompson comments:

However rigorous and systematic the methods of formal or discursive analysis may be, they can never abolish the need for a creative construction of meaning, that is, for an interpretive explication of what is represented or said. In explicating what is represented or said, the process of interpretation transcends the closure of the symbolic construction, puts forward an account which is risky and open to dispute.

(J. B. Thompson 1988; 369)

It is important to be perfectly plain about this. Not only is the kind of interpretation at issue here necessarily caught up in a realm of 'claim and counter-claim' (J. B. Thompson 1988: 373) but neither can the 'actual communicative effectiveness' (Eco 1972) of a particular mode of representation ever be treated as a given. Neither of these recognitions undermines the importance of attempting the interpretation of cultural forms and their associated practices. If, as Unger has it, society is both 'made and imagined' (1987: 1 ff) we are able to chart some features of these particular kinds of 'making' and 'imagining' and thereby to unfold some of the connections between 'formative frameworks' and the ordering of 'formed routines' (Unger 1987: 4) in everyday life, so as to lay them more open to discussion, evaluation and revision. The critical analysis of television and other media is not an arcane or unusual activity. It is not radically different in kind from what individuals already do in any case in everyday life, but it seeks to extend ordinary processes of interpretation in more than usually concerted, systematic and self-conscious ways. In so doing it seeks to deepen and refine the activities of interpretation and evaluation in order that we may 'engage in group life without becoming the victims of compulsions we do not master and hardly understand' (Unger 1987: 5).

A time for crime: scheduling and continuity

What positions do 'cop shows' occupy within the British broadcast television schedule? In my sample the largest number, roughly half the total, begin transmission between 9 and 10 p.m. By far the commonest positions are either on commercial television, beginning at 9 p.m. and occupying the hour immediately prior to *News at Ten* or on BBC1, beginning immediately after the *9 o'clock News*. These timings are clearly related to the traditional notion of a 'watershed' between 'family' and 'adult' programming at 9 p.m.

This is plainly 'prime-time'. Those series which do not observe this pattern tend also to be somewhat variant in other ways. Those which are broadcast earlier in the evening may be so either because they are aimed to a larger degree at children (and hence prefer vehicles and high-speed chases, clean-cut heroism, less menacing plotting: *CHIPS, Knight Rider*), or they are to some extent comedic (*Cover Up*), or they are 'whodunnits' rather than 'action series' (*Murder, She Wrote*). Those which are broadcast later in the evening are usually repeats of formerly important or popular programmes, and which thus offer a relatively cheap way of retaining a fairly large proportion of the insomniac audience (*The Sweeney, Streets of San Francisco, The Rockford Files*).

The vast majority of all crime dramas are one hour in length, or fifty minutes where imported programmes broadcast by the BBC have had commercial breaks removed. This in turn sets up a scheduling pattern for the BBC, such that its indigenously produced programming is often also of fifty minutes' duration. There were no crime dramas on BBC2 during my sample period. Meanwhile the only examples broadcast on Channel 4 were *Octopus: Power of the Mafia* (a serial, expensively co-produced with RAI) and a series of *Hill St Blues* which had already been shown on the other commercial channel (ITV). Each of these series had an imprimatur of 'quality television' (see Feuer et al 1984).

Scheduling is a matter of both economics and convention. 'Prime-time' is defined not only by numbers of viewers but also by the demographic composition or profile of the audience. The price of time for commercials, for example, varies in direct proportion to the attractiveness of the 'slot' for advertisers. Both advertisers, in buying space, and networks, in selling it, seek to make quite precise calculations in this regard, with predictive ambitions, in terms of the projected 'impacts' per unit of time in proportion to unit costs. These considerations therefore extend beyond the boundaries of any individual programme to include attention to the composition of the audience over the whole evening. Thus, weak or unpropitious programmes may be 'hammocked' between stronger ones, in an effort to gain or retain a sufficient audience share to make them viable. The BBC is only marginally less subject to these pressures than are commercial networks, not least in so far as it has to demonstrate to its governors and to Parliament its capacity to attract an adequate audience share. Thus the cost which can be devoted to either producing or buying any given programme is calibrated against the size and characteristics of its likely audience. Similarly, the cost of production of certain programmes may be justified by their 'serial marketability' in more than one country. Thus, the high 'production values' of, say, *Miami Vice* require that it be bought outside the United States by the BBC and other networks, just as its cost to the BBC demands that it be shown during prime-time.

Each of these considerations contributes to the regularity and predictability in the position of 'cop shows' within the television schedule. The primary dimension of this is the solidification of internal 'formulae', whose most visible consequence is the standardization of length (see Swidler et al 1986).

It is difficult to overstress the importance of these dynamics, but all too easy to oversimplify them. As I have noted above, generic fictions embody a tension between familiarity and novelty. They tend to fit an existing and recognizable format, while redeploying its elements in various ways. There is thus no particular paradox in insisting that the alluring and dazzling variety of scenarios and settings which entertainment television offers is nevertheless constructed out of a finite and prescriptive set of preoccupations, oppositions and possible resolutions. The closure which results is brought about (I have argued) partly by the presumption which the network makes of routine expectancies on the part of its audience.

The dynamics of scheduling and prediction have a range of consequences for the internal organization of narrative and mode of address in crime drama, to which I return below. Equally, they require that programmes be 'trailed', introduced or announced in advance in certain definite ways, so as to confirm and specify their attractiveness. Continuity announcements thus represent an effort both to secure viewers and to anticipate and direct the ways in which they are to view, through delineating aspects of what the episode's appeal (to whom and on what grounds) is supposed to be.

Continuity announcements as instructions to the audience

The instructions contained in continuity announcements thus all revolve around the priority of encouraging viewers to stay tuned. In performing this task they habitually call upon the dynamic of familiarity and novelty, placing the individual episode within the contexts both of the series or serial of which it is a member and its position within the evening's 'flow'.

This is most easily done in relation to serials, where successive announcements can track a developing story, reminding viewers of where it broke off the previous week and warning them that pleasures will be forgone by failing to continue to follow. Thus announcements introducing episodes of a serial observed the following sequence:

> Now on Channel 4 we continue the story of one man's fight against *Octopus: Power of the Mafia.*

> Now, the choices facing Inspector Cattani become fewer by the minute in *Octopus: Power of the Mafia.*

And finally,

> In a couple of minutes the final episode of our compulsive serial *Octopus: Power of the Mafia.* I'm not going to say anything more about it, but if you've seen the rest of the series you mustn't miss it and if you haven't, don't let that put you off. I guarantee it'll leave you wanting more.

These declarations have a repetitious and highly conventionalized character, especially in the flourishing of the name of the serial. Naming is also important in introducing episodes of series. Here the announcement typically both names the principal character or characters, thereby alluding to familiar elements of the appeal of the series as a whole, and prepares us for some key feature of the new particular episode. The latter is frequently encoded in the episode's title. Thus:

> Now, detection American-style with Danny and Jack on a 'Midnight Highway' in *Cover Up*.

Or again,

> Now there's murder and intrigue on a 'Mission in the Sun' for the *Cover Up* team.

Continuity announcements thus resemble newspaper headlines in the extent to which they both summarize what follows and invite us to continue. They are similar too in the skilful rhetorical compression through which this specification of appeal is achieved. The announcements have identified detection, murder, intrigue, heroes (but also sunshine) as things which interest us as viewers. Likewise to offer us

> first, a particularly savage and violent investigation for Tubbs and Crockett in this week's *Miami Vice*

is to waste no words in letting us know not only what to expect but also how we are supposed to stand in relation to both the episode and the series. On occasion the announcement takes on a jokier more inclusive flavour such that 'tonight *we* welcome back the hunky private eye *Magnum*'. This may be carried over into apostrophizing the audience directly:

> Now men, I understand that the open neck shirt and the gold medallion is terribly passé, but for *Magnum* it's still macho.

The most coercive examples of this technique occur late in the evening, where the announcement constitutes a specific exhortation not to switch off and go to bed. Hence the bossy tone in

> But we haven't finished with you tonight yet. . . . It's time to call in that boy in blue *T. J. Hooker*.

Each of these examples has said as much about the atmosphere which the series is intended to evoke as about the contents of the particular episode in a way which presumes familiarity. An extension of this mode of address occurs where the series announces itself using a voice-over within the credit sequence and which is repeated verbatim from week to week. Thus, *Knight Rider* employs the slogan 'In the world of criminals he operates above the law' (notwithstanding that he works for the 'Foundation for Law and Justice'). Each episode introduces itself as

> a shadow flight into the dangerous world of a man who does not exist . . . Michael Knight, a young loner on a crusade to champion the cause of the innocent, the powerless and the helpless.

It is apparent from these examples that the primary reference point in each case, in the process of presenting the 'narrative image' (Ellis 1982: 30) as something both familiar and exciting, is the personage of the hero or heroes. The play of positions between heroic figures and antagonists, victims, supplicants and onlookers (the basic dynamic of 'heroization, vilification and fool-making' as Klapp (1954) described it) is fundamentally constitutive of the genre. Before turning to the actions and interactions of these dramatis personae, however, it is first necessary to consider the backcloth of setting and locales against which the narrative is enacted.

Scenes, settings and locales

By far the largest number of cop shows within the sample both originate in and are set in the USA. In this programme category alone images of the United States permeate British experience on many if not most evenings. Unsurprisingly, almost all the remainder are British and set in Britain. The obvious exception to this is *Octopus*, which is set in Sicily: an exotic enough location even from the point of view of the bulk of an Italian audience, and one rich in resonance for crime and law enforcement.

The vast majority of both British and American series are set wholly or predominantly in great cities. In Britain this commonly means London and its environs (as it does in *The Sweeney, Minder, Bulman, The Detective, CATS Eyes* and subsequently to the sample in question also in *The Bill, Rockliffe's Babies* and *The Paradise Club*). Historically there have been exceptions as in *Shoestring* (Bristol), *Boon* (Birmingham) and of course *Z Cars* (Lancastrian new town). Nevertheless, the representation of crime and law enforcement in Britain is fundamentally also the representation of metropolitan experience. The salient exception to this among the present sample is provided by *Juliet Bravo*, whose particular characteristics (see pp. 132–3) are intimately connected to its small town setting. American images are also very largely of major cities: New York, Chicago, San Francisco, Los Angeles, Miami. American cities, as Knight observes (1980), and as the history of American literature and more particularly cinema attests (for instance in the novels of Raymond Chandler and Ed McBain and in films by Lang, Hawks, Coppola, Polanski, Hill and many others) have long provided especially fertile, if not archetypal, settings for crime stories.

The city

I cannot begin here to chart the development of the American fascination with the city. It evidently records, however, a deep sense of ambivalence, which Knight summarizes as its 'romance and anxiety' (1980: 171) and which Chandler held to constitute the sombre poetry of its streets. The city represents the site of aspiration and achievement as well as fear and degradation; situations of disorder as well as community (Tuan 1979; Berman 1983). In comic books the city, usually New York, takes on a mythic name and identity: Batman's *Gotham City*, Spiderman's *Metropolis*. The most alluring and representationally potent places within the city are also those regarded as the most dangerous: 'Chinatown', 'the waterfront'.

In television crime fiction the sheer size of the city and its geographical and social segmentation, its scale as a container of power and wealth, its polyglot diversity and ethnic divisions make it a place for inward exploration. For example in *Miami Vice* the main characters often spend time in contemplation of the city either through the venetian blinds of a high office window or from the harbour. The heroes know that the villain is out there in the city somewhere and that they must go in search of him. At moments of particular pathos the heroes on the other hand turn away from the city and look out to sea. The real cops are those who explore the city. Crockett and Tubbs go out from their office and down into the city's recesses and labyrinths: bars, pool halls, opium dens, flop houses, brothels on the one hand; the opulent homes, pools, yachts and parties of the super-rich on the other. They thus travel constantly around the city and between the extreme poles of its denizens. *Miami Vice* strangely resembles Balzac's vision of Paris in which the *demi-monde* of illicit pleasure is what links the social worlds of the very rich and the very poor, and the heroes' contemplation of the city similarly recalls Rastignac's contemplation of the lights of Paris from the cemetery in *Le Père Goriot*. As Knight shrewdly observes, to thus poeticize the city may at the same time represent a 'disavowal of knowledge of human causes' (1980: 179) of why it is as it is and where crime actually originates within it. The city becomes what Warshow calls the 'strange, sad city of the imagination' (1979) and the drama of crime and law enforcement is part of its aesthetic, its grandeur, pity and pathos.

The spheres of action of the crime story are thus contained in particular sites within the city, and the arch of the narrative characteristically describes the hero's journeys between them. If a general pattern can be discerned, it is one which begins from a known and familiar locale (a police station, office or home), moves outwards to encompass scenes of crimes and places of pursuit and combat and finally returns again to a point of safety (the police station again, or a bar or restaurant, for example). These movements frame and situate the 'action' as such.

The distribution of settings is thus a basic feature of narrative development. In many instances it seems to be premised upon some basic oppositions between the known and the unknown, safety and danger, indoors and outdoors, private and public. Most crimes take place either outdoors or in public and non-domestic buildings: warehouses, docks, car-parks, airports, hotels (see Gunter 1985; Grodal 1988). 'Indoors', on the other hand is usually the space of reflection, planning, discussion but also banter and intimacy. In a few cases crimes are committed within domestic spaces occupied by the hero himself, his own home or car or that of his female companion (this occurs in episodes of *Matt Houston, Hunter*). Meanwhile, at least one episode of *Miami Vice* turns on the terror which is engendered by a wave of invasions of comfortable family homes by a band of armed men, sneaking through the garden, breaking down doors and windows, killing dogs, terrorizing children, beating and humiliating women and men. Such crimes are established as being particularly wicked and frightening. They are also especially personal affronts and hence lay the ground for a very direct and intense antagonism between heroes and villains (see pp. 135–6).

The country

From time to time heroes also go on journeys outside the city, either into the countryside or abroad. The countryside seems to be able to carry a number of different significances: it is a place of quietness and nostalgic idyll, until such time as its order is disrupted and, as in the private home, that disruption seems particularly shocking and reprehensible; but the countryside can also stand for wilderness and primitiveness. It is characteristically a strange and unfamiliar place to the hero and one in which he is placed at a disadvantage. Cars break down there and cannot be mended (*Hunter*). Smart city shoes come off or break on rough terrain. Shirts and ties or tight skirts are conspicuous, inappropriate, constricting, too hot or too cold, emphasizing the hero's, and more particularly the heroine's vulnerability (*Matt Houston*). The hero is unsupported. His authority is not recognized, his technological back-up is not there. He is alone and forced to live off his wits (*Cover Up*). As Tuan shows (1979: chs 5 and 11), the countryside is equally amenable to being represented as a 'landscape of fear' as the city is.

'Country' characters include not only stout-hearted, honest farmers and other potential allies of the hero, but also corrupt sherrifs, violent rednecks, survivalist and religious cultists and strange, obsessive, rich recluses, the grounds of their mansions patrolled by Dobermanns and private armies and who exercise a feudal thraldom over the local population. In the country, even more than in the city, the principal form of villainy tends to arise from bossism, corruption and intimidation (see pp. 143–5).

To travel abroad, meanwhile, also disadvantages the hero, at the same time as extending the connection between crime, exoticism and situations of lawlessness and disorder. In general, the lesser the postulated realism of the series, the more travel it is likely to encompass. Thus, *Cover Up*, which lodges perhaps the slenderest reality claims of any programme within the sample, includes a large element of travelogue. In the episodes considered here the heroes not only visit a number of places within the United States (New York, San Francisco, New Orleans, as well as numerous resorts, spas and backwoods areas) but also the south of France (twice), Spain, Turkey and Mexico. These exotic locations in turn permit more various, strange and wonderful kinds of crime – espionage, smuggling, white slavery – at the same time as facilitating *Cover Up*'s fascination with sunshine, bodies and photographic voyeurism. *Miami Vice*, given its endless preoccupation with drug-smuggling, visits Colombia twice within the sample: a country whose association with drugs, violence and disorder is already well established from the point of view of an American audience. Meanwhile, in *Octopus* much depends on the fact that the hero is a newcomer in Sicily. His probity is established partly by virtue of his very isolation and the difficulty he faces in confronting the clannish, anti-modern mores of his new surroundings and their conspiracies of violence and silence.

Narrative structure, setting and 'tone'

The distribution of settings is also constitutive of narrative development in a further sense, providing for the weight, tone and significance of what happens where and the kind of conclusiveness which the narrative sets out to achieve. Thus one might identify a polarity between those stories which follow an orthodox narrative arch of danger framed by safety (i.e. those which are most 'closed') and those whose stories are less completely resolved and more continuous from week to week (and arguably more 'open'). I term these variants 'finished' and 'soap operatic' respectively. Those series which I call 'finished' include *Knight Rider, Cover Up, T. J. Hooker, Streets of San Francisco, Hunter, Matt Houston, Hardcastle and McCormick, The Sweeney, CATS Eyes, Murder, She Wrote* and *Bulman*. These are the clear majority. They are finished in the sense that the sequence of events which provides the narrative crisis or enigma for the plot of a particular episode, however simple or complex, is clearly signalled as being over at the end of that episode. The next episode will generally comprise a wholly separate sequence of events, and no reference will usually be made to anything at all that happened the previous week. In the 'soap operatic' form, which I take to include primarily *Hill St Blues* and *Juliet Bravo*, such resolution may not occur within the scope of the single episode, if at all, or may not be primary within it. In these instances the drama arises from problematic situations confronting a relatively large group of regular characters. These may include problems in their relations to one another as well as domestic and professional crises, and not just crimes to be solved. Crimes themselves also differ. 'Soap operatic' cop shows incorporate more petty and juvenile crimes, more domestic violence and other crimes indicated as arising from interpersonal, social and environmental strain. The actions of the familiar characters are co-ordinated by a morally commanding central figure, who is also the senior local officer – Captain Furillo in *Hill St Blues*, Inspector Kate Longton in *Juliet Bravo* – with supporting characters carrying variable amounts of plot from week to week.

The two variants differ markedly as between their use of time and place. On aggregate I have counted thirty-five to forty scenes per hour for the whole sample, where a scene is defined by a cut to another place or point of view. These tend to be more in classic action narratives where cutting signifies movement, detection and pursuit and where the excitement of the denouement is marked by ever more rapid cutting and decreasing length of shots and scenes. Scenes and changes of locale are far fewer in 'soap operatic' shows because of their greater degree of concentration on particular known spaces and on conversation. Thus in *Hill St Blues*, although there may be several lines of plot, a much larger proportion of time is spent inside the police station, or in the inner sanctum of Frank Furillo's own office or in Hill and Renko's patrol car. Captain Furillo indeed rarely leaves the office except to go home. Each episode is marked out and given form by certain fixed points beginning with early morning roll-call and ending with Frank and Joyce at home in the evening, with the episode often encompassing a single working day. The believability of the office, as the most important place, is corroborated by explicitly 'documentary' techniques such as the use of fixed cameras with people passing in and out of the field of vision.

The two serials (*The Detective* and *Octopus*), meanwhile, share a number of features in common with the 'soap operatic' style. This is partly because their greater length permits a more complex and less sequential narration, which by definition is unresolved until the final episode. It is also partly because of their greater interest in domesticity and in developing the characterization of the hero through his relations with others. In both cases the disruption of the hero's life by the investigation in which he is involved is mirrored by the disruption of his domestic life, further accentuating the hero's solitary and obsessive probity. The heroes of both serials are isolated from their colleagues. Both their families are threatened. Both are unfaithful to their wives. Each of them suffers stress in trying to reconcile his private and public commitments.

Miami Vice represents a problematic and intermediate case: it characteristically incorporates 'finished' narratives unfolding towards a final confrontation, but this resolution is not usually wholly satisfactory from the heroes' point of view. Something, generally a love affair, has been ended, lost or compromised along the way (often by the death of the loved one), suggesting a degree of irresolution and pathos. This is one aspect of what Grodal means by *Miami Vice*'s attachment to 'melancholia', because it often shows the heroes in moods of mourning and regret or experiencing crises of conscience and purpose (Grodal 1988). At the same time the plot remains schematic in the same proportion as the available time is deployed in these kinds of elegiac pauses or in the aesthetic contemplation of cars, people, cityscapes and erotic encounters.

In all these cases the evocation of place, and the distribution of time between places, is crucial to understanding what the narrative is doing and what responses it presumes to elicit from the viewer. The use of settings and scenes is central to the projection and perception of realism, and the depiction of conditions of danger and safety, that is in drawing the map of the world in which the actions of heroes, villains and others unfolds.

Heroes, villains and fools

Writing within the Durkheimian functionalist tradition, Orrin Klapp (1954) claimed to identify in the process of 'heroization, vilification and fool-making' what he regarded as socially central 'rituals of solidarity and norm-affirmation'. Through the actions of heroes, villains and fools, Klapp argues, 'common values are affirmed and potentially disruptive hostilities are sublimated by scapegoats' (1954: 61). Klapp thus regards folklore and popular culture as being centrally concerned with ways in which 'complex issues are personified as conflicts between champions and villains', thereby rendering them manageable and available for consensual judgement, 'familiar to all and indicating proper modes of response' (1954: 57). Heroes, villains and fools, Klapp argues, are first and foremost 'sanctions' (1954: 56).

Klapp's consensualism seems quaint beside subsequent developments in social theory, especially given the energy which has been devoted to the critique of functionalism (e.g. Mills 1959; Giddens 1984; Habermas 1987). Nevertheless it is difficult to deny that the clash of hero and villain is indeed pivotal in most popular narrative, or that the basic opposition between them is almost as primordially simple as Klapp describes. One might argue that where Klapp sees consensus as actively constructed and realized through heroization and vilification, we now see only an imaginative hankering after it, experienced as a nostalgic or fantastic possibility, and therefore undertaken with an ironic consciousness that things are otherwise. This is perhaps what Bourdieu means by the always failing attempt to 'restore the primal innocence of doxa' (1977: 169). It is clearly part of what Eco (1979) understands by 'the path of fable' in James Bond. It is related to what Knight intends when he speaks of crime fictions as being 'artificially and consolingly resolved' (1980: 5). It is also in large measure what I identify in saying that television crime fiction addresses a point of tension between anxiety and reassurance.

At one level there is very little complexity here at all. Heroes are heroic, villains villainous. We can all recognize them effortlessly. The good end happily (mostly) and the bad unhappily and, as Oscar Wilde (1960) has Miss Prism declare in *The Importance of Being Earnest*, 'That is what Fiction means'. Yet, in the ways in which these basic generative oppositions are in fact realized and elaborated in television crime fiction, and more particularly in the ways in which the construction of heroism and villainy also does or does not make referential claims about the way the world is, there is considerable variety.

Heroisms

Heroes are the pivotal figures of television crime fiction. In so far as the narratives which comprise the episodes of any given series are 'formulaic', they are constructed out of the repertoire of possibilities provided by the identity of the hero (or heroes) and the social position which he (or more rarely she) is designated as occupying. Stories are variable and evanescent, heroes constant. The marketing of the series necessarily depends on its constant elements – a hero, a style, a setting, an initial situation – rather than its contingent ones – the content of any particular story. Evidently the story must be sufficiently 'well-formed', interesting and exciting to hold the audience's attention: but the audience for that story is in a prior sense the audience for the series. This means, in the first instance, an audience for the hero or heroes and the dramatic possibilities (the 'scenarios') which the hero and his social world generate. The names of series record this rather clearly. The majority of cop shows suggest an identity between the persona of the hero and the 'narrative image' (Ellis 1982) of the series. The hero is eponymous, and the series is defined and marketed around the blunt, masculine surname: Bulman, Hunter, Magnum, Houston, Taggart, Rockford, Hooker. Heroines' names are similarly rendered assertive. 'Danny' is a more fitting partner for Jack Striker in *Cover Up* than Danielle. Didi McCall in *Hunter* is almost always simply 'McCall'. Matt Houston's female confederate is referred to only as 'C.J.'. The main exceptions to this arise when the series references a body of people in its title, usually in relation to a particular place. Hence the plural connotations of *Miami Vice* and *Hill St Blues*, or indeed of *The Sweeney*, which refers obliquely to London through the use of rhyming slang (Sweeney Todd/Flying Squad).

Cop shows incorporate a range of possible positions for their heroes. There are distinct versions of heroism and distinct roles for heroes as agents in stories. The nature of the hero's intervention in the story thus also varies in relation to the kinds of problems he confronts and the means at his disposal for addressing them: his powers and abilities, antagonisms and alliances. The crucial dimensions here may be summarized as including heroes' designated positions within or against institutional hierarchies, their relations to secular and moral law, their physical, intellectual and technological prowess, their class and gender positions. The character of heroism thus depends *inter alia* on whether the hero is a police-officer or a private citizen; if a police-officer then on his or her rank; on whether he or she works alone or in company with others. The establishment of the hero as heroic demands that we the audience be shown what would provide an honourable course of action under such initial conditions. I shall now summarize some such responses as they are suggested by the examples before me.

The hero as police-officer
Examples of heroes as police-officers include *Hill St Blues, Juliet Bravo, The Sweeney, Taggart, Miami Vice, Hunter, T. J. Hooker, Streets of San Francisco, CHIPS* and *Octopus: Power of the Mafia*.

In some of these cases the primary hero is a senior officer whose 'problem' centres on the proper exercise of authority. This is especially the case in *Juliet Bravo* and *Hill St Blues* (even though the latter tends to disperse its focus between a relatively large number of familiar characters). In both these cases the 'action' occurs largely within the police station. The station provides the hero's vantage point towards the world and is a place into which problems come. Because they are leaders the particular problems which these heroes confront centre largely on the sensitive and effective management and co-ordination of their subordinates. The heroes experience the loneliness and strain of command while continuing to provide guidance, counselling and direction to those for whom they are responsible. In *Juliet Bravo* Inspector Kate Longton confronts the special problem of being a female leader of male colleagues, and therefore of reconciling the effective exercise of authority with her status as a woman. This is achieved by indicating that in addition to strength and intelligence the qualities required for the proper fulfilment of her role include those which retain her femininity: sympathy, insight, intuition, patience and so forth. These capacities are especially appropriate to the kind of policing which the series envisions as existing in a small English town, emphasizing the service role and the mainly pacific resolution of human problems. In one episode of *Juliet Bravo* in my sample no crimes occur. *Juliet Bravo* thus furnishes the nearest approximation which the genre contemporarily allows of an example of what one might call 'organic' policing (see Clarke 1986: 231).

In *Hill St Blues*, however, Captain Furillo presides over a situation in which disorder always threatens, from the strain and antagonism between his subordinates as well as from 'the street'. Furillo is always in negotiation with somebody: the politicking Chief of Police, lawyers, community leaders, his ex-wife, his lover. Furillo is a stoic. His stoicism is indicated partly by the fact that he is a reformed alcoholic, one who keeps the tendency towards disorder within himself constantly in check. His 'problem' is indicative of the problem of leadership in American society: faced with plural conflicts he seeks the most equitable solution possible in each individual case, while acknowledging a severely constrained view of his own powers and possibilities. At the same time his presence is essential because it provides a moral anchor in an otherwise chaotically shifting world (Gitlin 1985: 313). This includes the restraint he imposes on the actions and responses of his subordinates. Thus in one episode Furillo finds a stock of unauthorized weapons (baseball bats in particular – the weapon of the street, not of the police force) concealed in the locker room, intended for use by some of his junior officers in revenge for having been beaten up. His response is unwontedly explosive. He poses the question: 'But if you go out there like a bunch of night riders what are we but another vicious street gang?' Furillo's job is to mark the boundaries between policing and vigilantism.

The charting of this boundary is a central preoccupation of the genre, although the dilemmas it postulates are variably defined and resolved. Crime stories return continually to the conditions under which the hero is or is not entitled to use force or to resort to extra-legal methods. The police-officer and the private citizen/investigator are differently situated in this regard. Membership of the police force implies both empowerment and constraint. Yet such constraints apply differentially depending on the police-officer's position within the institution, and on the depiction of legality and bureaucracy on which the story is premissed. When the institution is obstructive or corrupt, the police-officer, usually now a junior officer, can only rightly discharge his or her function for the story (i.e. the duty that the officer owes to a superordinate morality) by stepping outside its secular rules.

Such is the case in both *The Detective* and in *Octopus*. In *The Detective* the hero is a police-officer of senior rank, but one who is increasingly misplaced in the circles in which he moves. He is marked as old-fashioned in his personal and social attitudes as well as in his view of the proprieties of his job. He is regarded by his family and colleagues as a 'cold fish' and a 'miserable bastard'. His joyless probity isolates him from the more pragmatic outlooks of those around him. He is a 'detective' in the sense that he is committed to the implacable pursuit of wrong-doing, whereas his superiors (the highest echelons) recognize only *raisons d'état* and are preoccupied with counter-insurgency and the surveillance of civil disorder.

His relentless and insubordinate pursuit of a child prostitution scandal involving a Conservative Home Secretary is therefore undertaken from the vantage point of his inherited commitment to policing as it was, or as he held it to be, and in opposition against its current, debased condition. All does not go well for the hero. His exposures drive the politician to suicide. He becomes aware that he has been hoodwinked into precisely this course of action by those among the powerful who wanted to drive the Home Secretary out of office, on the grounds of his undue liberalism. The hero is pointed at his quarry 'like a guided missile', except that his implacable conscience has driven him to go further than his manipulators intend. *The Detective* is thus a sombre dystopian allegory, counterposing the contemporary (lawless) state of the police, and of social order, to one which is elegiacally evoked through the hero's reminiscences. The conspiracy theory on which the story is predicated also suggests a loss of moral direction and authority within the master institutions of the state. The hero's quest ends disastrously in both professional and personal terms, except that it retrieves for him the admiration of his children. Their youthful (and hence implicitly correct) moral judgement confirms that he has nevertheless acted rightly.

In *Octopus* somewhat similar dynamics apply. The hero is the new local police chief, but he is isolated from all but a few members of the local community, including those in positions of authority, either by their fear of or collusion with the mafia. His domestic life disintegrates under the strain of his isolation. His wife leaves him. His only alliances are with other heroic deviants (the drug-addicted heiress who becomes his lover, the priest). Standing almost entirely alone, he is forced to step outside due process. The step is further justified because personalized through his combat with the local mafia *capo* who both seeks to possess the same woman (and brings about her death by continuing to supply her with heroin) and kidnaps the hero's daughter. But the hero retreats from vigilantism by refraining from killing the adversary (thereby also permitting a sequel), and his successful resolution of his dilemmas is signalled by his eventual reunion and reconciliation with his family.

These are the more sophisticated cases. In simpler, more generically recognizable 'cop shows' the motif of extra-legality is broached continually, especially where junior officers are heroically insubordinate. Thus, both Regan and Carter in *The Sweeney* and Taggart in *Taggart* repeatedly continue to work on cases which they have been instructed to drop. In both series there is a suggestion of class antagonism in the refusal to recognize the legitimacy of bureaucratic imperatives. In both cases too the heroes' integrity is signified partly by their sheer mirthlessness and their joyless devotion to duty, relegating their private and personal lives to a secondary position (see Clarke 1986: 229).

In a few instances, acting extra-legally or in doubtfully legal ways is one of the hero's defining features. For example, the eponymous hero in *Hunter* is constantly in trouble with his superiors. This is clearly designated as intrinsic to his appeal, stemming from a ruggedly individualist and cheerful insouciance, combined with an incorruptible fidelity to the dictates of his own conscience. Hunter submits massive expenses claims. His car is damaged in every episode. He is scruffy and unconcerned with outward appearances. He repeatedly (in a familiar cinematic motif) hands in his badge, leaving him free to pursue the enemy outside institutional constraints. Yet at the same time, the series is preoccupied with differentiating Hunter's actions from those of a vigilante. There appears to be a recognition that Hunter's position is potentially ambivalent: hence the story must be resolved in such a way as to recuperate it. Thus, in the episode entitled 'The Avenging Angel', the villain is a vigilante who hero-worships Hunter and regards himself as meting out summary justice on occasions when Hunter's own cases have failed on technicalities. Hunter himself thus stands impugned, as when his antagonistic superior accuses him: 'As far as I'm concerned this "Avenging Angel" got all his bright ideas from you'. The story turns on Hunter's rejection of the vigilante's admiration, salvaging his own position as honest cop. Hunter is now both hunting and hunted. The vigilante places Hunter himself under surveillance (as the soundtrack plays a song about voyeurism and obsession, 'Every Breath You Take' by, loadedly, *The Police*). The final combat is thus between Hunter and one who has illegitimately claimed to represent his *alter ego* – a claim which cannot be allowed, and whose subversive implications are abolished through the vigilante's death by his own bomb.

Similar tropes recur in two other *Hunter* episodes within the sample. In one the vigilante figure is a parole officer, enraged at watching the guilty go free. In another it is a psychopathically cruel bounty 'hunter' (*sic*). In each case *alter ego* parallelisms are present. Thus, the parole officer/ vigilante's principal victim is an honest parole officer. In each case too the hero and villain engage in debate, whose terms are articulated around the notion of 'cleaning the street'. Thus, the vigilante/parole officer says of his victims 'They're garbage. I'm trying to keep the streets clean'. Likewise, the bounty hunter asserts, 'I go round cleaning up the things the cops can't'; to which Hunter's (faintly but crucially distinct) response is 'You know, we got laws in this borough. I'm just trying to keep the streets safe for everybody'. (Note the coincidence here with the preferred self-images of Peter Sutcliffe during his campaign of murder against women throughout the North of England. Sutcliffe sent taunting notes to the police signed 'The Street Cleaner', and later insisted to his brother Carl that he had been 'just cleaning up the streets' - see Burn 1984: 265.) In these ways the notion of taking the law into one's own hands fundamentally depends on whose hands they are, and on how the personal authority and entitlements of the hero are established, including in relation to his institutional authority. Vigilante villains claim to be able to take these judgements upon themselves, as only heroes can, and die for their presumption.

In each of these cases the difference between Hunter and his antagonists is established partly by reference to psychological states, encoded especially in their treatment of women, particularly Hunter's female partner Didi McCall. Hunter and McCall are a bonded pair. Although they have no sexual liaison they are 'partners', and routinely jealous of one another's other relationships. McCall is the widow of a police-officer – an ambiguous position, designating her as both a sexual free agent and under Hunter's chivalrous protection. McCall's male escorts (who are smart where Hunter is dowdy) always turn out to be unreliable or inadequate, so that McCall is always finally returned to Hunter's protection. McCall always stands in danger of being attacked or taken prisoner. She is often used in entrapment, usually dressed as a prostitute (see Liebman 1986).

Each of Hunter's vigilante antagonists are specifically misogynist. They menace women, including McCall. Hunter's self-sufficient masculinity allows him to act as a chivalric rescuer, at the same time as the attack on McCall is a directly personal affront to him. The equation between villainy and misogyny is a device whereby Hunter's position is distinguished and justified. Vigilantism proceeds from a specific personal failing and lack, and the vigilante's attempts at self-justification are negated by his irrationality and ulterior motivations. Hunter has no such inadequacy. He thus gathers no emotional satisfaction from violence as such. His judgement is unclouded, his actions disinterested and necessary ones.

The boundaries of legality are trodden in another way in cases where the heroes are members of agencies other than the police as such. Such agencies are clandestine and specialized. Their sphere of operation is arcane and exotic. Having no clear real-world referent, the tone and content of such stories is more plainly fanciful, and therefore less compromised by 'realist' constraints or inhibitions. The conventions of the 'cop show' thus blur with those of the espionage story and the comic book. Heroes and villains are drawn in larger, simpler strokes in such stories, and their actions take place on a more freely imagined canvas, because their claim on our attention is directed towards an interest in the bizarre rather than the plausible. The suspension of disbelief which is called upon in these stories is more complete and unambiguous, and hence the more easily achieved. Where the crime story opens out into super-heroism it sells itself both through the promise of wish-fulfilment and through presenting itself as camply knowing pastiche (thus inviting, like Eco's reading of James Bond, both 'naive' and 'smart' responses).

At the same time, the distancing of heroism from the realm of the real and familiar also provides for a more extravagant and casual use of violence. Permission to use violence freely also represents permission to watch it freely, because its seriousness is disclaimed in advance. Thus, the two series I have particularly in mind here, namely *Knight Rider* and *Cover Up*, are precisely those which are broadcast in the early evening, before the 9 p.m. 'watershed' (see also *The A-Team*, which does not occur in the sample, but of which the same is true; see Hodge and Tripp 1986).

The techniques of excitement in such series are at the same time those of 'de-realization'. Heroes use hi-tech and secret weapons rather than mundane policing methods, such as the computerized, talking super-car in *Knight Rider*. They use martial arts rather than simple fisticuffs, machine-guns and grenades rather than pistols. The 'violence' is thus marked as unreal by virtue of its very extravagance and its observation of a stylized choreography, so that it retains its signification of 'excitement' while being freed from any disturbing force. It is thereby established as appropriate for an audience including large numbers of children. In the main it is 'hardware violence', signified through speed of movement, crashing and exploding vehicles and so forth, rather than violence against the body as such.

Jack Striker in *Cover Up* is more obviously a super-hero than any of his televisual contemporaries. His 'actual' and his 'cover' occupations (secret agent and male model) are equally removed from the realm of the real for the everyday audience. His perfect musculature resembles that which is drawn on the body of Superman or Captain Marvel. The montage of the credit sequence shows him successively as commando, cowboy, model and man about town, so that it is unclear whether he is actually occupying these roles or simply modelling the clothes. Meanwhile, the sexily parodic theme song also marks him as a fantasy figure:

Where have all the good guys gone and where are all the gods?
Where's the street-wise Hercules, to fight the rising odds? . . .
I need a hero, I'm holding out for a hero till the end of the night.
And he's got to be cool, and he's got to be strong, and he's got to be
    dressed for the fight.

Striker's is one of the most wholly objectified male bodies in television history. More homo-erotic pin-up than a figure who claims to be emblematic of law enforcement in its more commonplace senses, he is assimilated to the known unreality of the convention of the half-clothed male hero in *Tarzan, Flash Gordon, Conan the Barbarian* and *Rambo*.

Cover Up is thus sophisticated and schematic in equal proportions, because the schematization itself is a marker of unreality which attempts to pre-empt any attempt to take it seriously. This achieves a number of objects. It allows the *mise-en-scène* to linger over lithe bodies, sunshine, exotic locations, expensive clothes and the paraphernalia of a shadowy institutional world (to be, in this sense, discursive) at the same time as projecting monumentally straightforward narrative categories of arch-heroism and arch-villainy. *Cover Up* is thus in a number of ways a very perfectly constructed commodity. Its lack of recognizable contexts takes it outside the limitations provided by parochial references. It makes itself internationally marketable because its syntax is simplified to the lingua franca of Bond movies and Martini commercials, and at the same time it is available to both adults and children at different levels of 'smartness' in the decoding of its games. Striker is a hero who is free to disregard due process because he is outside a world in which it is relevant. His job is to secure order from without and in secret; and because we cannot affirm his existence, we can imagine it as we please.

The hero as private citizen

Since police-officers in television crime stories sometimes act in a quasi-private capacity, the boundary between their heroic agency and that of the hero as private citizen or investigator is not completely sharp. However, there are a number of important distinctions to be drawn between heroisms established in fulfilment of public and private obligations.

'Private eyes' constitute a somewhat more varied and differentiated set of social types than police-officers do, and the kinds of stories in which they are involved likewise range somewhat more widely among the *faits divers* of human deviance and wrongdoing. The crimes which private eyes confront conventionally include those of which the police are un-aware or on which they cannot or will not take action. These include crimes which take place in private and domestic spaces: crimes of passion and family dramas, blackmailing and kidnappings which must be kept secret, recondite conspiracies behind the apparent impunity provided by wealth and social position. The story is also more likely to include signifi-cant victim figures, in the person of clients who entrust their troubles to the private investigator in the first place. Private investigation can thus provide a double opportunity for identification, both in the person of the hero and through the position of the victim, so that the contract between them also becomes a matter of specifically personal obligation.

It also tends to follow that the private investigator's story is more importantly predicated on the existence of a puzzle or enigma than is often the case in the police story. Private investigators exist to discover that things are not as they seem. The detective detects that which is hidden or unacknowledged – secret jealousies, ambitions, obsessions or corruptions beneath the surface of ordinary society. His or her special point of vantage on such hidden actions and motivations is furnished by particular deductive or intuitive powers, the exercise of which requires that the hero stands outside institutions and is beholden to no one. This can be achieved in various ways. Thus, Matt Houston in *Matt Houston* is independently wealthy. He wants for nothing and is therefore incorruptible. He is at the same time a plain, straightforward Texan (as his name implies) and a natural aristocrat. In other cases the reverse applies. Jim Rockford in *The Rockford Files* is an ex-con, living physically and symbolically apart from mainstream society in a trailer on the beach, the contemporary equivalent of the frontiersman's log cabin. He is a rogue and master of disguises, so that his infiltration of the worlds of the wealthy and villainous depends on his sheer insouciance and cheek. Yet he is also fallibly flat-footed and prone to being beaten up in the course of his investigation. It is a version of heroism which the audience is encouraged to feel they might almost, but never quite, emulate. Magnum in *Magnum P.I.*, meanwhile, lives in some style because he lives with Higgins at the country club, but he has no visible means of support of his own and is always chided by Higgins for his feckless disregard for property and propriety (see Haralovich 1988).

In each case the detective cares for morality but is careless of convention, including those conventions which are seen as restricting the effectiveness of the police. Such characters thus enjoy a special freedom as well as a special capability. For example, George Bulman in *Bulman* is a retired policeman, disaffected by the trend of modern policing away from classic detection and towards bureaucracy and technology. He lives in near-penury in a small antique shop with Lucy McGinty, his partner in detection and surrogate daughter. George and Lucy are specifically an odd couple, whose unorthodox domestic arrangement also makes possible their particular mode of detection. George's status as a retired policeman permits him to carry a number of heroic resonances. He continues to enjoy a certain regard from police-officers and crooks, who recognize his experience and expertise. He perseveres in acting as a detective should, and is able to do so because he is free of institutional fetters. The series implies that there once was an individually heroic, intuitive mode of policing which George formerly inhabited but that since this is no longer the case his continuing activity of detection must now be conducted from the outside. George's sense of his responsibilities as a citizen, which used to provide the rationale for the implicitly remembered heroic mode of policing, now serves as the basis for private action. Thus, he growls while apprehending a villain: 'Citizen to citizen, pillock, you're nicked'.

The notion of citizenship can provide the basis for both more and less bellicose postures. Thus, in *Hardcastle and McCormick* Hardcastle is a retired judge whose mission is to track down criminals who walked free from his court 'on technicalities'. Violent pursuit is already justified for the active citizen by foreknowledge of guilt. Legality has already failed. The pathologist Quincy in *Quincy*, whose forensic skills enable him also to function as a detective, adopts a more cerebral and pacific mode of operation. Quincy admonishes one villainous character: 'You choose to live your life through violence. But I choose civility. And in the end I'll win.'

Heroes and the legal order

In all these cases, for both police-officers and private eyes, the problem of heroism is defined by the hero's relation to the legal order and, by extension, the problem of whether legality provides a sufficient guarantor for social order. Heroes stand in a variety of positions which range between stoical resistance to circumstances (Captain Furillo in *Hill St Blues*) and magical intervention from without (Jack Striker in *Cover Up*). These positions roughly correspond to the postulated 'realism' of the series. Broadly speaking, police-officers occupy a more recognizable institutional world than do private eyes. Violence is tempered in some degree by a need to maintain the dignity of the force. Hence we find Furillo's sternness in the face of the passions of his subordinates; T. J. Hooker's *apologia* 'Because I care about that badge and what it stands for'; Hunter's basic 'We got laws . . .'. Even Sonny Crockett in *Miami Vice* accepts the admonition of his former teacher and mentor: 'Sonny, you let me show you when to take your gun out of its holster, now let me show you when it's time to put it back.'

Hill St Blues and *Miami Vice* are both fictions about the threat of anomie. They are premissed pessimistically on a particular vision of the city, containing an indefinitely large pool of crimes (the 'dark figure' of criminological theory). The world is only provisionally and momentarily made safe by heroic intervention. Hence, however, the absolute necessity of a hero, in order to confer dignity on the process. The dilemmas of policing are salvaged by the relentless probity of Captain Furillo, and also by the acceptance of suffering signified by the melancholic dandyism of *Miami Vice*, as it is identified by Grodal (1988).

In less realist settings less equivocation is necessary. The demand for plausibilty is attenuated. The crime itself answers only to intra-narrative demands, namely that it be heinously culpable and amenable to resolution. In such cases resolution is more final, problem-solving more optimistic. Yet this is achieved only by placing the hero outside a sphere where the law obtains at all, or indeed in opposition to its secular manifestations. An optimism about individual heroism and a cynicism about institutions can thus easily be combined. One is forced to resort to oxymorons in order to capture this paradox of the jolly pessimism or merry cynicism of the moral tale about extra-legal heroes.

Crimes, criminals and their victims

Murder is the primary crime. This is unsurprising given the commitment of popular narratives to basic and emotionally effective moral distinctions and oppositions. Enzensberger (1976) argues that, however relative and contingent a matter the definition of most crimes might become, the prohibition against killing has a special character (Enzensberger 1976: 72–97; see also S. Cohen 1988: 236–40 on 'Primal Crime'). The detection and pursuit of murder is basic, in Enzensberger's view, to the 'palliative' effect of fables and moral tales: 'The murderer's fate makes it apparent that "there are still judges". . . . By punishing the criminal society sustains its conviction that its legal order is intact' (1976: 89).

The majority of cop shows incorporate at least one unlawful and deliberate killing, or attempt, and often several more. Most of these killings are committed ostensibly for greed or gain, but a simple pattern of instrumental crime followed by the apprehension or death of the culprit rarely fulfils all the narrative's purposes. Thus, while killing for gain is the most frequent starting-point in these stories they characteristically also elaborate a range of subsidiary crimes and motivations. Thus there are very few simple robberies or thefts in television crime drama. Rather there are a range of more elaborate and devious criminal campaigns and conspiracies in the course of which killings occur. These most often involve drugs and other forms of contraband. The distancing of the action from reality also makes available a panoply of more recondite and ingenious crimes. Within the body of stories under discussion here these included political subversion; various forms of fraud, extortion and blackmail; white slavery and so forth. This in turn also provides for the use of similarly varied and ingenious methods and techniques. Almost all stories involve the use of physical force and usually also firearms; but they also incorporate numerous other less workaday kinds of lethal force – poisoning, explosions, crashing vehicles and sabotage, trained or poisonous animals, gassing, martial arts.

Villainies

By the same token, criminal motivations are also ramified and various. The instrumentalism of the initial crime is complicated and supplemented by the introduction of further kinds of motivation and personal oddity among villains, as though the simple connection between crime and greed were felt to be insufficiently interesting or plausible or, perhaps most importantly, reprehensible. Indeed, as Klapp (1954) insists, villains must be no less extraordinary than heroes, in order that their monstrous character should both oppose and justify the hero's deeds. Thus, as I have already begun to suggest above, the narrative must specify aspects of the villain's personality, appearance and prowess, often in a highly specific counterpoint to those of the hero. Villainous motivations thus include sadism, the desire for vengeance, delusions or compulsions, and megalomania. The desire for gain through crime is thereby explained as a symptom or expression of an unbridled will to power or other passion, coupled with unusual ruthlessness in pursuit of that desire or passion.

There are of course many variations in the deployment of these themes. Stories which tend towards the model of classic detection (*Bulman, Murder, She Wrote, Streets of San Francisco*) commonly refer offences to directly personal causes, often in familial settings: hate, jealousy, distorted senses of honour and duty, obsession. These are the humanly intelligible passions, and in the investigation of them the detective is established as one who has special insight into the vagaries of the human heart. The domestic murder story allows for pity and pathos as well as pursuit and retribution, and it permits the depiction of the improbable killer, who provides the greatest test of the detective's art and intuition.

At a distant point on the criminal spectrum stand the arch-villains: corrupt business people and politicians, mafia bosses, big-time drug barons and so forth. Like the vigilantes to whom I have already referred, the arch-villain may threaten or intimidate the hero or his female confederate, but he does so using powers and prowess which resemble or even seem to exceed those of the hero himself. In this respect the arch-villain may be the most fitting match for the hero. Like the vigilante he stands in a relation not only of opposition but also competition to the hero, implicitly mocking or impugning the hero's capabilities. This also makes for the possibility of an intimate and long-standing enmity, in line of descent from that between Sherlock Holmes and Professor Moriarty. So, the most appropriate enemy for Jack Striker in *Cover Up* is the old Vietnam buddy gone to the bad and who resembles him in strength and cunning. More particularly, in two episodes of *Miami Vice* the arch-villain is 'General Lao Lee', greatest of drug smugglers and old adversary of Lieutenant Castillo. Lao Lee seeks to intimidate Castillo by threatening his lost love, brought from Asia to Miami for that express purpose. Lao Lee thus embodies a remarkable overcoding of villainies: he is an alien, bringing with him the alien contagion of drugs, threatening not merely Crockett and Tubbs (whose business it is to undergo danger routinely) but rather their superior officer, thereby attacking the integrity of the Miami Police Department at its root, and doing so by playing upon the hero's chivalric protection of a pure woman whom he loves. Even in less paradigmatic cases than this some element of these devices of direct and personal opposition between hero and villain is usually present in some degree: the initial offence takes place; the pursuit begins; the villain knows he is being pursued and by whom; he commits further crimes in order to evade capture; the hero's desire to capture or kill the villain is intensified and justified by this compounding of the initial offence.

In neither of these variants, which seem to me to be predominant ones, is any systematic connection made between crime and need or poverty. Criminals who are poor are rarely more than the minions or victims of criminals who are rich. This is one of the most interesting and curious features of the cop show form: it continually stresses social disturbance, sited in the city, in the bars and car-parks and tenement buildings, yet the lumpenproletarian threat exists only in so far as it is co-ordinated by some sort of shadowy criminal ruling elite. This is perhaps one of the most revealing levels of analysis of these stories because it suggests – as Knight (1980) has also suggested – that the narrative itself is predicated upon a particular set of assumptions about the character of urban life; that is it suggests an implicit social theory. One can easily spot and choose to decline the narrative and stylistic conventions of any particular story; but this is not so easily achieved in relation to the underlying assumptions about social life which in turn generate that discourse (Gouldner 1976), especially if these resemble our own common sense.

Crime myth and conspiracy theory

Television crime stories thus address themselves to our ambivalent and anxious feelings about urban life through a version of conspiracy theory. They call upon the kind of suspicion that 'something is going on' to which Brecht draws attention (see Chapter 2). So, the majority of criminal protagonists (those to whom the trail of detection finally leads) are rich, male, white and outwardly respectable. They are businessmen, corrupt policemen and politicians. The manifest world of crime, drug-taking, prostitution, extortion and so forth, is one over which these super-rich, super-criminals secretly preside, hence the moral and social contiguity of the worlds of opulence and the *demi-monde* to which I have already alluded.

Thus, although murder is the cardinal offence, criminality is in large measure the pursuit of wealth and power, most commonly by those who are already wealthy and powerful. For some crime is the extension of business or politics, and their wickedness partly consists in the masquerade of respectability itself. Others, especially in *Miami Vice* and *Octopus*, are known to both audience and police as crooks (drug barons in particular), but they have been shielded from retribution by their sheer power and influence – their clever lawyers, their use of graft and intimidation. This is one way in which the unorthodox or extra-legal means used by the hero are justified, as a strategy for overcoming such impunity. The frustration felt by the heroes is a spur to their ingenuity as well as a test of integrity and daring.

The pursuit of wealth and power by criminals is not rational and instrumental: it is obsessive, neurotic. It is connected not only to ruthlessness but also to eccentricity. It is encoded in excessive consumption, physical handicap, sexual inadequacy, reclusiveness, often deploying the motif of the opulent home, with its grounds patrolled by private armies of retainers and savage guard dogs. Again this reflects upon the nature of heroism. In *Matt Houston* criminals pursue wealth obsessively; Matt inhabits it effortlessly. In *The Rockford Files, Hunter, Bulman, The Sweeney* or *Taggart* the hero is either indifferent to the seductions of affluence or actively antagonistic towards the rich.

These are ingenious narrative devices. In the first place they accentuate the element of travelogue and exploration. Through the trail of detection we can not only take a walk on the wild side down in the streets, but also have the pleasure of looking on at scenes of great opulence and style, carrying connotations of erotic and other pleasures (see Grodal 1988). At the same time, the hero in carrying his integrity into these settings takes with him the *ressentiment* of the audience against the very wealthy and corroborates their suspicion that they are not to be trusted. Moreover, the sense that there is something rotten in the state of the super-rich contrasts with and emphasizes the hero's integrity and chimes with the cynicism about institutions which requires him to stand on the margins of respectable society, because respectability itself is morally suspect. Hence also the allocation of heroic attributes either to maverick cops and private eyes or to undercover agencies: heroism consists either in individual probity or in superordinate guardianship from outside the compromised and tarnished everyday institutions of law enforcement. However, there is not usually any politically radical implication in this mistrust of wealth and spectacular consumption. It is mainly a technique for accentuating the personal wickedness of the rich villain. The ruthless pursuit of wealth and power by the already wealthy and powerful suggests obsessiveness, excess, driven by personal inadequacy. Criminals in general are *arrivistes*: they are vulgar and showy, incapable of handling wealth responsibly.

The prevalence of corruption and arch-villainy does suggest, however, as a number of commentators have noted (Knight 1980; Mandel 1984; Gitlin 1985), a persistent trope of cynicism and disillusion, in which vague anxieties and mistrusts seek personal embodiment in villains. This is perhaps most deliberately and consistently marked in *Miami Vice*. In *Miami Vice* drug-running is the primary crime. Drugs and drug-runners both come in from outside, from Asia or Colombia. Drugs provide an especially charged motif of social and moral chaos, unusually amenable to being thought of in terms of metaphors of tides and epidemics, threatening to overwhelm civil society. As Jeudy (1979) notes using the analogy of public responses to rabies, once the disease metaphor has gained currency the attribution of specially frightening, wicked and dangerous characteristics to the carriers of the contagion is both usual and particularly forceful. Miami is thus both corrupted within and besieged from without. Drugs are the Trojan Horse of an insidious invasion. This in turn bears upon the ethnic politics of the genre. The heroes themselves, especially in *Miami Vice* and *Hill St Blues*, may be ethnically and socially diverse.

Their differences in dress and styles of speech reflect the plural unity of American society, and they are united by common purpose and allegiance. Villains on the other hand, especially in *Miami Vice*, are recent arrivals, if not actually foreign. They are different and unassimilated. Thus, the explanation for the crisis of the American city, as it is depicted in *Miami Vice*, can be not only personified but also turned outwards, and the war on drugs made literally into a matter of the repulsion of the invaders.

Victims

Crimes also have victims. This is the guise in which ordinary people who are neither heroic nor villainous mostly appear, if at all. There are a number of dimensions of vulnerability to victimization within the conventions of the genre. Some victims are either culpable or pathetically unfortunate – junkies and small-time dealers, for example. Many victims are in some sense foolhardy or rash. They may be at risk by being members of particular subcultures and having dealings with villains. Or they may be too plucky and show resistance to villains, or co-operate with heroes. It is well worth laying odds that any young woman, member of ethnic minority, reformed crook, old soldier or other sympathetic non-heroic character who assists or forms a friendship with the hero will be threatened, hurt or killed before the narrative ends.

Victims thus tend to be socially proximate to both villains and heroes. Indeed they constitute the connection between the two. Many more women appear as victims than in other roles; though a woman may both be victimized and act as helper and confederate to the hero. The victimization of women allows heroes to display not only chivalry but also emotion (especially grief: see Grodal 1988). Women appear to be especially vulnerable if they are not only young and attractive but also outside marriage and working in occupations connected with their sexuality. Thus female victims in my sample include prostitutes, masseuses, beauticians, waitresses, rock singers, models, beauty queens and criminals' mistresses. Women in these roles often form relationships with heroes, sometimes turning away from peripheral involvement in crime in the process. Their relationships with heroes may rehabilitate them morally but also place them in great danger. Thus the socially disreputable damsel in distress is the likeliest single category of victim. Grodal (1988) considers the consequences of this for the narrative economy. It provides for romance, grief and vengeance within a remarkably short span of time, but it also leaves the hero free from commitment at the end of each episode. (Meanwhile stout-hearted little old ladies are also much at risk of attack but are well known to be preternaturally immune to injury, if not actually immortal.)

Conclusion: the crime drama as moral tale

In this chapter I have undertaken a preliminary and conjectural discussion of what seem to me to be some of the more important and characteristic features of a set of television 'cop shows'. This discussion makes no pretence at quantification (except in that descriptive language always quantifies through the use of comparative and emphatic terms). Neither therefore does it claim to have given conclusive demonstration of any of its arguments. It is not, that is to say, a content analytic inventory of items and events. Rather, it concerns the distribution and ordering of moral and other emblematic categories within narratives. As such it cannot help but concern itself with matters of metaphor and resonance. It is in the nature of such tropes and figures to be open and ambiguous (Ricoeur 1977), and hence of the discussion of them to be inconclusive and disputatious. None the less, I do not conclude that televisual images are therefore without 'intrinsic meaning' (Hartley 1984: 120). I am indeed claiming that the tendencies and occurrences that I identify are really there, and I have set out to indicate both the intriguing variety and the common preoccupations of the body of material before me. On the other hand I know of no canon of proof which would demonstrate beyond argument that I am right (see J. B. Thompson 1988). Validation of such interpretations lies finally in the agreement of other viewers or readers that they constitute a gain in awareness. The point has been to sketch some of the boundaries of the moral world which the cop show depicts, and the contours of its landscape.

Moral tales, again

The stories under consideration here are, for the most part, moral tales of a relatively familiar and easily recognizable sort. As such they do display common features not only with one another but also with heroic stories of other kinds. This is the sense in which they are not only 'generic' but also 'fabular' (Eco 1979), if not in fact loosely 'mythological' (Silverstone 1981; 1988). To this extent it is worth emphasizing their similarities in that they are composed out of a common and finite set of discursive resources which provide for the presence of pattern and order at the levels of plot and of the relations between characters. Thus, in all but a few cases, there is a narrative sequence of danger and pursuit, framed at either end by a return to familiar and safer conditions. Again, in most cases the depiction of heroism is central. The stories are capable of being viewed perhaps primarily as pretexts for the demonstration of heroic agency. Heroism is a matter of integrity, capability and decision and of the overcoming of tests and adversities. It is mainly, though not exclusively, a masculine attribute. It connects with qualities of independence, individualism, self-possession and ingenuity, as well as courage and force of arms. It is a matter of agency in that heroes intervene to ensure that justice is done where otherwise it would not be done. Within these conventions institutions of justice without heroes are insufficient (even where the hero is not in opposition to them). Heroes, not organizations, are the guarantors of justice. If the hero is a policeman it is he who validates the organization, rather than the reverse. Given the primacy of the hero, villains and their villainies may be relatively incidental. They are 'plot functions', to borrow Propp's (1984) expression. Criminals characteristically appear only once. It is in their nature to have been disposed of in a quite final sense, by death or capture, by the end of the story. Indeed, the resolution towards which the narrative tends is usually identical with that death or capture.

Plots do not compel or require belief. Heroism and triumphalism are part of what marks the story as fictive. Conventionality is the condition on which the bargain of the suspension of disbelief is struck with the audience. The recognition of a convention is itself pleasurable: it permits the audience the satisfactions both of 'smartness' and of familiarity, as Eco notes. It also allows the use of stylistic and narrative shorthand through techniques of editing and compression. Grodal goes so far as to claim, plausibly but rather too emphatically, that the plot of *Miami Vice* is in fact not followable by anyone not familiar with its particular syntax, and that this works to the exclusion of many older viewers in favour of an appeal to youth. (This begs the question of variant readings: it would be more prudent just to say that it may be differently received, and differentially enjoyed.) As has often been observed, the tendency towards the form of a fable stipulates relatively simple oppositions between characters and the qualities they embody, even though the 'game-space' of the plot may be quite complicated, and crowded with incident. It is as a product of this format, which is expedient for producers and perhaps preferred by audiences, that the stories produce so much redundancy, resulting in the continual reiteration of broadly similar categories of heroism and villainy and which are then the dominant ones within the relevant frame.

Story and discourse

However much it sets out merely to tell a story, every narrative, as Genette has observed (1982: 134), also produces discourse, in the sense of description, allusion and commentary. The narrative cannot help but project a view of the world (see Ricoeur 1981). The fictive world both resembles and differs from the world we inhabit. Yet, however much we know the television image to result from the operation of codes and conventions it is also in the nature of those codes that the image looks very like the real thing. Television need make no strong presumption as to the believability of the story: that appeals to other conditions of plausibility, interest and excitement. Nevertheless, it does, it seems to me, make a rather strong 'request of conformity' (Eco 1979) at the level of discourse. That is, it does require that we recognize that the world it depicts looks like our world, in its physical features and attention to detail – that it is, in this sense at least, realistic – and that this is a generally acknowledged criterion of its adequacy. In this sense there is inherently a blurred or 'dirty' boundary (Hartley 1984) between the fantastic and the realistic, the magical and the mundane. Television drama is thus perhaps inherently 'liminal' (Silverstone 1988) in that it partakes both of realism and wish-fulfilment seamlessly and without apparent contradiction. The settings for crime drama – the way that we as audience receive 'New York' or 'Los Angeles' or even 'The East End' – are at the same time real cities and cities of the imagination (see Warshow 1979). The world which is depicted is indeed a dangerous one, and Gerbner is to this extent correct. It is a mean, nasty, insecure world; but it is also a providential world in which a form of wild and poetic justice is usually at hand. The analysis of narrative always has to confront, as Eco makes clear, the problem of its cognitive status. There is no contradiction in saying that something we do not believe nevertheless clearly has the power to move, excite and engage us and that it is on occasion more affectively powerful than a documentary depiction of similar real events.

Too familiar and routinized really to shock, too fabulous to compel belief, these stories nevertheless exercise some degree of resonance and emotive force. They do so, I have tried to show, by addressing some rather fundamental anxieties in ways which are familiar, manageable and intelligible but still involving and exciting. There is a basic narrative trajectory, but it is not so rigidly programmed and invariant as to foreclose the possibility of surprise and novelty or to prevent the narrative performing a variety of 'functions' for its audience (S. Hall 1984). The basic meanness and nastiness of the world is countered provisionally and sometimes imperfectly by heroism. This provisionality is something that I have sought to emphasize. Rather than by virtue of the 'content' of any individual story television works by placing its stories within routines, setting up a demand for its own continuity and reiteration. It is thus inherent that the narratives revolve around a play of anxiety and reassurance and the disruption and restoration of order which is continual and which itself provides the context for any particular story.

Anxiety, reassurance and ideology

Of course I have not resolved the 'pesky problem of validity' which besets studies of the mass media (Rowland and Watkins 1984: 28), nor is anyone imminently likely to do so. Validity is inherently problematic at the levels both of 'reading' and 'effect'. I have not tried to shirk the fact that the activity of reading in which I have been engaged here is conjectural and open to dispute (see J. B. Thompson, 1988). Equally, I have tried to avoid conflating the terms on which the stories I have studied seem to address their presumed audience with the way in which they are actually received by the real audience. Perhaps there is a genuine uncertainty principle at work in communication studies. Just as physicists are unable to measure velocity and position with equal accuracy students of communication may be unable to speak equally convincingly about texts and audiences at the same time. One of the most important of a number of problems in Gerbner's account of these matters, for example, is that it generates no real understanding of why people should wish to view these stories, which are taken to frighten and disturb them, and hence no analysis of the techniques and devices which make it pleasurable to do so. Nevertheless, Gerbner's initial insight that the primary point at issue regarding the representation of crime and law enforcement is its relation to the audience's anxiety, and in turn of anxiety to politics, has provided the necessary starting-point for all subsequent work in the field. My understanding is that what Gerbner's 'message system analysis' ought really to be doing is to specify the features of the underlying discourse upon which the events of any particular narrative rely for power or plausibility. For, if these stories do indeed carry any ideological weight, such that they do relate in any way worth mentioning to the feelings, sympathies and attitudes of their audiences, they can do so only by first being sufficiently successful in gaining attention, holding interest and providing pleasure. I believe that a crucial element in this is the routine reiteration of a known narrative economy in which the audience's anxieties are both invoked and assuaged, on terms which the narrative tends to dictate.

The really tricky question then is how exactly does the demand for reiterative and consoling fictional television stand in relation to more didactic formats and veridical representations – in short to real belief? As Genette points out narrative is not free from discourse. As Ericson et al (1987) conversely show neither is news discourse innocent of narrative. Perhaps it is television's practice to frighten and demoralize its audience with one hand (the news) and console it with the other (the drama)? Wherever the effects of these practices are to be located they are subtle and oblique: they relate to the use of media as formative of daily routines and as points of reference in conversation and shared activity, and to the density of reference and connotation in ordinary vocabulary.

Heroic stories affirm rather than contradict the passions and sentiments involved in punitive justice. Cop shows do not presume that we believe the world to be divided neatly into heroes and villains: but they do presuppose that at some level we would like it to be so. Whether this habit of thought is so endemic as to carry over into other spheres of life is a further question. Do the rhetorics, metaphors and images at work in political campaigns and other public discussions of crime and punishment in fact call upon discursive resources which are similar to those common in fiction, or betray the same paleo-symbolism beneath their manifest claims? I believe that they do, but the demonstration of that view would await a further and more extensive investigation than I have been able to undertake here.

7 A long goodbye

But you are, perhaps, ready to ask, 'What has this to do with the perpetuation of our political institutions?' I answer, it has much to do with it. Its direct consequences are, comparatively speaking, but a small evil, and much of its danger consists in the proneness of our minds to regard its direct as its only consequences.

Abraham Lincoln (27 January 1838) Speech at Springfield
Illinois, quoted in Hartogs and Artzt

I began by identifying a sense of dissatisfaction with the ways in which a number of issues regarding societal responses to crime, law and punishment have hitherto generally been posed and addressed. I have taken a view similar to that which Garland (1990a) has recently expressed, namely that the adequate discussion of these issues demands attention to their expressive as well as to their instrumental character and that neither theory nor policy can properly be developed in ignorance of their inherent rhetorical and emotive nature:

> In other words, it is the values and sentiments intrinsic to social relations – and the passions aroused when these are violated – which form the broad context within which legal punishments operate. These sentiments and passions help shape penal institutions, giving them their form as well as their force.
>
> (Garland 1990a: 8)

Garland does not ignore the instrumental and purposive aspects of punishment, but he declines to presuppose that they are primary. Equally, he argues, however instrumental, strategic or 'disciplinary' punishment may become, it is always also a bearer of meaning, whose action takes place before an audience. 'Consequently, we should conceive of the elements of punishment . . . as being a condensation of instrumental purpose and rhetorical significance' (Garland 1990a: 10). It follows that:

> Ideological work in the realm of punishment can succeed in connecting with popular emotions and individual sentiments precisely because punishment does have a deep resonance and a fundamental social importance. People are, in a sense that we have barely begun to understand, mentally and emotionally involved in the business of punishing law-breakers – even when they delegate the actual task to institutions behind the scenes – and this is why they can be addressed by political ideologies which operate in the penal realm. If we are to understand the ideological force of law and order policies, or of the kind of capital punishment politics which have featured in recent U.S. elections, then we have to come to terms with the cultural meanings of punishment and the emotional involvement of individuals in the process.
>
> All of this makes punishment incapable of being understood within a purely instrumental framework. Myths and symbols and contradictory emotions form part of the cultural context within which penal policy is developed and upon which it relies for support. The forms and limits of penal control are thus styled by cultural demands as well as by rational strategy – and one should not assume that these amount to the same thing.
>
> (Garland 1990a: 12)

This is not altogether a novel view, but it is none the less one which stands in need of further development and exploration. Among the most important 'social sentiments' which crime, law and punishment can evoke, I have argued, are fear and anxiety; and one way in which fear and anxiety are commonly represented and invoked in contemporary culture is in television crime stories. I have thus sought to use a case study of the characteristic features of such stories as a way of broaching some larger questions about public perceptions of crime and justice, the conceptualization of fear and its consequences, and the import of these issues for theory.

Theoretically, my main interest has been in the place which fear and other related emotions occupy in criminological thought. Criminology has not in general shown itself particularly willing or well-equipped to explore the mundane, experiential aspects of its subject matter. Larger explanatory and systematic questions about the great public problems of crime and law enforcement tend to crowd out reflection on the place they occupy in ordinary, private experience. Yet, as we are beginning to learn, through more sophisticated surveys and the impact of feminist and other ethnographies, no such sharp separation between the public and the private is tenable in the face of the flow of information and imagery in our times. This fact has been known to social theory and the sociology of communications for some time, but until quite recently most criminologists have continued to act with a naive understanding of their purely public concerns.

The fear of crime has recently become an increasingly important focus of attention, albeit one which is often construed in limiting ways. As Downes remarks:

> That the 'fear of crime', in itself a growth area of interest following the British Crime Surveys, remains most developed in relation to certain forms of street crime is probably more to do with collective representations of unpredictable violence than that which more frequently occurs in the home, or that which is normalised as accidental, or where victimisation is indirect and dispersed, as with corporate crime.
>
> (Downes 1988: 182)

Fear is a bone of contention both substantively and theoretically. Indeed, I have argued, disputes about the determination of fears have become central to the division of the field into competing schools of thought. If, as Bennett argues (1989: 6), most positions on the subject fall either into 'victimization' or 'social control' perspectives, then left realism has so far stood four-square in the 'victimization' camp. Realism, as exemplified in Young's recent writing (1987; 1988), objects to the 'social control' premises of both 'left idealism' and 'administrative criminology' on the grounds that such emphases distract from the analysis of the strong relationship, for relevant publics, between actual risks and the distribution of fears.

I think that a proper understanding of the evidence about the relationship between television viewing and fearfulness suggests the possibility of a lateral approach to the vehement but ultimately frustrating dispute between 'realism' and 'idealism' in contemporary criminology. At the outset I raised some difficulties in the realists' assumption that fear is usually, and with the possible exception of the so-called 'suburban soul', a predominantly *rational* response to actual and accurately known dangers. I did not do so in order to propose that fear is in general *irrational*, nor to dispute the important realist emphasis on the groundedness of fear in experience and sense of place. I have, moreover, explicitly rejected Gerbner's view of paranoid perception engendered or fabricated by mass media. Rather, I have objected to the use of the notion of a 'rational fear' on the grounds that it is an untenable category. It denies that fear and anxiety interact with or inform other dimensions of social being, and this is a mistake about the nature of social sentiments in general and the distribution of fear and anxiety about crime in particular. It is unproductive for 'realists' to make the denial of the 'Great Denial' the primary mode of theoretical argument.

When we speak about fear and anxiety we are using shorthand terms which incorporate a range of possible states of mind and of social being. Part of what I have tried to establish in this argument is that it is important to address these as dimensions of experience and subjectivity, a task which is not assisted by assuming that they are always simple products of calculable risks. Even a fear which was wholly 'rational' in Young's sense of the term would still have personal, social and perhaps political consequences which would not have been accounted for by fitting it under that description. Among these is the potentiality for fear as a 'social sentiment' to provide the motive power for ideological work of the kind that Garland mentions (1990a: 11; see also I. Taylor 1988). If this seems like a reinvention of the criminological wheel it is none the less necessary. The realms of representation, depiction and narration are not adjuncts or afterthoughts to these processes and experiences in this area any more than in any other. They are part of the way in which life is *really* lived (and most recent social theory has objected to the kind of dualist thinking which holds discourse and representation to be secondary and subsidiary rather than seeing them as involved in the constitution of action and perception as such).

I find it difficult enough, therefore, to attribute rationality to my own or anyone else's responses to crime, law and punishment not to want to introduce it as a theoretical a priori, but rather to restrict the use of the term to circumstances in which it seems relevant and attainable. However, this only leads me to endorse that part of Young's argument which objects to the weight of condescension which allows technocratic 'administrative criminology' conversely to presuppose *irrationality* on the part of the benighted and gullible public. What we know from introspection is that what are called rational responses to crime, law and punishment are hard to achieve or sustain, if what we mean by 'rational' in this context is getting our private and emotional responses to relate to our public behaviour and expressed beliefs in some coherent way. It seems to me, therefore, if criminology is seriously interested in the way that 'fragments of reality are recontextualised' by social actors, as Young says it should be (1987: 337), that the analysis of the place of fear and anxiety in television narratives suggests that the boundaries between reality and representation, experience and imagination, are always likely to be fuzzier and more perplexing than the terms of a debate between 'realism' and 'idealism' would seem to allow. I thus tend towards the view that Young and other 'realists' are in danger of succumbing to that 'proneness of our minds' to think that direct consequences are the only ones to which Abraham Lincoln alluded. Realism itself at times glides over other facts that have real existence, namely the embeddedness of crime, law and punishment in discourse, talk and rhetoric in routine and institutionalized ways. It is far from impossible to be mistakenly fearful, or 'rationally' fearful on the basis of misinformation. It is possible for anxieties about crime to blur with other sources of anxiety, both collective and personal. Once such anxieties have assumed a determinate form in accustomed modes of discourse, narration and imagery it is possible for them to be taken up and used for ulterior purposes, demagogic or commercial.

One of my main intentions has therefore been, through the review of the evidence about how television viewing relates to fearful public perceptions, to suggest some ways of looking at the private 'trouble' of fear and anxiety (see Mills 1959), and in so doing to draw attention to at least some of its public consequences. What the literature on television and fear does show, however inconclusive it might be in other respects, is the mundane presence of images of crime at many moments of our lives. Such images, however familiar and routinized they may be in the way they enter our domestic spaces, are never self-evident in either meaning or effect. They are co-ordinated in stories and discourses of particular kinds. They demonstrate particular preoccupations. They postulate problems, explanations and resolutions. They invite certain responses, often in ways which are difficult to refuse. One of the ways in which they make a claim upon our attention is through the kinds of fears and anxieties which we experience in daily life, whether simply to incite or also to console those feelings. Thus I have suggested, in response to Gerbner, it is neither very interesting nor very plausible to argue that such stories *cause* fear in any important degree. However, it is both interesting and plausible to think that they can address fears, play upon them, exploit or reassure them. It is also interesting and important to wonder what consequences follow for a culture which builds into its routine forms of communication and exchange, and its representations of itself to its members, such an abiding preoccupation with crime, law and punishment, organized in a particular and characteristic moral structure.

One such possible consequence is the one I have suggested in Chapter 3 with regard to censorship campaigns. Television makes itself a plausible target for moral enterprise because its own preoccupations with crime, law and punishment speak to the anxieties of the moral entrepreneurs in a sufficiently powerful way. The argument is largely about the medium itself, but it tends to be warranted by allegations of further consequences for behaviour and civility. There follows a conflation between talk about law and order and talk about their representations which it is quite difficult to disentangle. It is an irony that the only effect of 'violence on television' which is truly and conclusively demonstrable is the demand for its own more stringent regulation. Unsurprisingly, television producers have often shown more insight into these processes than social scientists have. As one BBC executive comments on the endless recurrence of 'violence on television' as a campaigning issue, 'Perhaps it is the nerve of anxiety which really concerns us in this debate' (Powell 1988: 48).

In large measure this view also forms the basis of my misgiving about and exploratory critique of television crime fiction. I have not concluded, on the strength of extended reflection on the subject, that it is wise to attribute a direct and determining influence from television imagery over anybody's perceptions. Watching entertainment television is more basically a way of passing an idle hour in search of distraction than it is a means of finding out about the world. There is a necessary element of inconclusiveness in any way of studying the topic which is sensitive to the complexity of its relations to other dimensions of experience. I understand perfectly well why Pearson (1983: 239) half apologizes for having 'laboured' the point about the metaphorical and figurative resonances of crime and fear. Yet it is also clear that the subject is not really a trivial one. Crime fiction on television does for the most part address us as fearful 'privatists' rather than contented social beings. Its narrative devices commonly use our anxieties as the hook on which to capture an audience. It does routinely register a level of social anxiety about crime and law enforcement, and in so doing tends to reproduce its cultural salience. In so doing it does also let us off the hook of the effort to strain for rationality. It does muddy and jumble rather than clarify and illuminate our experiences. If it has 'effects' these do tend more towards distraction from rather than confrontation with the sources of our social sentiments, more towards consolation than transcendence, and more towards punitiveness than generosity. It is not incidental that more fearful populations may be more 'anti-heterodox' (Corbett 1981) and more given towards authoritarianism than less fearful ones, nor that they make more demands for the simplification of experience, the maintenance of boundaries and the castigation of outcasts. It is not a trivial matter that 'crime scarers' such as *Crimewatch UK* do in a very real and particular sense employ the same syntax of depiction, narration and editing as crime fictions do, nor that newspaper reports similarly use television fiction as a point of reference in their narration of real events (see Carriere and Ericson 1989; Schlesinger et al 1989).

It may therefore be the case, and I do not wish to put it any more strongly than this, that if, as Garland (1990a) advocates, we need to continue looking for the preconditions for ideological work to take place in the arena of crime, law and punishment then television fiction is a place in which it remains worthwhile looking. It may be that habituation to a paleo-symbolic structure (Gouldner 1976) of fear followed by reassurance predicated on heroic force 'makes us fond' of punishment in Eco's sense (1979: 160) and that this is not a particularly healthful or helpful involvement. It does suggest a level of emotional investment in seeing punishment done which we may be unable or reluctant to acknowledge publicly, and about which it is at least precautionary to be aware. At the least it is enabling and illuminating to seek a degree of self-consciousness about the nature of our involvement with these stories, if only in order to guard against the tendency for the relevant levels of discourse, of fact, opinion, sentiment and mythology, to collapse into one another in a great experiential jumble – and to resist political projects predicated upon an appeal to these feelings. As the research which I have reviewed in Chapter 4 attests, none of this has proven conclusively demonstrable or quantifiable by conventional methods; but this is at least in part because those who have deployed the conventional methods have looked for 'effects' which were always implausibly simple and stark, as some of the harshest critics of Gerbner, for example Hughes (1980) and Hirsch (1980; 1981), have readily acknowledged. If Gerbner had been content to say that what is at stake here is an issue in the quality of publicly exchanged discourse about crime and law enforcement, and that the routine domination of this discourse by a preoccupation with images of fear and threat is distracting and unhelpful, then his 'Cultural Indicators Project' would have retained more plausibility and been truer to its name.

I am conscious also that my critical review of the argument about television and fear has led me back into the realms of discourse and representation and narrative, obliging me to adopt a language which does not easily lend itself to translation into practical intervention in, say, fear reduction. I can offer no apology for this. Discourse and narrativity are, really, integral dimensions of social life. This being so there is a sense in which some discussion of the kind I have undertaken is probably a necessary preliminary to work of a more directly empirical or interventionist kind, or is necessary to the assessment of such work. It is also part of my argument, however, that the activity of critique is itself a beneficial one. The discussion and 'disruptive evaluation' (Giddens 1987: 233) of familiar vocabularies and imageries, the 'unconsidered trifles' of mass culture, is itself a contribution to rational self-awareness. It thus presents a certain defence against the taken-for-grantedness of cultural forms (their 'doxicity' in Bourdieu's terms). It aims to clarify some sources of perplexity and confusion in ordinary life. This is at least a benign and perhaps a truly necessary and sufficient aim.

The growing importance of the issues of fear and anxiety in criminology, and the question of the role of the mass media in relation to them, has now achieved some recognition as a policy problem, including in official discourse. A critical posture of the kind I have advocated is important in evaluating, and where necessary challenging, this work. I shall take as an example the *Report of the Working Group on the Fear of Crime* (also known as the Grade Report: Home Office 1989). This document takes up and elaborates some now orthodox criminological views: that the fear of crime is a problem in itself because it is constraining and unpleasant for those who experience it (Home office 1989: 1); that it is 'only partly' related to victimization (1989: 1, 9, 15, 23); that it also relates to 'incivility' and to the nature of the built environment (1989: 10, 46); that those crimes which are most feared are not necessarily those which are most risked (1989: 25–32); that mass media may be implicated in sustaining this distribution of fear (1989: 23–34); that fear disproportionately afflicts Asian people, elderly people and women living in inner urban areas (1989: 15–19); that there are a range of possible dispositions from complacency to terror, some of which are more cogent and manageable than others (1989: 11–13); and that people find ways of responding to their fear, for example by buying big dogs, not all of which are likely to reduce the general distribution of fearfulness (1989: 18–19). Some of these views are unexceptionable, indeed helpful and interesting, especially inasmuch as they call for reflexivity from policy-makers about the balance of intended and unintended consequences of their interventions. For example, the document is genteelly critical of 'the hyping of crime prevention' (1989: 20). In so saying it begins to broach some moral dimensions of its subject matter, which are also issues about representation and depiction – for example in relation to Government advertising strategies (1989: 21). Equally, while some of its views (which it does not recognize as being controversial) will have outraged 'realist' criminologists by stressing determinants of fear other than victimization, some of its recommendations regarding street lighting, the policing of public transport and stringent opposition to racist graffiti and harassment will not have been uncongenial to them. Moreover, the Grade Report demonstrates the permeation of orthodoxy with themes which were the erstwhile prerogatives of radical criminology – domestic violence, racial attack, the under-reporting of rape, rape by acquaintances and 'dates', the hyping of danger for commercial advantage (for example in advertisements for personal alarms) and so forth.

The Report includes a separate chapter on 'The Rights and Responsibilities of the Media' which concentrates in particular on the so-called 'crime scarers' such as *Crimewatch UK*, *Crime Stoppers* and *Crimebusters*. The terms in which the Report defines the potential 'irresponsibility' of these formats include 'decontextualization', 'selectivity', inflammatory vocabulary and stereotyping. These certainly look like a familiar group of concepts, known to us from another time and another vantagepoint (S. Cohen and Young 1973; Chibnall 1977; S. Hall et al 1978). Yet, unlike its radical precursors, the Grade Report attributes such problems to inadequate training, failures of awareness among journalists and editorial misjudgement (Home Office 1989: 27–29). This is where it differs from that earlier radical project in media studies, and from mine. What it does not say is that the fanning of fear need not be inadvertent or mistaken. It may on the contrary be quite purposive and deliberate. Equally it may not be extraneous, disposable, the outcome of simple misjudgement. Rather it may be integral to a whole rhetoric, a whole conception of salience and interest, a whole body of domain assumptions about the relation between the media and their audiences. Fear may not be optional for either reporting or fiction. Rather the invocation of fear is deeply integrated in both the discursive structures and the saleability of cultural goods. Neither, therefore, notwithstanding its liking for the expression 'research has shown that' (Home Office 1989: 15, 18), does the Report make any mention of numerous things that research has also shown (or rather suggested), namely the prospect that the sense of living under an emergency either fosters the demand for stronger public authority (S. Hall et al 1978) or engenders a withdrawal from citizenship and into 'privatism' (Lasch 1980).

Much interesting recent theoretical activity has addressed itself to problems and tensions arising at the boundary between the public and the private spheres. The American psychiatrist James Glass considers relevant problems in his *Private Terror: Public Life* (1989). Glass illuminates the question of what it means to live in a state of terror or panic through the analysis of stories recounted by patients. He goes on to reflect on the sense in which such inward states of being impinge upon our capacities to act as public beings. In their more extreme forms, in delusive and psychotic states, Glass argues, fear and anxiety

> seriously alter one's sense of freedom, one's scope of participatory citizenship; they interfere with the psychological conditions necessary even to begin to perceive oneself as a political being, a citizen.
>
> (Glass 1989: 1)

The relevance of Glass's point is not confined to those whom we consider to be mentally ill. Rather, it concerns the preconditions for participation and 'communal attachment' (Glass 1989: 1) in modern societies and for the reconciliation of public and private worlds (which Glass also takes to be the preconditions for his patients to be cured). The question, as Glass poses it, is what is the 'self's habitat' (1989: 2) to be? On this view the 'habitat' of the anxious and isolated self 'is a politics' because it bears upon the difference between 'being a subject and being a participant in community' (1989: 5). Glass argues, following Ricoeur (1977), that the language in which these issues are discussed cannot be purged of metaphor and symbolism. Rather, Ricoeur argues, it is through the understanding of these figurative forms of speech that one 'opens the largest view' (1977: 302), because to look at metaphorical and figurative language is to open up a world in which 'we find ourselves already rooted' (1977: 306). Perhaps then, as Glass goes on to suggest, it is not through formal, factual language but rather through 'discourse that overwhelms and invades the senses' that one can 'reveal connections between the private and the public that more mediated forms of rational or scientific discourse obscure' (1989: 21).

This is to some degree the view I have taken of the place of fictional representations of crime and law enforcement in attempting to reach a more general understanding of the expressive and emotive qualities of these themes (and thereby aspects of their political potency) in contemporary culture. Crime, law and punishment involve real, material social facts. Prisons, police forces and courts are as thing-like as any positivist might wish. But, as Garland has argued (see also S. Cohen 1985; 1988), they are real and forceful partly in virtue of the language in which they are 'already rooted'. It makes no sense for criminology and the sociology of social regulation to disregard these aspects of its subject matter. Indeed to do so would be to falsify its nature and to remain unaware of a basic issue, namely the place of crime and punishment both in our public culture and in our private sentiments.

I have tried, through the analysis of the narration of crime, law and punishment in television fiction, to address these issues, however obliquely. If these narratives are in any sense revealing (but also perplexing, distracting and given to authoritarianism) it is because they depict an orientation to law enforcement in which anxiety is endemic and the relation between public and private spheres chronically problematic. Within such a world crime fictions can only offer magical and contrived solutions, in which the liminality (Silverstone 1988) of heroic agents allows them to bring wild justice from outside (from some moral universe in which vengeance and providence still make sense). Yet the pleasure in seeing retribution exacted which they thereby offer serves to stave off a degree of cynicism about a dangerous and corrupt social world. In that world ordinary people (people who are like us) are not agents, only victims or onlookers. The capacity for action must be delegated to heroes.

Thinking seriously about crime in the accustomed ways of gathering information, analysing policy outcomes and so forth remains vitally important. However, as Glass comments, 'Thinking involves feeling as well as cognition or ratiocination' (1989: 24). The kinds of vocabularies in which crime, law and punishment are 'already rooted' in our kind of society are at least as prone to find their most powerful expression in stories, fables, anecdotes, tall tales and rumours as in more plainly 'discursive' registers of language and depiction. The way in which these topics enter ordinary language and everyday life – the forms in which we are habituated to speaking about them unless we make a special effort of interpretation – are ones which tend to accept the existence of what Cohen has called 'primal crime' (1988: 236). Those who make narratives for us have found it expedient and successful to rely in the main on variations on already known themes and oppositions. The key to understanding how television is used and viewed in this respect lies, first and foremost, in its deployment of a language in which its audience is 'already rooted'.

Thus, one level of critique of the contemporary crime story might be that, to borrow Glass's terminology again, it is one of the routinely provided cultural forms which tend to render the 'self's habitat' more problematic and uncongenial than it need be, by simplifying without also clarifying our relation to troubling experience and by subsuming the complexity and contingency of contemporary crime problems within a fabular moral structure.

Whether this has any marked, demonstrable or direct political consequence is uncertain – and the question may in any case suffer from too strong a wish to draw analogies between such fictions and more plainly propagandist and didactic modes of representation. Television belongs to the realm of culture which, as Raymond Williams held, is 'ordinary'. It finds its place in everyday practice and exchange because television accompanies, and in some degree thereby also structures, the rhythms and routines of everyday life. For all that one may watch entertainment television in a wide variety of ways (casually, ironically, bored, distracted, dozing, drunk, cheerful, excited) some kinds of depiction will have a higher degree of what Hodge and Tripp (1986) call 'modality' because they attend, in however light and conventional a way, to things which actually concern us a good deal. It is also true, following Eco's argument about readers' responses that one cannot engage wholeheartedly with any story without, at least conditionally, accepting some of the discursive preconditions which generate it.

The attempt has been made many times (Gerbner and Gross 1976b; S. Hall et al 1978; Gitlin 1979; Knight 1980; Murdock 1982; Mandel 1984; Scheingold 1984; Clarke 1986 – to name only some of the more important instances) to suggest specific ideological effects of the depiction of crime in the media. If such attempts have proven inconclusive this has more to do with the deep evidentiary problems in demonstrating with certainty any specific effect of mass media on public perception than with the plausibility of the basic idea. My consideration of the subject has been no more conclusive than any predecessor, indeed in some ways less so in that I have not looked for simple effects and correspondences.

Nevertheless, this book raises issues which deserve further serious consideration. First, one should consider seriously whether the moral structure of the fable can be detected in other registers of discourse (in news, in speeches from public platforms or in the dramatic reconstructions of the 'crime scarers', for example). One must therefore entertain the possibility that the plausibility of fictions and facts are mutually constraining, and that stories and entertainments contribute to the setting of parameters on what rhetorics, political postures and policies we are inclined to believe or accept. If we have grown fond of heroism and simplicity and have become accustomed to taking pleasure in seeing retribution done is it easier for us to accept rhetorics which divide the world of crime and law enforcement into simple categories, rather than those which tax us with more heterogeneous distinctions? Is this therefore a way in which the punitive preoccupation is kept alive? Second, it seems to me inescapable that one has to take in earnest the expressive and emotive character of the themes of crime and punishment. This is perhaps most obviously visible in fiction, which is why I have used fiction as a point of entry into the discussion of the place of crime, law enforcement and punishment in public and private life. The fact that expressiveness and emotiveness seem inherent does not however mean that certain of their manifestations may not be damaging – distracting, excessively simplified, anachronistic, illiberal. The question is thus not whether people have emotional responses to crime and punishment, but rather whether the uses made of the emotiveness of the topic are exploitative, ulterior, sectional, and in this sense ideological. Yet the notion of a rational response to crime, purged of social sentiment, is equally a distraction. The question thus concerns in what kind of language we should seek to address one another about crime and punishment, and what to guard against. To this extent criminological analysis is necessarily about more than providing information, correcting misperception and advocating policy; it is also about refining sensibilities and promoting vigilant and self-conscious critical awareness. Unless this forms part of the criminological enterprise it matters little how much one might complain about misinformation and cliche in public talk about crime and punishment, because the intellectual tools with which to contest the reduction of problems of crime and punishment to primal categories and to check the growth of punitive obsessions will be lacking.

Notes

2 Moral tales and social theory

1 This, of course, underlines the argument made by Hebdige which I discuss in this chapter. Dramatic tropes are most to be used for events which at some level matter, which unnerve or threaten, and where ordinary discursive language seems inadequate (see Glass 1989). This lays open the possibility of a real confusion where a narrowly conventional dramatic idiom simplifies complex processes and assimilates them to essentialist categories of good and evil. One possible further outcome of this is the slippage in some recent social criticism in which it becomes unclear whether the real object of concern is the medium or the things it represents or both (see Chapter 3; see also Pratt and Sparks 1987).

2 The notion of universal narratives, deriving from early folklorism, was certainly more current in the heyday of structuralism than today. It is severely problematic in so far as it seeks to make observed variations into merely contingent matters, thereby obscuring their relation to the contexts of their production and use (e.g. Zipes 1979). It is useful only to the extent that it traces real historical continuities between primordial myth and modern 'myth' (see Jacoby 1985).

3 I have already alluded to the clear historical succession between Westerns and crime shows in US television and cinema. The preoccupation in US popular culture, to which Martin Williams (1982) and Gitlin (1985) refer, with individual integrity in the face of the violence and corruption of social life (which in turn is a preoccupation with masculinity) perhaps finds its purest realization in the classic Western. One of the primary concerns of the genre is the foundation of the law, and many Westerns are thus located in moments of historical transition between gun-law and civil society. In the classic Western the final showdown bespeaks an end of the age of lawlessness; thereafter guns are no longer toted.

High Noon and *Rio Bravo* fit this pattern. The wistfulness which many observers identify in the later Western springs in part from the recognition that the hero too belongs to the earlier age. To the extent that the foundation of the law is also an end of the heroic age it signifies a moment of disenchantment. Where the law is founded by force yet also seeks to prevent or contain the use of force it may find no place for its own founder who, being 'caught between two worlds' may be called upon to die (*Guns in the Afternoon*) or to return to the wilderness (as was already the case in *Shane* and *The Searchers* and which Clint Eastwood gave a late elegiac revival in *Pale Rider*). Hence in part the presumption of kinship between outlaw and lawman in the later Western, and the apparent fluidity between the two roles: this wears a sunny interpretation in *The Magnificent Seven*, a much darker one in *The Missouri Breaks*. Hence also the fact that virtually all Westerns set after 1900 are either camp or tragic: *The Shootist; The Long Riders*. For some accounts of Westerns see Kitses (1969), French (1977) and Parks (1982).

3　Entertaining the crisis? Television and moral enterprise

1　There is an evident connection here with twentieth-century fictional dystopias. The novels of Orwell, Huxley, Kosinski, Pohl and others all take as their premise the erosion of the will and of civic virtues in the face of monolithic control over the means of communication. Perhaps the plainest example of this is given by Anthony Burgess's (1962) *A Clockwork Orange*, in which the diminution of moral responsibility is represented by the regression of language itself. The protagonist, Alex, cannot distinguish in his fantasies between his adoration of Beethoven and his addiction to violent pornography; he is turned on by both, thereby reducing the former to the level of the latter. Alex's primary hobby is 'ultra-violence'. The zeal with which he pursues violence is the only outlet he can find for his creativity. *A Clockwork Orange* is *par excellence* a 'mass society' book.

2　Bourdieu (1985) gives an account of the 'genesis of groups' which describes rather well some aspects of the relations between Whitehousian conservatism and recent Conservative administrations in Britain. A subaltern group is forced to seek rapports with better 'capitalized' spokespersons, but in so doing is forced to accommodate more to their position than they to its. Hence, whereas many aspects of recent Conservative policy, especially the neo-liberal preference for deregulation and its associated moral agnosticism about consumption, run directly counter to Whitehouse's desires she is none the less incorporated within the umbrella of Conservative politics. Conservative politicians on the other hand are not constrained to observe Whitehouse's priorities in any thoroughgoing way, though they are able to call upon its rhetoric as and when it seems to them strategic or appropriate. Thus the Government may be happy enough to exclaim against violence on television, but only faintly interested in legislating against it, especially if this contradicts impulses towards deregulation.

References

Adler, R. P. (1975) *Television as a Social Force*, New York: Praeger.

Adorno, T. W. (1954) 'How to look at television', *Quarterly of Film, Radio and Television* 8: 213–35.

Adorno, T. W. (1967) *Prisms*, London: Neville Spearman.

Allais, M. (1953) 'Le comportement de l'homme rationnel devant le risque', *Econometrica* 21: 503–46.

Altheide, D. (1984) 'Media hegemony: a failure of perspective', *Public Opinion Quarterly* 48: 476–90.

Althusser, L. (1969) *For Marx*, London: Allen Lane.

Althusser, L. (1971) *Lenin and Philosophy and Other Essays*, London: New Left Books.

Anderson, D. and Sharrock, W. (1979) 'Biasing the news: technical issues in "media studies" ', *Sociology* 13, 3: 365–85.

Ang, I. (1985) *Watching Dallas*, London: Methuen.

Annan, N. (1977) *Report of the Committee on the Future of Broadcasting*, Cmnd 6753, London: HMSO.

Arendt, H. (1970) *On Violence*, London: Allen Lane.

Auden, W. H. (1948) 'The guilty vicarage' in *The Dyer's Hand*, London: Faber.

Baggaley, J. and Duck, S. (1976) *Dynamics of Television*, Westmead: Saxon House.

Ball-Rokeach, S. and Cantor, M. (eds) (1986) *Media, Audience and Social Structure*, London: Sage.

Barker, M. (1984a) *A Haunt of Fears*, London: Pluto.

Barker, M. (1984b) *The Video Nasties: Freedom and Censorship in the Media*, London: Pluto.

Barnouw, E. (1975) *Tube of Plenty*, Oxford: Oxford University Press.

Baron, J. and Reiss, P. (1985) 'Mass media and violent behavior', *American Sociological Review* 50, 3: 347–63.

Barthes, R. (1972) *Mythologies*, London: Jonathan Cape.

Barthes, R. (1985) 'On the subject of violence' in *The Grain of the Voice*, London: Jonathan Cape.

Bateson, G. (1972) *Steps to an Ecology of Mind*, London: Intertext.

BBC (1972) *Violence on Television: Programme Content and Viewer Reception*, London: BBC.

BBC (1979) *The Portrayal of Violence in Television Programmes*, London: BBC.

BBC (1988) *Violence and the Media*, London: BBC.

Becker, H. (1963) *Outsiders*, New York: Basic Books.

Belson, W. (1978) *Television Violence and the Adolescent Boy*, Westmead: Saxon House.

Benjamin, W. (1970) *Illuminations*, London: Jonathan Cape.

Benjamin, W. (1979) 'Critique of violence' [1922] in *One Way Street and Other Writings*, London: Verso.

Bennett, T., Boyd-Bowman, S., Mercer, C. and Woollacott, J. (eds) (1981) *Popular Film and Television*, London: British Film Institute.

Bennett, T. H. (1989) *Tackling Fear of Crime: A Review of Policy Options*, University of Cambridge, Institute of Criminology.

Berger, A. (1982) *Television as an Instrument of Terror*, New Brunswick, NJ: Transaction Inc.

Berman, M. (1983) *All That is Solid Melts into Air*, London: Verso.

Bernstein, R. (1978) *The Restructuring of Social and Political Theory*, Philadelphia, PA: University of Pennsylvania Press.

Best, J. and Horiuchi, G. (1985) 'The razor blade in the apple: the social construction of urban legends', *Social Problems* 32: 488–99.

Biderman, A. (1967) *Report on a Pilot Study on Victimization and Attitudes towards Law Enforcement*, Washington, DC: US Government Printing Office.

Bigsby, C. W. E. (ed.) (1976) *Approaches to Popular Culture*, London: Edward Arnold.

Billig, M. (1987) *Arguing and Thinking: A Rhetorical Approach to Social Psychology*, Cambridge: Cambridge University Press.

Bottomley, A. K. and Coleman, C. (1981) *Understanding Crime Rates: Police and Public Roles in the Production of Official Statistics*, Farnborough: Gower.

Bottomley, A. K. and Pease, K. (1986) *Crime and Justice: Interpreting the Data*, Milton Keynes: Open University Press.

Bourdieu, P. (1971) 'Intellectual field and creative project' in M.F.D. Young (ed.) *Knowledge and Control*, London: Collier-Macmillan.

Bourdieu, P. (1977) *Outline of a Theory of Practice*, Cambridge: Cambridge University Press.

Bourdieu, P. (1980) 'The production of belief', *Media, Culture and Society* 2, 3: 224–54.

Bourdieu, P. (1985) 'The social space and the genesis of groups', *Theory and Society* 14: 723–44.

Bourdieu, P. and Passeron, J.-C. (1977) *Reproduction in Education, Society and Culture*, London: Sage.

Box, S. (1971) *Deviance, Reality and Society*, London: Holt, Rinehart & Winston.

Box, S., Hale, C. and Andrews, G. (1988) 'Explaining Fear of Crime', *British Journal of Criminology* 28, 3: 338–56.

Boyanowski, E., Newtson, D. and Walster, E. (1974) 'Film preference following a murder', *Communication Research* 1: 32–4.

Braudel, F. (1980) *On History*, London: Weidenfeld & Nicolson.

Brecht, B. (1967) *Gesammelte Werke*, vol. 16, Frankfurt: Suhrkamp.

Bremond, C. (1966) 'La logique des possibles narratifs', *Communications* 8: 60–77.

Browne, N. (1982) *The Rhetoric of Filmic Narration*, Ann Arbor, Mich.: UMI Research Press.

Bruckner, P. (1975) *Sigmund Freud's Privatlekture*, Koln.

Burgess, A. (1962) *A Clockwork Orange*, Harmondsworth: Penguin.

Burn, G. (1984) *Somebody's Husband, Somebody's Son*, London: Heinemann.

Campbell, T. (1980) 'Chemical carcinogens and human risk assent', *Federation Proceedings* 39: 2467–84.

Canetti, E. (1986) *The Conscience of Words*, London: André Deutsch.

Carey, J. (1990) 'Revolted by the masses', *Times Literary Supplement* 12–18 January.

Carey, J. W. and Kreiling, A. (1974) 'Popular culture and uses and gratifications' in J. Blumler and E. Katz (eds) *The Uses of Mass Communications*, Beverly Hills, Calif. and London: Sage.

Carlson, J.M. (1985) *Prime-Time Law Enforcement: Crime Show Viewing and Attitudes Toward the Criminal Justice System*, New York: Praeger.

Carriere, K. and Ericson, R. (1989) 'Crime stoppers'. Paper presented to British Criminology Conference, Bristol, July.

Carroll, J. (1980) *Towards a Structural Psychology of Cinema*, The Hague: Mouton.

Cater, D. and Strickland, S. (1975) *TV Violence and the Child: The Origin and Fate of the Surgeon General's Report*, New York: Russell Sage.

Caulfield, M. (1975) *Mary Whitehouse*, Oxford: Mowbrays.

Chandler, R. (1944) 'The simple art of murder', *Atlantic Monthly* December.

Chaney, D. (1977) 'Fictions in mass entertainment' in J. Curran, M. Gurevitch and J. Woollacott (eds) *Mass Communication and Society*, London: Edward Arnold.

Chatman, S. (1978) *Story and Discourse: Narrative Structure in Fiction and Film*, Ithaca, NY: Cornell University Press.

Chibnall, S. (1977) *Law and Order News*, London: Tavistock.

Chomsky, N. (1959) 'Review of B. F. Skinner, *Verbal Behaviour*', *Language* 35: 26–58.

Christians, C. and Carey, J. W. (1981) 'The logic and aims of qualitative research' in G. H. Stempel and B. H. Westley (eds) *Research Methods in Mass Communication*, Englewood Cliffs, NJ: Prentice-Hall.

Christie, N. (1981) *Limits to Pain*, London: Martin Robertson.

Cicourel, A. V. (1970) 'Negotiation of status and role' in H. P. Dreitzel (ed.) *Recent Sociology 2*, London: Macmillan.

Clarke, A. (1983) 'Holding the blue lamp: television and the police in Britain', *Crime and Social Justice* 19: 44–51.

Clarke, A. (1986) 'This is not the boy scouts: television police series and definitions of law and order' in T. Bennett, C. Mercer and J. Woollacott (eds) *Popular Culture and Social Relations*, Milton Keynes: Open University Press.

Clarke, A. H. and Lewis, M. J. (1982) 'Fear of crime among the elderly', *British Journal of Criminology* 22, 1: 49–61.

Cohen, J. (1977) *The Probable and the Provable*, Oxford: Clarendon Press.

Cohen, J. (1981) 'Can human irrationality be experimentally demonstrated?', *Behavioural and Brain Sciences* 4: 317–70.

Cohen, P. (1979) 'Policing the working-class city' in B. Fine (ed.) *Capitalism and the Rule of Law*, London: Hutchinson.

Cohen, S. (1972) *Folk Devils and Moral Panics*, Harmondsworth: Penguin.

Cohen, S. (1985) *Visions of Social Control*, Cambridge: Polity Press.

Cohen, S. (1988) *Against Criminology*, New Brunswick, NJ: Transaction Inc.

Cohen, S. and Young, J. (1973) *The Manufacture of News*, London: Constable.

Comstock, G., Chaffee, S., Katzman, N., McCombs, M. and Roberts, D. (1978) *Television and Human Behavior*, New York: Columbia University Press.

Conrad, P. (1982) *Television: The Medium and its Manners*, London: Routledge & Kegan Paul.

Corbett, M. (1981) 'Public support for "Law and Order" ', *Criminology* 19: 328–43.

Counihan, M. (1975) ' "Reading Television": notes on the problem of media content', *Australian and New Zealand Journal of Sociology* 11: 31–6.

Coward, R. (1987) 'Violent screen play', *Marxism Today* December: 24–7.

Crawford, A., Jones, T., Woodhouse, T. and Young, J. (1990) *Second Islington Crime Survey*, Middlesex Polytechnic, Centre for Criminology.

Critchley, T. A. (1978) *A History of Police in England and Wales*, London: Constable.

Culler, J. (1973) 'The linguistic basis of structuralism' in D. Robey (ed.) *Structuralism: An Introduction*, Oxford: Clarendon Press.

Cumberbatch, G. (1988) 'The incidence and nature of violence on television' in *Violence and the Media*, London: BBC.

Cziczentmihalyi, M. and Kubey, R. (1982) 'Television and the rest of life', *Public Opinion Quarterly* 45: 317–28.

Dahrendorf, R. (1985) *Law and Order: The Hamlyn Lectures*, London: Stevens and Sons.

Davis, J. (1980) 'The London garrotting panic of 1862' in V. Gatrell, B. Lenman and E. Parker (eds) *Crime and the Law: the Social History of Crime in Europe since 1500*, London: Europa.

Davison, P., Meyersohn, R. and Shils, E. (eds) (1978) *Literary Taste, Culture and Mass Communications* (14 vols). Cambridge: Chadwyck-Healey.

Devlin, P. (1965) *The Enforcement of Morals*, Oxford: Oxford University Press.

Dewey, J. (1927) *The Public and its Problems*, London: Macmillan.

Ditton, J. and Duffy, J. (1983) ' "Bias" in newspaper reporting of crime news', *British Journal of Criminology* 23: 159–65.

Dominick, J. R. (1973) 'Crime and law enforcement on prime-time television', *Public Opinion Quarterly* 37: 241–51.

Dominick, J. R. (1978) 'Crime and law enforcement in the mass media' in C. Winick (ed.) *Deviance and Mass Media*, London: Sage.

Doob, A. and Macdonald, G. (1979) 'Television viewing and the fear of victimization: is the relationship causal?', *Journal of Personality and Social Psychology* 37: 170–9.

Douglas, M. (1986) *Risk*, London: Routledge & Kegan Paul.

Downes, D. (1988) 'The sociology of crime and social control in Britain, 1960–87' in P. Rock (ed.) *A History of British Criminology*, Oxford: Oxford University Press.

Dunn, J. M. (1985) 'Identity, modernity and the claim to know better' in *Rethinking Modern Political Theory*, Cambridge: Cambridge University Press.

Eagleton, T. (1976) *Criticism and Ideology*, London: Verso.

Eco, U. (1972) 'Towards a semiotic enquiry into the television message', *Working Papers in Cultural Studies 3*, Birmingham: Centre for Contemporary Cultural Studies.

Eco, U. (1979) *The Role of the Reader*, London: Hutchinson.

Eliot, T. S. (1948) *Notes towards the Definition of Culture*, London: Faber & Faber

Elliott, P. (1982) 'Intellectuals, the "information society" and the disappearance of the public sphere', *Media, Culture and Society* 4: 243–53.

Ellis, J. (1982) *Visible Fictions*, London: Routledge & Kegan Paul.

Ellul, J. (1968) 'Terrorisme et violence psychologique' in J. Onimus (ed.) *La Violence dans le monde actuel*, Nice: Brouwer.

Ellul, J. (1980) *The Technological System*, New York: Continuum.

Ennis, P. H. (1967) *Criminal Victimization in the United States*, Washington DC: US Government Printing Office.

Enzensberger, H. M. (1976) *Raids and Reconstructions*, London: Pluto.

Ericson, R. (1991) 'Mass media, crime, law and justice: an institutional approach', *British Journal of Criminology* 31, 3: 219–49.

Ericson, R., Baranek, P. and Chan, J. (1987) *Visualizing Deviance*, Milton Keynes: Open University Press.

Feuer, J., Kerr, P. and Vahimagi, T. (eds) (1984) *MTM: Quality Television*, London: British Film Institute.

Fishman, M. (1978) 'Crime waves as ideology', *Social Problems* 25: 531–43.

Fiske, J. (1987) *Television Culture*, London: Methuen.

Fiske, J. and Hartley, J. (1978) *Reading Television*, London: Methuen.

Foucault, M. (1975) *Surveiller et punir*, Paris: Gallimard (trans. A. Sheridan, 1979, *Discipline and Punish*, Harmondsworth: Penguin).

Foucault, M. (1984) *The Foucault Reader* (ed. P. Rabinow), Harmondsworth: Penguin.

Fraser, J. (1974) *Violence in the Arts*, Cambridge: Cambridge University Press.

French, P. (1977) *Westerns: Aspects of a Movie Genre* (2nd edition), London: Secker & Warburg.

Fried, C. (1970) *An Anatomy of Values*, Cambridge, Mass.: Harvard University Press.

Fromm, E. (1956) *The Sane Society*, London: Routledge & Kegan Paul.

Fussell, P. (1977) *The Great War and Modern Memory*, Oxford: Oxford University Press.

Fyvel, T. R. (1961) *The Insecure Offenders*, London: Chatto & Windus.

Gans, H. J. (1970) *Deciding What's News*, New York: Vintage Books.

Garland, D. (1987) 'Review of R. Kinsey *et al.*, *Losing the Fight Against Crime*', *Contemporary Crises* 11, 2: 198–200.

Garland, D. (1990a) 'Frameworks of inquiry in the sociology of punishment', *British Journal of Sociology* 14, 1: 1–15.

Garland, D. (1990b) *Punishment and Modern Society*, Oxford: Clarendon Press.

Garland, D. and Young, P. (eds) (1983) *The Power to Punish*, Aldershot: Gower.

Garnham, N. (1973) *Structures of Television*, London: British Film Institute.

Garnham, N. (1986) 'The media and the public sphere' in P. Golding, G. Murdock and P. Schlesinger (eds) *Communicating Politics: Mass Communications and the Political Process*, Leicester: Leicester University Press.

Garofalo, J. (1980) 'Victimization and the fear of crime' in E. Bittner and S. Messinger (eds) *Criminology Review Yearbook*, vol. 2, London: Sage.

Garofalo, J. (1981) 'Crime and the mass media: a selective review of research', *Journal of Research in Crime and Delinquency* 18: 319–50.

Gatrell, V., Lenman, B. and Parker, E. (eds) (1980) *Crime and the Law: the Social History of Crime in Europe since 1500*, London: Europa.

Genette, G. (1982) *Figures of Literary Discourse*, Oxford: Basil Blackwell.

Gerbner, G. (1970) 'Cultural indicators: the case of violence in television drama', *Annals of the American Academy of Political and Social Science* 338: 69–81.

Gerbner, G. (1972) 'Violence in television drama: trends and symbolic functions' in G. Comstock and E. Rubinstein (eds) *Television and Social Behavior*, vol. 1, Rockville, Md: US Department of Health, Education and Welfare.

Gerbner, G. and Gross, L. (1976a) 'Living with television: the violence profile', *Journal of Communication* 26: 173–199.

Gerbner, G. and Gross, L. (1976b) 'The scary world of TV's heavy viewer', *Psychology Today* April: 89–91.

Gerbner, G., Holsti, O., Krippendorf, K., Paisley, W. and Stone, P. (eds) (1969) *The Analysis of Communication Content*, New York: John Wiley.

Gerbner, G., Gross, L., Morgan, M., Signorielli, N. and Jackson-Beeck, M. (1978) 'Cultural indicators: violence profile no. 9', *Journal of Communication* 28: 176–207.

Gerbner, G., Gross, L., Morgan, M., Signorielli, N. and Jackson-Beeck, M. (1979) 'The demonstration of power: violence profile no. 10', *Journal of Communication* 29: 177–96.

Gerbner, G., Gross, L., Morgan, M. and Signorielli, N. (1980) 'The mainstreaming of America: violence profile no. 11', *Journal of Communication* 30: 19–29.

Gerbner, G., Gross, L., Morgan, M. and Signorielli, N. (1984) 'Political correlates of television viewing', *Public Opinion Quarterly* 48: 283–300.

Geuss, R. (1981) *The Idea of a Critical Theory*, Cambridge: Cambridge University Press.

Giddens, A. (1976) *New Rules of Sociological Method*, London: Hutchinson.

Giddens, A. (1984) *The Constitution of Society*, Cambridge: Polity Press.

Giddens, A. (1987) *Sociology and Modern Social Theory*, Cambridge: Polity Press.

Giddens, A. (1990) *The Consequences of Modernity*, Cambridge: Polity Press.

Giner, S. (1976) *Mass Society*, London: Martin Robertson.

Gitlin, T. (1979) 'Prime-time ideology: the hegemonic process in television entertainment', *Social Problems* 26: 251–66.

Gitlin, T. (1985) *Inside Prime Time*, New York: Pantheon.

Glass, J. (1989) *Private Terror: Public Life*, Ithaca, NY: Cornell University Press.

Glucksmann, A. (1965) *Violence on the Screen*, London: British Film Institute.

Golding, P. and Murdock, G. (1979) 'Ideology and the media: the question of determination' in M. Barrett, P. Corrigan, A. Kuhn and J. Wolff (eds) *Ideology and Cultural Production*, London: Croom Helm.

Golding, P., Murdock, G. and Schlesinger, P. (1986) *Communicating Politics: Mass Communication and the Political Process*, Leicester: Leicester University Press.

Goldmann, L. (1977) *Cultural Creation*, Oxford: Basil Blackwell.

Gould, P., Johnson, J. and Chapman, G. (1984) *The Structure of Television*, London: Pion.

Gouldner, A. W. (1976) *The Dialectic of Ideology and Technology*, London: Macmillan.

Graber, D. (1980) *Crime News and the Public*, New York: Praeger.

Gramsci, A. (1971) *Selections from the Prison Notebooks* (ed. and trans. Q. Hoare and G. Nowell-Smith), London: Lawrence & Wishart.

Griffiths, E. (1988) 'The fine art of murder', *The Independent* 27 September, p. 30.

Grodal, T. (1988) '*Miami Vice*, melancholia and post-modernity'. Paper presented to the International Television Studies Conference, London, July.

Grossberg, L., Curthoys, A., Patton, P. and Fry, T. (1988) *It's a Sin: Essays on Post-Modernism, Politics and Culture*, Sydney: Power Publications.

Gunter, B. (1985) *Dimensions of Television Violence*, Aldershot: Gower.

Gunter, B. (1987) *Television and the Fear of Crime*, London: John Libbey.

Gunter, B. and Wakshlag, J. (1986) 'Television viewing and perceptions of crime among London residents'. Paper presented to International Television Studies Conference, London, July.

Gunter, B. and Wober, J.M. (1982) 'Television and personal threat: fact or artifact?', *British Journal of Social Psychology* 21: 239–47.

Gunter, B. and Wober, M. (1983) 'Television viewing and public trust', *British Journal of Social Psychology* 29: 177–96.

Gunter, B. and Wober, M. (1988) *Violence on Television: What the Viewers Think*, London: John Libbey.

Habermas, J. (1974) 'The public sphere', *New German Critique*, vol. 3.

Habermas, J. (1976) *Legitimation Crisis*, London: Heinemann.

Habermas, J. (1987) *The Theory of Communicative Action*, vol. 2, Boston, Mass.: Beacon Press.

Hall, R. (1985) *Ask Any Woman: A London Enquiry into Rape and Sexual Assault*, London: Fallingwall Press.

Hall, S. (1971) 'Television as a medium and its relation to culture'. Occasional Paper, Birmingham: Centre for Contemporary Cultural Studies.

Hall, S. (1975) 'Encoding and decoding in the television discourse'. Occasional Paper, Birmingham: Centre for Contemporary Cultural Studies.

Hall, S. (1976) 'Violence and the media' in N. Tutt (ed.) *Violence*, London: HMSO.

Hall, S. (1980a) 'Reformism and the legislation of consent' in National Deviancy Conference (eds) *Permissiveness and Control*, London: Macmillan.

Hall, S. (1980b) 'Drifting into a law and order society' (Cobden Trust Human Rights Day Lecture, 1979), London: Cobden Trust.

Hall, S. (1984) 'The narrative construction of reality' (interview), *Southern Review* 17.

Hall, S., Clarke, J., Jefferson, T., Critcher, C. and Roberts, B. (1978) *Policing the Crisis: Mugging, Law and Order and the State*, London: Macmillan.

Halloran, J. and Croll, P. (1972) 'Television programmes in Great Britain' in G. Comstock and E. Rubinstein (eds) *Television and Social Behavior*, vol. 1, Washington, DC: National Institute of Mental Health.

Hanmer, J. and Saunders, S. (1984) *Well-Founded Fear*, London: Hutchinson.

Hanmer, J., Radford, J. and Stanko, E. (1989) *Women, Policing and Male Violence*, London: Routledge.

Haralovich, M. (1988) 'Champagne taste on a beer budget: Magnum PI'. Paper presented to International Television Studies Conference, University of London, July.

Harari, J. V. (ed.) (1980) *Textual Strategies*, London: Methuen.

Hart, H. L. A. (1963) *Law, Liberty and Morality*, Oxford: Oxford University Press.

Hartley, J. (1984) 'Encouraging signs: television and the power of dirt, speech and scandalous categories' in M. W. D. Rowland and B. Watkins (eds) *Interpreting Television: Current Research Perspectives*, London: Sage.

Hartogs, R. and Artzt, E. (1970) *Violence: Causes and Solutions*, New York: Dell Publishing.

Hawkins, R. and Pingree, S. (1982) 'Television's influence on social reality' in D. Pearl, L. Bouthilet and J. Lazar (eds) *Television and Behavior*, vol. 2, Rockville, Md: National Institute of Mental Health.

Heath, S. (1981) *Questions of Cinema*, Bloomington, Ind: Indiana University Press.

Hebdige, D. (1974) 'The Kray Twins: a study of a system of closure'. Occasional Paper, Birmingham: Centre for Contemporary Cultural Studies.

Hirsch, P. (1976) 'The role of television and popular culture in contemporary society' in H. Newcomb (ed.) *Television: The Critical View*, Oxford: Oxford University Press.

Hirsch, P. (1980) 'The "scary world" of the non-viewer and other anomalies: a reanalysis of Gerbner *et al*.'s findings, part 1', *Communication Research* 7: 403–56.

Hirsch, P. (1981) 'On not learning from one's own mistakes: a reanalysis of Gerbner *et al*., part 2', *Communication Research* 8: 3–37.

Hodge, R. and Tripp, D. (1986) *Children and Television*, Cambridge: Polity Press.

Holbrook, D. (1976) 'Television and the new brutality', *The Listener* 16 October.

Holdaway, S. (ed.) (1979) *The British Police*, London: Edward Arnold.

Home Office (1957) *Report of the Committee on Homosexual Offences and Prostitution* (Wolfenden Committee), London: HMSO.

Home Office (1979) *Report of the Committee on Obscenity and Censorship*, Cmnd 7772 (Williams Report), London: HMSO.

Home Office (1989) *Report of the Working Group on the Fear of Crime* (Grade Report), London: HMSO.

Hough, M. and Mayhew, P. (1983) *The British Crime Survey*, London: HMSO.

Hough, M. and Mayhew, P. (1985) *Taking Account of Crime: Key Findings From the 1984 British Crime Survey*, London: HMSO (HORS 85).

Howitt, D. (1982) *Mass Media and Social Problems*, Oxford: Pergamon.

Howitt, D. and Cumberbatch, G. (1975) *Mass Media Violence and Society*, London: Elek Science.

Hubbard, J. C., DeFleur, M. and DeFleur, L. (1975) 'Mass media influence on public conceptions of social problems', *Social Problems* 23: 22–34.

Hughes, M. (1980) 'The fruits of cultivation analysis: a re-examination of some effects of television watching', *Public Opinion Quarterly* 44: 287–302.

Hurd, G. (1979) 'The television presentation of the police' in S. Holdaway (ed.) *The British Police*, London: Edward Arnold.

IBA (1971) *The Portrayal of Violence on Independent Television*, London: Independent Broadcasting Authority.

Jacoby, S. (1985) *Wild Justice: The Evolution of Revenge*, London: Collins.

Jaspers, K. (1951) *Man in the Modern Age*, London: Routledge & Kegan Paul.

Jefferson, T. (1987) 'The Police', in Open University, D310 *Crime, Justice and Society* (Block 3, Part 1a), Milton Keynes: Open University.

Jeudy, H.-P. (1979) *La Peur et les média: essai sur la virulence*, Paris: Presses Universitaires de France.

Jones, T., MacLean, B. and Young, J. (1986) *The Islington Crime Survey*, Aldershot: Gower.

Kappeler, S. (1986) *The Pornography of Representation*, Cambridge: Polity Press.

Katz, E. and Liebes, T. (1986) 'Dallas and Genesis: primordiality and seriality in popular culture'. Paper presented to International Television Studies Conference, University of London, July.

Katz, J. (1988) *Seductions of Crime*, New York: Basic Books.

Keane, J. (1984) *Public Life and Late Capitalism*, Cambridge: Cambridge University Press.

Kermode, F. (1967) *The Sense of an Ending*, Oxford: Oxford University Press.

Kermode, F. (1979) *The Genesis of Secrecy*, Cambridge, Mass.: Harvard University Press.

Kerr, P. (1981) 'Watching the Detectives', *Prime Time* 1, 1.

Kinsey, R. (1985) *Merseyside Crime and Police Surveys: Final Report*, Liverpool: Merseyside County Council.

Kitses, J. (1969) *Horizons West*, London: Secker & Warburg.

Klapp, O. (1954) 'Heroes, villains and fools as agents of social control', *American Sociological Review* 19, 1: 56–62.

Klapper, J. (1962) *Effects of Mass Communication*, New York: Free Press.

Knight, S. (1980) *Form and Ideology in Crime Fiction*, Bloomington, Ind: Indiana University Press.

Kracauer, S. (1971) 'Der Detektiv-Roman. Ein philosophische Traktat' in *Schriften 1*, Frankfurt: Surhkamp.

Kraus, S. and Perloff, R. (1985) *Mass Media and Political Thought*, London and Beverly Hills, Calif: Sage.

Kreiling, A. (1984) 'Television in American ideological hopes and fears' in W. D. Rowland and B. Watkins (eds) *Interpreting Television: Current Research Perspectives*, London: Sage.

Kress, G. (1976) 'Structuralism and popular culture' in C. W. E. Bigsby (ed.) *Approaches to Popular Culture*, London: Edward Arnold.

Krippendorf, K. (1980) *Content Analysis*, Beverly Hills, Calif: Sage.

La Fontaine, J. de (1974) *Fables*, Paris: Gallimard.

Larkin, P. (1964) 'Reference Back' in *The Whitsun Weddings*, London: Faber & Faber.

Lasch, C. (1977) *Haven in a Heartless World: The Family Besieged*, New York: Basic Books.

Lasch, C. (1980) *The Culture of Narcissism*, London: Sphere Books.

Lasswell, H. (1953) 'Why be quantitative?' in B. Berelson and M. Janowitz (eds) *Reader in Public Opinion and Communication*, Glencoe, Ill.: Free Press.

Lea, J. and Young, J. (1984) *What is to be Done about Law and Order?*, Harmondsworth: Penguin.

Leavis, F. R. (1943) *Education and the University*, London: Chatto.

Leavis, F. R. and Thomson, D. (1942) *Culture and Environment*, London: Chatto.

Lévi-Strauss, C. (1966) *The Savage Mind*, Chicago: University of Chicago Press.

Lewis, D. (1980) *Sociological Theory and the Production of a Social Problem: the Case of Fear of Crime*, Chicago, Ill., Northwestern University, Center for Urban Affairs.

Lewis, D. and Salem, G. (1986) *Fear of Crime*, New Brunswick, NJ: Transaction Inc.

Lichter, S. and Lichter, S. R. (1983) *Prime-Time Crime: Criminals and Law Enforcers in TV Entertainment*, Washington, DC: Media Institute.

Liebman, S. (1986) 'Female dicks'. Paper presented to the International Television Studies Conference, University of London, July.

Lovibond, S. (1990) 'Reply to Elizabeth Wilson', *New Left Review* 180 (March/ April) p. 190.

Macaulay, S. (1987) 'Images of law in everyday life: the lessons of school, entertainment, and spectator sports', *Law and Society Review* 21, 2: 185–217.

MacCabe, C. (1985) *Theoretical Essays*, Manchester: Manchester University Press.

McCann, G. K. (1986) 'The keys to dreamland: Marxism, aesthetics and film', unpublished PhD thesis, University of Cambridge.

MacDonald, D. (1981) 'A theory of mass culture' in P. Davison, R. Meyersohn and E. Shils (eds) *Literary Taste, Culture and Mass Communication*, Cambridge: Chadwick-Healey.

MacIntyre, A. (1981) *After Virtue: A Study in Moral Theory*, London: Duckworth.

MacLean, B. (1989) 'In partial defence of socialist realism'. Paper presented to British Criminology Conference, Bristol, July.

MacLuhan, M. (1964) *Understanding Media*, London: Routledge & Kegan Paul.

McQuail, D. (1984) *Communication* (2nd edition), London: Longman.

MacRae, D. (1974) *Max Weber*, London: Woburn Press.

Mandel, E. (1984) *Delightful Murder*, London: Pluto.

Mannheim, H. (1965) *Comparative Criminology*, London: Routledge & Kegan Paul.

Mannheim, K. (1940) *Man and Society in the Age of Reconstruction*, London: Routledge & Kegan Paul.

Marcuse, H. (1964) *One Dimensional Man*, London: Routledge & Kegan Paul.

Mark, M. (1984) 'Review of R. Milavsky *et al.*, *Television and Aggression*' *Public Opinion Quarterly* 48: 701–5.

Marx, K. (1968) *Theories of Surplus Values*, vol. II, Moscow: Progress Publishers.

Maxfield, M. (1984) *Fear of Crime in England and Wales*, London: HMSO.

Mead, B. (1974) 'Media – breeder reactors', *Viewer and Listener* summer/autumn: 4.

Mead, G. H. (1968) 'The psychology of punitive justice' [1917] in J. W. Petras (ed.) *George Herbert Mead: Essays on his Social Philosophy*, New York: Teachers' College Press.

Mercer, C. (1986) 'Complicit pleasures' in T. Bennett, C. Mercer and J. Woollacott (eds) *Popular Culture and Social Relations*, Milton Keynes: Open University Press.

Merton, R. K. (1957) *Social Theory and Social Structure*, Glencoe, Ill.: Free Press.

Metz, C. (1974) *Film Language*, Oxford: Oxford University Press.

Meyrowitz, J. (1985) *No Sense of Place*, Oxford: Oxford University Press.

Michaels, E. (1986) 'Hollywood iconography: a Warlpiri reading'. Paper presented to the International Television Studies Conference, University of London, July.

Milavsky, J., Kessler, R., Stipp, H. and Rubens, W. (1982) *Television and Aggression*, New York: Academic Press.

Mills, C. W. (1943) 'The professional ideology of social pathologists', *American Journal of Sociology*, 46, 2: 165–80.

Mills, C. W. (1956) *The Power Elite*, Oxford: Oxford University Press.

Mills, C. W. (1959) *The Sociological Imagination*, Harmondsworth: Penguin.

More, T. (1967) *The Essential Thomas More* (ed. J. Greene and J. Dolan), New York: New American Library.

Morley, D. (1980) *The Nationwide Audience*, London: British Film Institute.

Morley, D. and Silverstone, R. (1988) 'Domestic Communication'. Paper presented to the International Television Studies Conference, London, July.

Morris, T. (1989) *Crime and Criminal Justice Since 1945*, Oxford: Basil Blackwell.

Muccigrosso, R. (1979) 'Television and the urban crisis' in F. Coppa (ed.) *Screen and Society*, Chicago: Nelson Hall.

Murdock, G. (1980) 'Misrepresenting media sociology: a reply to Anderson and Sharrock', *Sociology* 14: 457–68.

Murdock, G. (1982) 'Disorderly images' in C. S. Sumner (ed.) *Crime, Justice and the Mass Media*, Cambridge: Institute of Criminology.

Murdock, G. (1984) 'Figuring out the arguments' in M. Barker (ed.) *The Video Nasties*, London: Pluto.

Murdock, G. and Golding, P. (1977) 'Capitalism, communications and class relations' in J. Curran, M. Gurevitch and J. Woollacott (eds) *Mass Communication and Society*, London: Methuen.

Murray, J. and Kippax, S. (1979) 'From the early window to the late night show' in L. Berkowitz (ed.) *Advances in Experimental Social Psychology*, New York: Academic Press.

Newcomb, H. (1976) *Television: The Critical View*, Oxford: Oxford University Press.

Newcomb, H. (1978) 'Assessing the violence profiles of Gerbner and Gross. A humanistic critique and suggestion', *Communication Research* 5, 3: 264–82.

Newman, G. (1979) *Understanding Violence*, New York: Harper & Row.

Nietzsche, F. (1914) *Beyond Good and Evil*, London: Foulis.

Nisbet, R. (1970) *The Sociological Tradition*, London: Heinemann.

Ong, W. J. (1982) *Orality and Literacy*, London: Methuen.

Ortega y Gasset, J. (1976) *La Rebelion de las Masas*, Madrid: Selecciones Austral.

Packer, H. L. (1969) *The Limits of the Criminal Sanction*, Stanford, Calif: Stanford University Press.

Pandiani, J. (1978) 'Crime-time TV: if all we knew is what we saw . . .', *Contemporary Crises* 2: 437–58.

Parks, R. (1982) *The Western Hero in Film and Television*, Ann Arbor, Mich.: UMI Research Press.

Pateman, T. (1983) 'How is understanding an advertisement possible?' in H. Davis and P. Walton (eds) *Language, Image, Media*, Oxford: Basil Blackwell.

Pearl, D., Bouthilet, L. and Lazar, J. (eds) (1982) *Television and Behavior*, Washington, DC: National Institute of Mental Health.

Pearson, G. (1983) *Hooligan: A History of Respectable Fears*, London: Macmillan.

Pearson, G. (1984) 'Falling standards: a short, sharp history of moral decline' in M. Barker (ed.) *The Video Nasties*, London: Pluto.

Pecheux, M. (1982) *Language, Semantics and Ideology*, London: Macmillan.

Pepinsky, H. (1987) 'Justice as information sharing' in J. Lowman, R. Menzies and T. Palys (eds) *Transcarceration: Essays in the Sociology of Social Control*, Aldershot: Gower.

Phillips, D. (1986) 'Natural experiments on the effects of mass media violence on fatal aggression' in M. Berkowitz (ed.) *Advances in Experimental Social Psychology* 19: 207–47.

Postman, N. (1986) *Amusing Ourselves to Death*, London: Heinemann.

Poulantzas, N. (1973) *Political Power and Social Classes*, London: New Left Books.

Powell, J. (1988) 'Making drama for television' in M. Redfearn (ed.) *Violence and the Media*, London, BBC.

Pratt, J. D. and Sparks, J. R. (1987) 'New voices from the ship of fools: a critical commentary on the renaissance of permissiveness as a political issue', *Contemporary Crises* 11: 3–23.

Pringle, A. (1972) 'Review of Glucksmann', *Violence on the Screen*', *Screen* 12, 3: 152–6.

Propp, V. I. (1984) *Theory and History of Folklore* (ed. A. Liberman), Manchester: Manchester University Press.

Reddy, M. (1979) 'The conduit metaphor' in A. Ortony (ed.) *Metaphor and Thought*, Cambridge: Cambridge University Press.

Reiner, R. (1985) *The Politics of the Police*, Sussex: Harvester Wheatsheaf.

Reiner, R. (1988) 'British criminology and the State' in P. Rock (ed.) *A History of British Criminology*, Oxford: Clarendon Press.

Riches, D. (ed.) (1986) *The Anthropology of Violence*, Oxford: Basil Blackwell.

Ricoeur, P. (1967) *The Symbolism of Evil*, Boston, Mass: Beacon Press.

Ricoeur, P. (1970) *Freud and Philosophy*, New Haven, Conn. and London: Yale University Press.

Ricoeur, P. (1974) *Political and Social Essays*, Athens, Ohio: Ohio University Press.

Ricoeur, P. (1977) *The Rule of Metaphor*, Toronto: Toronto University Press.

Ricoeur, P. (1981) *Hermeneutics and the Human Sciences* (ed. and trans. J. B. Thompson), Cambridge: Cambridge University Press.

Robertson, G. (1979) *Obscenity*, London: Weidenfeld & Nicolson.

Rock, P. (ed.) (1988) *A History of British Criminology*, Oxford: Clarendon Press.

Roshier, B. (1973) 'The selection of crime news by the press' in S. Cohen and J. Young (eds) *The Manufacture of News*, London: Constable.

Ross, N. and Cook, S. (1987) *Crimewatch UK*, London: Hodder & Stoughton.

Rowland, W. (1983) *The Politics of TV Violence*, London: Sage.

Rowland, W. and Watkins, B. (1984) 'Introduction: beyond mass culture and normal science in television research' in W. Rowland and B. Watkins (eds) *Interpreting Television: Current Research Perspectives* (Sage Annual Reviews of Communication Research) vol. 12, London: Sage.

Said, E. W. (1980) 'The text, the world and the critic' in J.V. Harari (ed.) *Textual Strategies*, London: Macmillan.

Sartre, J.-P. (1976) *Critique of Dialectical Reason*, London: New Left Books.

Scannell, P. (1986) 'Radio Times: the temporal arrangements of broadcasting in the modern world'. Paper presented to the International Television Studies Conference, University of London, July.

Scannell, P. (1988) 'The communicative ethos of broadcasting'. Paper presented to the International Television Studies Conference, University of London, July.

Scannell, P. (1989) 'Public service broadcasting and modern public life', *Media, Culture and Society* 11: 135–66.

Scheingold, S. A. (1984) *The Politics of Law and Order*, New York: Longman.

Schiach, M. (1988) *Discourse on Popular Culture*, Cambridge: Polity Press.

Schlesinger, P., Tumber, H. and Murdock, G. (1989) 'The media politics of crime law and justice'. Paper presented to British Criminology Conference, Bristol, July.

Scraton, P. (ed.) (1987) *Law, Order and the Authoritarian State*, Milton Keynes: Open University Press.

Seneca, L. A. (1985) *Seneca's Thyestes* (ed. R. J. Tarrant), Atlanta, Ga: Scholar's Press.

Sennet, R. (1970) *The Uses of Disorder: Personal Identity and City Life*, New York: Alfred Knopf.

Serres, M. (1980) 'The algebra of literature: the wolf's game' in J. V. Harari (ed.) *Textual Strategies*, London: Macmillan.

Shils, E. (1978) 'Mass society and its culture' in P. Davison, R. Meyersohn and E. Shils (eds) *Literary Taste, Culture and Mass Communications*, Cambridge: Chadwick-Healey.

Shuttleworth, A. (1978) 'Two working papers in cultural studies' in P. Davison, R. Meyersohn and E. Shils (eds) *Literary Taste, Culture and Mass Communications*, Cambridge: Chadwick-Healey.

Silverstone, R. (1981) *The Message of Television*, London: Heinemann.

Silverstone, R. (1988) 'Television myth and culture' in J. W. Carey (ed.) *Media Myths and Narratives* (Sage Annual Reviews of Communication Research) vol. 15, London: Sage.

Skogan, W. (1987) 'The impact of victimization on fear of crime', *Crime and Delinquency* 33: 135–54.

Skogan, W. and Maxfield, M. (1981) *Coping with Crime*, London: Sage.

Skolnick, J. and Woodworth, J. (1967) 'Bureaucracy, information and social control' in D. Bordua (ed.) *The Police: Six Sociological Essays*, New York: John Wiley.

Smith, A. (1974) *British Broadcasting*, Devon: David & Charles.

Smith, S. J. (1986) *Crime, Space and Society*, Cambridge: Cambridge University Press.

Sparks, J. R. (1987) 'Crimewatch UK', *New Socialist* April p. 51.

Stanko, E. (1985) *Intimate Intrusions: Women's Experience of Male Violence*, London: Routlege & Kegan Paul.

Stanko, E. (1990) *Everyday Violence*, London: Pandora.

Steiner, G. (1984) *George Steiner: A Reader*, Harmondsworth: Penguin.

Sumner, C. S. (1979) *Reading Ideologies*, London: Academic Press.

Sumner, C. S. (ed.) (1982) *Crime, Justice and the Mass Media*, Cambridge: Institute of Criminology.

Sumner, C. S. (1990) 'Rethinking deviance: towards a sociology of censures' in C. S. Sumner (ed.) *Censure, Politics and Criminal Justice*, Milton Keynes: Open University Press.

Surgeon General's Scientific Advisory Committee (1972) *Television and Growing Up*, Washington, DC: US Government Printing Office.

Surette, R. (1984) *Justice and the Media*, New York: Alfred Thomas.

Swidler, A., Rapp, M. and Soysal, Y. (1986) 'Format and formula in prime-time TV' in S. Ball-Rokeach and M. Cantor (eds) *Media, Audience and Social Structure*, London: Sage.

Swingewood, A. (1977) *The Myth of Mass Culture*, London: Macmillan.

Taylor, I. (1987) 'Violence and video: for a social democratic perspective' *Contemporary Crises* 11: 107–127

Taylor, I. (1988) 'Left realism, the free market economy and the problem of social order'. Paper presented to the American Society of Criminology meetings, Chicago.

Taylor, T. J. (1980) *Linguistic Theory and Structural Stylistics*, Oxford: Pergamon.

Thompson, E. P. (1965) 'The peculiarities of the English' in R. Miliband and J. Saville (eds) *Socialist Register 1965*, London: Merlin Press.

Thompson, E. P. (1978) *The Poverty of Theory*, London: Merlin Press.

Thompson, J. B. (1984) *Studies in the Theory of Ideology*, Cambridge: Polity Press.

Thompson, J. B. (1988) 'Mass communication and modern culture: contribution to a critical theory of ideology', *Sociology* 22, 3: 359–83.

Tobias, J. (1979) *Crime and Police in England, 1700–1900*, Dublin: Gill.

Tonnies, F. (1971) *On Sociology: Pure, Applied and Empirical* (ed. W. Cahnman and R. Heberle), Chicago: Chicago University Press.

Toplin, R. B. (1975) *Unchallenged Violence: An American Ordeal*, Westport, Conn: Greenwood Press.

Touraine, A. (1984) *Le Retour de l'acteur*, Paris: Fayard.

Tracey, M. and Morrison, D. (1979) *Whitehouse*, London: Macmillan.

Tuan, Yi-Fu (1979) *Landscapes of Fear*, Oxford: Basil Blackwell.

Turner, B. S. (1990) 'Outline of a theory of citizenship', *Sociology* 24, 2: 189–217.

Tyler, T. R. (1980) 'The impact of directly and indirectly experienced events – the origin of crime-related judgements', *Journal of Personality and Social Psychology* 39: 13–28.

Tyler, T. R. (1984) 'Assessing the risk of criminal victimization: the integration of experience and socially transmitted information', *Journal of Social Issues* 40: 27–38.

Unger, R. M. (1987) *Social Theory: Its Situation and its Task*, Cambridge: Cambridge University Press.

Von Neumann, J. and Morgenstern, O. (1953) *The Theory of Games*, Princeton, NJ: Princeton University Press.

Wakshlag, J., Bart, L., Dudley, J., McCutcheon, J. and Rolla, C. (1983) 'Viewer apprehension about victimization and crime drama programs', *Communication Research* 10: 195–217

Wakshlag, J., Vial, V. and Tamborini, R. (1983) 'Selecting crime drama and apprehension about crime', *Human Communication Research* 10: 227–242.

Wallas, G. (1920) *Human Nature in Politics*, London: Constable.

Wallis, R. (1976) 'Moral indignation and the media: an analysis of the NVALA', *Sociology* 10: 271–95.

Warshow, R. (1979) *The Immediate Experience*, New York: Atheneum.

Weaver, J. and Wakshlag, J. (1984) 'Perceptions of personal vulnerability to crime, criminal victimization experience and television viewing'. Paper presented to Broadcast Education Association, Las Vegas, April.

Weber, M. (1930) *The Protestant Ethic and the Spirit of Capitalism*, London: George Allen & Unwin.

Weber, M. (1958) *From Max Weber* (ed. and trans. H. Gerth and C. W. Mills), New York: Galaxy.

Weigel, R. and Jessor, R. (1973) 'Television and adolescent conventionality', *Public Opinion Quarterly* 37: 76–90.

Whitehouse, M. (1974a) 'Mental pollution', *Viewer and Listener* Spring, p. 4.

Whitehouse, M. (1974b) 'Inverted censorship', *Viewer and Listener* Spring, p. 5.

Whitehouse, M. (1978) 'The corruption of culture', *Books and Bookmen* May, p. 15.

Whitney, J. (1985) 'Crime and broadcasting', Address by the Director-General, IBA to AGM of NACRO, 8 November.

Wilkins, L. (1964) *Social Deviance, Social Policy, Action and Research*, London: Tavistock.

Williams, M. (1982) *Television: the Casual Art*, Oxford: Oxford University Press.

Williams, R. (1958) *Culture and Society*, Harmondsworth: Penguin.

Williams, R. (1973) *The Country and the City*, London: Hogarth Press.

Williams, R. (1974) *Television: Technology and Cultural Form*, London: Fontana.

Williams, R. (1976) *Keywords*, London: Fontana.

Wilson, J. Q. (1975) *Thinking About Crime*, New York: Basic Books.

Wilson, J. Q. and Kelling, G. (1982) 'Broken windows', *Atlantic Monthly* March: 29–38.

Winn, M. (1977) *The Plug-In Drug*, New York: Viking Press.

Wright, K. (1985) *The Great American Crime Myth*, Westport, Conn.: Greenwood Press.

Yeats, W. B. (1950) 'Meditations in Time of Civil War' in *Collected Poems of W. B. Yeats* (2nd edition), London: Macmillan.

Young, J. (1971a) 'The role of the police as amplifiers of deviancy, negotiators of reality and translators of fantasy' in S. Cohen (ed.) *Images of Deviance*, Harmondsworth: Penguin.

Young, J. (1971b) *The Drug-Takers*, London: MacGibbon & Kee.

Young, J. (1987) 'The tasks facing a realist criminology', *Contemporary Crises* 11: 337–56.

Young, J. (1988) 'Radical criminology in Britain: the emergence of a competing paradigm', *British Journal of Criminology* 28: 159–83.

Young, J. (1989) Inaugural lecture, Middlesex Polytechnic, March.

Zillman, D. (1980) 'Anatomy of suspense' in P. Tannenbaum (ed.) *Entertainment Functions of Television*, Hillsdale, NJ: Erlbaum.

Zillman, D. and Wakshlag, J. (1987) 'Fear of victimization and the appeal of crime drama' in D. Zillman and J. Bryant (eds) *Selective Exposure to Communication*, Hillsdale, NJ: Erlbaum.

Zipes, J. (1979) *Breaking the Magic Spell: Radical Theories of Folk and Fairy Tales*, London: Heinemann.

Index